CONVERSATIONS WITH
PERFECT
STRANGERS

CONVERSATIONS WITH
PERFECT STRANGERS

MEMOIRS OF A PSYCHOLOGIST

PHYLISS SHANKEN

TATE PUBLISHING
AND ENTERPRISES, LLC

Published by Tate Publishing & Enterprises, LLC
127 E. Trade Center Terrace | Mustang, Oklahoma 73064 USA
1.888.361.9473 | www.tatepublishing.com

Tate Publishing is committed to excellence in the publishing industry. The company reflects the philosophy established by the founders, based on Psalm 68:11,
"The Lord gave the word and great was the company of those who published it."

Book design copyright © 2013 by Tate Publishing, LLC. All rights reserved.
Cover design by Rtor Maghuyop
Interior design by Jomel Pepito

Published in the United States of America
ISBN: 978-1-62510-325-3
1. Psychology / General
2. Self-Help / Personal Growth / General
13.05.01

Other books by Phyliss Shanken:

Silhouettes of Woman

Laughter is a StressBuster

Heart of Boynton Beach Club

Eye of Irene

DEDICATION

To Will

My Life, Love, and Professional Partner

ACKNOWLEDGMENTS

This book, which is a virtual culmination of my life's work, took thirteen years to be published. Before I wrote it and during the years I waited to be "discovered," I had lots of supportive and loving cheerleaders by my side.

My husband, Will, a psychiatrist, eagerly shared his admiration and respect for my clinical and written work. My children, Greg and Lisa, Ross and Lori, and Rachel, periodically checked in to inquire about my publishing progress and encouraged me to stay with it. I carry with me the memory of the generous, warm, and most loving faces of my buddies and surrogate sisters: Pat McGettigan, Nancy Mellon, Kathi Eichman, and Donna Monk, some of the most competent and humanistic clinicians in their own right. Nancy and Pat co-designed and facilitated our Women's Enrichment Series at INTROSPECT. They had input in one of the exercises mentioned in the Strangers No More chapter: "Do I Have To Change the Past In Order To Take Charge of the Present?"

Carolyn Shanken-Kaye: You have rubbed off on me in countless ways and applauded my risk taking ability, which merely enhanced my confidence.

John Shanken-Kaye: You have a way of getting right to the meat of the matter and have helped this techie novice get up to speed. One of these days I might even figure out how to tweet you my appreciative words!

Thank you, Vicki Bogle, for your never-ending curiosity and enthusiasm about my creative works, Carol and Bill Tilles for your smiling support (Bill, if I ask for feedback, you really put in the time – a great commodity that you so selflessly share) and to Florence Seidelman who can sell anyone anything including belief in herself!

To my colleagues, many of whom professionally reside at our psychological/psychiatric practice at INTROSPECT in Colmar, PA who mutually exchange your experience, theory and practical issues in psychotherapy, especially you, Frank Sergi, our Associate Medical Director, who conveyed a reverence for my work that matches my admiration for your own clinical capability.

I cherish the supportive members of the Ventnor Library Book Club in Ventnor City, New Jersey. Thank you for your feedback when I asked for it!

To Steve Ferber, author of *21 Rules to Live By: A Pathway to Personal Growth*, who tracked me down after ten years, having retained my laughter article and asked to include it in your book. Then you opened up your most valued expertise and time, to provide among other gifts, your marketing tips.

Thanks to the participants of the 2012 Cape Cod Institute seminar on Masculinity, especially Anne Driscoll, who spurred me to seek publication of a book I had shopped around a dozen years ago and had put aside unable to find a publisher because the going feedback had been, "The only memoirs we publish are about famous people and you are not famous!" The professionals at the seminar listened to excerpts from *Conversations* and strongly encouraged me to renew my pursuit. I can still hear your applause after the reading and see your smiling faces. The echo of your laudatory phrases still rings so sweetly in my ears! I also recall fondly my response, "Really?! *Really?!*"

To my patients, who opened up your hearts to me, expressed your secrets, trusted me with your unique and precious histories, gave me feedback, and permitted yourselves to form our mutual bond. Along with my children, you have taught me just about everything I know. I feel privileged to have been invited into your lives.

—Phyliss Shanken
2013

All names, histories, and treatment of patients are totally fiction except where people have given me permission to *anonymously* share specific anecdotal information.

All information about myself, the therapist, is totally true, except when I temporarily go bananas and say wacky things! Well, the wacky words might be right on but don't hold me to them!

TABLE OF CONTENTS

INTRODUCTION: EVERYTHING I EVER HEARD BUT COULDN'T SAY

I live in the secret world of other people's pain and suffering. I'm a psychologist, and I'm not permitted to tell you anything about the people I treat. Even though you might like to be a fly on the wall and view my patients' sagas complete with lights and sound, alas, I am necessarily committed to those who first consulted me as strangers yet trusted me to hold their stories sacred forever even after death has done us part.

The memories of many people resonate inside me. I remember every single person I've ever treated. They've imprinted themselves in my mind's visual field. I have registered their pain in a special place deep within my heart. I can still hear their silent whimpers, their muffled screams of terror, or their secrets of guilty pleasures. I have relived with them the early traumas they've suffered at the hands of adults who had control over their survival. I have loved them with my whole being. I carry their spirit within me. I am changed because of them.

I have been taught about various life styles: what it's like to be a priest or a nun, a nurse, a chief executive officer, or business owner. I have gone inside the personality of a truck driver, a ballet dancer, a policeman, a physician, a psychologist, a wife, a mother, a bachelor, a homosexual, an artist, a twin, a triplet, an alcoholic, an abuser, and a victim of abuse. I have walked in the footsteps of professional athletes, hairdressers, schoolteachers and administrators, secretaries, newspaper reporters, and psychiatrists. I have experienced the joys and frustrations of being African American, Native American, Asian, Indian, or having been raised as the offspring of immigrants. I have pondered the conflicts along side of my patients who were adopted at birth. I have sat between husbands and wives, parents and grown children, employer and employee, all wanting to work out the aches that kept them apart. I have spent an entire day at a work environment helping employees deal with guilt, fear, and anger over an unsuspected co-worker's suicide.

If I die tomorrow, what happens to the memories of all the personal portraits I've colored with my own experience? At my cremation, my life's work will be puffed up in smoke. Where will the spirit of all those human beings reside? Yes, they have families and others to mourn their loss and to remember them, to mark their lives with a tombstone of love, but no one knows them as I do.

Yet I'm not permitted to tell you a thing. Nada. Zip. Zero. How many ways can I say "nothing?"

What does this reality do to a woman whose mind never stops imbibing one's pain, sifting it around with my own understanding of life, trimming the edges to get to the core, passionately enduring silence while surreptitiously viewing films of the mosaics of other people's lives? What do I do with the wisdom that has grown in me because I've had the privilege of knowing someone who pushes through his or her own fear to entrust precious secrets to me?

I fudge. That's what I do. Temporarily I "forget" them all. I transform myself into another psychologist in a parallel world where no one knows anyone's name.

Here's how I'm going to solve my dilemma: everything I've said so far is a lie. All I will say in the future is a falsehood. I'll have you coming and going. You're not going to know where I discovered my tales of woe and how I could possibly conjure up such weird and crazy stuff. You won't know if the psychologist in this story is I or some figment of a creator's mind. You shouldn't allow yourself to be taken in by me anyway. I'm someone else's psychologist. I'm a plastic wind-up shrink ready to fool the pants off of you. So don't believe me.

Even at the risk of being redundant, for emphasis, and in the name of being an ethical and responsible psychologist, I feel the need to further spell out my plan to you. In order to insure that I don't betray the confidences my patients have placed in me, and at the same time to be able to present interesting stories, I have fictionalized every believe-it-or-not story presented here. In other words, the people in this saga don't exist except in my imagination. I totally made up their lives, their therapy with me, and their happily-ever-after resolutions.

Pretend everything that is really true is in my large handbag, but the satchel is misplaced forever. In the lost world, in a sanctuary of souls, all their information is decoded and presented to you in a different lifetime. Based on my experience, I conjured up sound fibs that could possibly have occurred but did not. A person might have actually lived this life but did not. As astounding as his or her confabulated history is, in the altered world I present to you, this person presents himself or herself as real but only on this written page.

Clever, you say? Has any psychologist ever pulled this off? It's the only way. How else do I release myself from all the years of restraint while I sat in that chair, the poet who was sifting, sorting, soaring, singing songs of love within the caverns of my bongo drum heart and my only relief being to write love letters solely for my own eyes?

So many people have contributed to my learning about multiple ways of life, of varying religions, cultures, and occupations—they all have histories. Consider these to be accounts that never were yet will always be. Their spirit resides in me, so now their stories are mine. I alone transformed their stories. Stir all the people I've known into cross-sectional composites, and you have new beings who will become the novel characters in my tale.

Just in case something you hear from me sounds familiar, as if maybe you know the person or maybe you even see yourself in it and you might have had contact with me, trust me, because many of my patients have given me permission to write about them as long as I disguise the material. So I've already lied about this being a total lie, because intermingled among the falsehoods are some of those permitted anecdotes.

Why am I carrying on like this about confidentiality? One would say I'm a nutcase when it comes to my sticking to the rules. I believe you don't talk about anyone without his or her permission, even if you don't use the real person's name. The words people share are their words and belong to no one else. Some therapists say it's okay to talk about someone as long as you don't use his or her name. Phooey. Baloney. That's a lot of hullabaloo. Just a way to justify acting out on the part of the professional who can't keep his mouth shut!

I've been out socially where other therapists were present. I winced as soon as the first words come spewing forth from their lips, "I have a patient who…"

Yuck. What do I do now?

I have two choices: I either correct this person and shut him or her up, or I leave the room because I believe if someone is doing something that I wouldn't do, if I stay in the room and don't do anything about it, I am just as guilty as the person who commits the indiscretion. If I leave the room, sometimes I speak to the therapist afterward, because I believe this is my obligation to myself, to my profession, and to the patient who is the unknowing victim here.

If I do confront someone about his negligence, most often the therapist will say, "But I didn't say his or her name." Even if it were okay to refer to your patients anonymously, there's still the risk of recognizable details slipping out and into the ears of an unsuspecting person at the party. Remember, six degrees of separation? Think of all the coincidences in your life. Why would any respectful and ethical therapist want to increase the chances of causing harm? Besides, how many people who are in the room are in therapy themselves? Imagine if one of them had just told her therapist this very morning she had been sexually abused at age five and she has never before told another living soul. She goes to a party and hears a psychologist talking about his patient. Oh boy. She had trusted her own therapist, but this observation of another therapist who is part of the same professional society turns her whole morning experience into a travesty.

On the other hand, as in my case, my artistic talents could burn holes in my heart if I spend my entire professional life fearing I might inadvertently betray my patients by telling a story I thought came from my imagination, and without realizing it, I related a saga about a real someone. Isn't this what we authors go through? Our characters come out of our unconscious. While writing the novel, we psychologists must necessarily hold back certain details and run the risk of stifling our own creativity. If we close off one idea, we must then shut down all ideas that pop up for fear these will be the "wrong" ones, which might hurt someone else. If we're always keeping guard over our own slip-ups, we have to keep watch over everything. Hence, we're in for a whopper of a depression. This limiting process is very difficult for me, the one who goes into an altered state of maddening numbness when my creative mind is stifled.

Alongside of the confidentiality issue, I have stringent rules for myself about truth. Ah, truth: I almost always tell it. I'll explain more about this as we go along but for now, suffice to say, I have real conflicts about the fibbing process. When I do take the easy way out by distortion, stretching or omitting the truth, I'm not taking good care of myself. The fact that this whole book is a lie—presenting the tales as if they were true—shakes me up inside.

It is for these reasons this writing project has taken me a lifetime to prepare. Time is running out.

Keeping secrets has always been fine with me. I enjoy connecting with human beings. I'm compassionately watching real life "videos" all day in my office. I'm feeling what I'm supposed to feel as a fellow human being. I'm not an automaton who spouts out theories or fits people into cookie-cutter molds. Each person is unique, and I feel honored to learn his or her story and feel his or her pain.

Do you know how I feel about listening to people all day? Rather than enduring the process, I become invigorated. Instead of putting up a wall to protect myself, I choose to immerse myself into their inner world. I feel privileged that people allow me into their lives. I wouldn't have it any other way.

It's always been enough for me to have these bonding experiences, and I haven't felt compelled to tell anyone else about it. Like undercover cops, my patient and I are partners in covert operations.

Let's get going. You want the details of the patients' sessions to which I keep referring. I'm getting there. I promise. But before I get into the lives of my psychotherapy partners, I'll tell you a little more about me. (It's all about me, me, me, right?) This information will be helpful when you do enter my office so you'll have some idea as to where I'm coming from when I make an intervention.

Okay, I'm an optimist. Do you want to know why? Because I face reality, and I truly believe that even though I didn't ask for bad or unexpected things to happen, when awful stuff happens, I will be able to manage the frustration, pain, anger, and sorrow that accompanies the crises. This is the attitude I want my patients, and now *you*, to absorb.

Not to put words in your mouth, but let's just imagine that you say: "You're stronger than I am. After all, you're a psychologist. You help people who are so messed up; they can't deal with anything. If your husband deserted you suddenly, or you were robbed at gunpoint, you would merely come to terms with the tragedy. Nothing bad happens to psychologists." Referring to yourself, you would say: "I couldn't handle any of that stuff."

Do you think I want tragedy to befall me? Do you think I actually like it when things beyond my control take over and my heart feels like a hard ball being pounded in baseball practice? Do I relish the adjustments I have to make or the stretching beyond what I know to be safe? Do I enjoy feeling like a clock with arms that don't move just at the time I'm in a hurry to feel better, or clock arms that move too fast when I'm afraid to face risky endeavors? I'm as frightened as you are.

And when I'm not with you in my office, I'm living my life! If bad stuff happens there, you won't know about it, but I will. I'll have to compartmentalize my life to keep it distinct from yours.

Here's the rub: I'm aware that stuff can, does, and will happen. I'd love to whisper some mantra and magically ensure that the unexpected wouldn't come about. Since I'm a realist, I do not hesitate to spout out the truth. This very song I sing of potential crisis helps me in my own healing. The more I accept the realities of life, the better chance I have to deal with what comes with it. Also, the more I look fate in the eye, the more likely I can live in the here and now. Yes, I could worry myself sick as some of my patients do, but no matter how much I fret and pace in an attempt to prevent the tragedy, it's gonna happen anyway. Because I know that something bad can and most likely will happen during my lifetime; therefore, I have more fun. The more I live as if this minute is my very last moment on earth, the more peace I attain.

And that's why I am writing to you. Yep, I may be dead tomorrow. If I don't do something about it, I will not have reported to you a record of all my experiences and the thoughts I've thunk (and the words I've created!).

I have put aside other important activities because this one takes priority. Consider yourselves fortunate. If I hadn't started this memoir, I had planned to begin a different book project, one that didn't put stress on my adherence to ethical conduct but that "just had to be written!" It is called *On the Rodent: True Stories of Mice and Men*, a reality book about people's encounters with mice.

Thanks, you say? Thanks for not writing said book? My retort: you're welcome, but this is just a reprieve for you. The cute little mice who lived in my house as well as others in the world deserve to have their stories told.

I told you a little bit of the fairy tale so far. There's so much more to tell. Consider what follows as one long psychotherapy session— only in this instance, I am the patient. It's as if you are asking me the questions, and I am relating to you my life as a psychologist. To complete the task, I'll need help, and here's where the patients from my practice come in. These are the extraordinary people who have made me what I am now. The analysis cannot be conducted without them.

I see myself in your living room by the fireplace, all comfy and safe. What an arrangement! I recommend this set up to everyone—if you can afford it. The fee here is different though. As a writer, for a mere outlay of the *time* it takes me to write the account, I attain your undivided attention. For a change, I am the one who sits in the chair across from you, the therapist, who probes for clues as to what makes this particular psychologist tick.

We are now ready, my friends, to move on…

STRANGERS NO MORE

One of my favorite quotes is from Maya Angelou's poem *On the Pulse of the Morning*, read at President Clinton's inauguration:

> History, despite its wrenching pain, cannot be unlived, but
> if faced with courage, need not be lived again.

Because I immerse myself in people's emotional pain, I am particularly in touch with the impact of early hurts on people's lives. Many times, as people share their personal stories, I relive with them their fears of being abused by a parent: their terror over watching their parents quarrel, their scary trips to the doctor, their reluctant temper tantrums that only brought them grief, their loss of a loved one through death, their agony over being teased as a young child, or their disappointment over not being chosen for a sorority.

None of these recollections is trivial. To those of you who experienced the "crush" of these never-to-be-forgotten traumas, your memory of these nightmarish scenes assumes an indelible place in your mind.

As I look back on my clinical life, I recall accounts of school cafeteria scenes. Scores of people have embarrassedly related a story similar to the one I'm about to recount. Some of those people wept as if the event had taken place just yesterday.

Maybe something like this has happened to you. The details of the situation may be different, but there's a familiarity in the real or imagined words that are spoken behind your back and the false phrases that are dispassionately hammered forevermore into the defenseless gelatin part of your brain.

DONNA

Here's Donna's teary rendition of this almost universal adolescent trauma:

"For some reason, they all decided I was wild and 'fast.' One day they were my friends, and the next day, when I walked toward my table in the lunchroom, they were all pointing and whispering. I overheard someone say the word 'slut.' I kept telling myself, *Don't cry. Don't cry.* I don't know how I held my tears back. My eyes were watering. I couldn't let them see how hurt I was. I never found out who started the rumor. I ate in silence. Until the end of the school year, I was alone. I'll never forget it."

And I'll never forget how Donna expressed this to me. She started with one tear, which she caught in her protruded tongue as it dripped down her mascara-stained cheek. Then her lower lip quivered. And soon, she couldn't turn back to feigned quiescence. Her chant of "I'm sorry," was periodically coincident with my tranquil chant of reassurance: "Donna, this is a painful memory. It's so real, as if you are still there in the cafeteria, as if it happened today."

I wanted to be there with Donna, but I didn't want to drown her out by trying to eradicate her secondary feelings of shame over being upset about being upset, so I abstained from further comment. Anyway, between gulps, Donna argued, "I'm a grown woman. It happened over thirty year ago. This is silly."

I didn't counter her protestations. Why don't people give themselves a break? The unrelenting unconscious mind that stokes a lifetime of hurts into the flaming pit doesn't know time. Everything recalled feels as if it's in the present day. It was clear to me I shouldn't take away Donna's original pain as well as her embarrassment over continuing to feel it.

Later, we would work on why she begrudged herself a nourishing cry in a safe place alongside a non-judgmental person. This discharge of emotion erupted after a thirty-year postponement, and look at all the damage the submersion had caused. It was as if she were back there pretending she didn't hear and telling herself, *Don't cry. Don't cry!* Donna was so intent on hushing herself, she didn't see the droplet that I surreptitiously wiped away from my own eyes.

As we learned from Donna, being in touch with your adolescent feelings can haunt you but ultimately help you in your adult life. Try a little shortcut I devised and taught my patients: When you are feeling blue, allow yourself to reminisce or daydream, and see what images emerge. Dollars to donuts (whoever came up with that phrase anyway?), you will return to your temporarily tortured teenage years (seems that's where we all end up sooner or later) and you will learn plenty about yourself in present day.

For example: you are at a party. Suddenly, you start perspiring. Everyone else looks cool, and now that you think about it, they appear calm and collected in sharp contrast to despondent, dizzy you. Take a deep breath (rather than a drink) and search for the pictures in your brain to help you understand why, without provocation, your surroundings suddenly seem so dark.

In your daydream, you "see" yourself on the first day of school proudly wearing a dress you so thoughtfully selected from the closet amidst your assortment of fresh new what-you-thought were up to date clothes. You overhear one of those cruel girls whisper, "I know where she bought that. Wasn't it from the vintage thrift store?"

Is there a ditch to fall into, one that you have been digging deeper many times in your life since then?

Emotions that materialize from you without warning and seem unfitting for the occasion should not be shooed away but embraced so you can learn what is going on inside your mind at the moment. Feel the emotion. Allow it to take you over. Use your internal camera to capture a snapshot. Look in your album for the scene's origin. Then re-apply what you felt at that time to what you are feeling here-and-now. Do this and you will almost never be in a quandary as to how you feel or why you feel it.

Now you are in a position to help yourself move through your discomfort. Why, in a usually friendly, fun place, do you suddenly feel down and anxious? You know from where the strange emotion originates—from your early social anxiety emerging out of your need to be accepted and liked by everyone. Are you, today, making the same internal plea from yesteryear? *If only I had the formula for how to dress and what to say. Then I could reel those caddy teenagers in and* make *them accept me…*

To help yourself out of the doldrums, you could ultimately tell yourself: *This is not that horrid first day of school. I'm at an adult celebration among friends.* Or *those kids don't live here anymore.* Or *even if those kids have come to call, their regard for me has lost all its power.* You may even figure out that you've been feeling insecure lately with this present day crowd because last time you were together you refused to go along with a joke they were playing on someone and you worried afterward that they would probably reject you for your rebelliousness against the status quo.

Okay. Take what I just said as the first of many tips to appear in the advice column of this psychologist who learned so much from her patients. To review: Think of other times when your emotion that is presently out of synch with the occasion was appropriate to that earlier experience. Try the *internal camera method.* Force yourself to question your strange emotion. Observe the pictures that emerge. Relate to the emotion that goes with the picture. Bring the historical photo back to real life today and you will have a shortcut to solving many mysteries. Never again will you say, "Feel? Feel? How do I feel? How am I supposed to know. All I know is I'm shaking inside!"

Later you will see how I do this with my patients. Yes, if I'm feeling something in a session and I don't know why it came up at this moment in our discussion, I use abbreviated pictures from my own life. I attach the feeling from my memory of that event and apply it to what the patient is conveying. In that way, if the person seems blocked or speaks without expressing the emotion that goes with it, I have a neat way of travelling to their hidden heart as if we have a wifi connection: my unconscious mind to my patient's unconscious! Say I "see" a picture of a leaky faucet, yet this guest in my office is speaking in a neutral way, might he be holding back tears? If seemingly out of nowhere, I remember when my mother lied about my age to a cashier, might this person be feeling guilty about some distortion?

Of course, I can't take my picture journey as an absolute truth for the patient and will have to check it out with him or her, but it's a nice start. Stay tuned for how I use the information I glean from my in-house camera.

For now, though, practice what I recommended because there will be a test at the end of the session! (Smiley face.)

KEVIN

Kevin, a man I will tell you more about soon (I promise) lost his father when Kevin was four, and his mother was in and out of hospitals for treatment of alcoholism. I wished I could take him home to my house to live. I wanted to wipe away his history and give him a new mother who was consistent, steady, honest, and clear. He would never be confused again as to whether I loved him or hated him, whether he had pleased me or was responsible for turning me away. His existence wouldn't have depended on whether I was drunk or sober. But if I could have successfully executed my magic and changed his past, in essence, I would have been the culprit in the assassination of his specific spirit. He wouldn't be Kevin any more. He would be someone else with a different kind of misery. This new man might have affected me in a totally dissimilar way.

Although I keep people company as they relate their painful memories, in order for them not to have to live the same themes all over again in their adult life, I try to help them face these agonizing remembrances with "courage." We don't go past the past; we must go through the past to get to the "now" and to allow for the future. As we engage in this process, it is painful for both of us, and we feel pressured to make it go away forever. We must resist this urge to numb the pain, so we can achieve the long-term goal of arriving at self-acceptance.

A friend of mine recently suggested that, in order for youngsters not to have to go through the pain of adolescence, when physical appearance is all important, perhaps we could provide plastic surgery for all teens who weren't born beautiful.

I immediately objected, saying, "Oh no, then they would turn out to be different people from those who they were meant to be! We would be robbing them of their unique spirit and character. We'd be manipulating their future by trying to redo their inevitable past!"

This idea may seem cruel to you. After all, if we can save people from suffering, why not do it? But just think about all the great people who have endured disabilities and how they inevitably reversed their handicaps and sculpted them into assets: Helen Keller, Albert Einstein, Ludwig Von Beethoven, to name a very few. We find some kind of mental torment in the histories of most of the great thinkers and artists, and it was out of this misery they created their art. My need to write to you today emerges from my struggle with the constraints on me to withhold words that didn't necessarily belong to me. My finding a way to surmount the conflict and writing about it has been my artful expression. What kind of world would this be if we took away our human right to meet and surpass the challenges of living?

Some of you are telling me to hurry up and get on with it, to get to the real life, storybook stuff. Patience please. This is not about you. It's about me, and I alone hold the secrets for which you are digging. I am your stranger, and I must feel safe before I'll open myself up to you. You want to know about my patients? They reside in the sanctuary I fashioned for their souls and buried under layers of my time and experience.

I try to help face their past hurts, appreciate how these have shaped them, and then make use of the strengths they have acquired because of and in spite of their deprivation. In chorus with this acceptance of their early life anguish, I encourage them to move on. As their personal plots unfold, my hope is always that I can open myself up like a flower and allow them in. They are the experts in their own records. My patients are artists who brush their emotions onto scenic canvases. I don't want to tell you *about* them. I would rather you board the time machine and enter their lives.

CHRISSY

I'm ready now to tell you about Chrissy. Within minutes of meeting her, at first a perfect stranger to me, I could sense her turmoil behind a mask-like cartoon smile, which betrayed her fear. We were off and running. The adventure had begun, and she was a stranger no more. After the first few sessions and having learned a great deal about her, I imagined how her life must have been when she was growing up:

Red. Even though there are snippets of recall for other events, her first complete visual memory is of red: oozing rivulets of blood streaming down her mother's arms and onto the pink and black tiles, the tiles she always followed with her little fingers to make a road. Now the red liquid tagged along her make-believe trails and moved toward her toes, the same toes her father had kissed just last night.

For a moment, she stood there in the airless room, fixated on the new floor design. Then she roused, certain now she wasn't dreaming. The scream that had been lurking in her chest began to erupt, and her hands with wide-open fingers lunged forward, but for certain, not touching the human grown-up doll in front of her, which was just about at eye level. Her muffled screech designed to stop the eventuality of what she presently saw sounded as if her lips had been sewn up by a monster who emerged from the closet, the same closet in which her father had hidden one night after Mommy and he fought with fists over Daddy's coming home late.

As an adult looking back, she didn't recall exactly what happened next except for a montage of sounds and shapes such as shattering sirens, father's curses, and her younger sister's and brother's sobbing as they huddled together to be "out of the way!" of father who was orchestrating her mother's rescue. When Daddy had come in to see what she was fussing about, he brutally pushed her aside, and she took this to mean that he was angry with her. But instead, as she learned later, Daddy was furious with Mommy for "pulling this stunt," yet again. Even after Chrissy figured out the truth, she still was unable to shed the notion that she was responsible for the turmoil in the house and at the very least, she was the bad little girl who was somehow the cause of her mother's self-induced violent actions.

In her memory, Chrissy had saved her mommy's life. And she was to be responsible for her mother ever more. She didn't have to say it aloud. She didn't even say it to herself, but it became her internal commandment: no matter what befell her in her own life, Chrissy would never let down on the job of being her mother's guardian again.

This event and others to follow were the precursors to Chrissy's need to help others. It went beyond help. "Rescue" would be a better word. She became a nurse. But that was to be expected. What caused Chrissy much of the distress in her life was that she was everyone's nurse even if she hadn't been given the assignment.

In terms of Chrissy's father's affection, how was she to determine what was proper? Although Daddy favored her younger sister—it was obvious to everyone; even Mommy said so—whenever Chrissy was upset, Daddy consoled her. He did so hours after her bathroom discovery of Mommy when he came to her room and sang her lullabies and told her not to be troubled any more; everything would be all right.

The same night as her Mommy's blood letting, Daddy quietly tiptoed into her room and whispered, "Chrissy, are you asleep?"

Always confused about whether or not to answer the recurrent question, particularly the evening when she had saved her mother's life and after Daddy had returned from the hospital, she managed a muffled groan. Her eyes were stinging, and her face had swelled up with hives, which emerged through her ordinarily sallow skin. To Daddy, she looked like a clown. At least, that's what he said when he lifted her in his arms and boosted up her chin with his massive hands. Whenever he conducted himself like this, she always remembered the touch of his thick, hairy fingers.

"Is Mommy dead?" She covered her eyes as if the momentary blindness would expunge any possibility of affirmation.

"No, no, no," Daddy said with irritation. "Mommy is in the hospital and will be back after they make her better." Then Daddy hugged her tightly while rubbing her back and patting her rhythmically, saying, "Poor Chrissy. There. There."

Her back tickled, and it felt good. His hands moved to the rear of her neck. He lifted her hair and ran his fingers through it, curling the strands around and clutching on a little too tightly.

Something told her not to complain. Even though the room was dark, the room got darker as if chocolate clouds had embraced her, yet hemmed her in at once. She didn't remember much more than that. Maybe in her relief, she had fallen asleep in Daddy's arms.

The next day, Daddy was brusque with her again as if his hugs last night had been lies. She never understood why Daddy got so mad at her, but not at Sunny, her little sister.

Mommy eventually came home from the hospital. She had convinced the doctors it was all a big mistake, and they should let her go. Life went back to the usual hum of routine.

As she grew older, sometimes Chrissy would awaken to the sound of breathing, which came from her nearby her closet. She always thought she had been dreaming. By the time she reached adolescence, she figured out it was her father who was in the closet, gazing at her. But the closet shared a common wall with her sister's room. Chrissy knew there was a hole in that closet, because she had used it herself to spy on her sister, especially when they played hide and seek and her sister counted to ten while Chrissy determined which direction Sunny was headed. Sunny never knew why Chrissy was so good at that game.

What was father doing in the closet? Chrissy wanted father to be looking at her, not at his precious Sunny. She never found out for sure which one he chose, but deep down, she knew it had to be Sunny.

There were more suicidal episodes by her mother, and always Chrissy felt responsible. It was as though Chrissy had eyes all around her head, because she learned to keep a close watch on Mommy. And Mommy knew it. Mommy used it.

When Chrissy balked at something Mommy told her to do, Mommy would say, "I don't know if I have the will to live any more; my daughters are so ungrateful." Oh yes, the ploy worked all right. On cue, Chrissy always reversed her stance.

If Chrissy were upset, Mother might say, "Oh, Chrissy, you look so unhappy. It's because I'm a bad mother. If a mother can't keep her children happy, she has failed. You really don't even need me around any more. All I do is cause you harm."

"No, Mommy, no. I am happy. I just had some dust in my eye. See!" And Chrissy put a smile on her face so broad, her mommy would settle down and beam bountifully.

Mother sent Chrissy to do errands for other people. "We have to be good to others," she would say, "and remember, if Mrs. Salfor tries to give you money for helping her, don't you take it. It would be a mortal sin. God doesn't want you to be good just because you expect something in return."

These simplistic edicts from Mommy sustained Chrissy until she reached her adolescence when she began to distrust and resent her mother's machinations. In addition, Chrissy became frightened of her father and blamed Mother for staying with him.

Father's odd behavior had increased, and one night he produced a gun and pointed it at Mommy. "So you want to die! I'll put you out of your misery!"

Once again, Chrissy, her sister, and brother clustered together on the second floor landing, screaming, "No, Daddy, no! Please, Daddy, don't shoot her!"

Daddy eventually put the gun down.

I am always intrigued that despite their unhappy childhood, high-functioning people, meaning those who can manage their lives, go to work, achieve great milestones in their profession, or carry on well as a homemaker, inevitably had someone in their past to help them through it. There had to be a "fairy godmother" somewhere on the scene. I'm looking for one redeeming person who didn't have to be around continually but who had an opportunity to make an impact on the youngster. It could be a grandparent, neighbor, teacher, or family friend. I don't believe little guys can make it unless they have some positive validation of their inherent worth.

True, Chrissy did have her oddball father who both loved and perhaps abused her, and on occasion, he did show her tenderness, even though when others were present, he offered her no special treatment. Perhaps her father's attentiveness would have been enough.

But I searched further, and a few sessions after the initial visit, I asked Chris (as an adult, she used a more sophisticated nickname) directly, "There must have been someone in your life who gave you something special, who endeared you to him or her. I say this because with all the negative things that befell you in your childhood, there is no way you could have turned out to function as well as you do today without some abiding experience to help you. Okay, even with your early training in 'rescue missions' that inspired you to become a nurse, you couldn't have pulled it off without having ego strength. Was there someone in your life who provided this for you?"

Dear Reader, look back on your own life? Yes, do it now. Who was your fairy godmother or godfather (and I don't mean the Soprano's kind!)

In a few minutes, after we finish this installment of the account of Chrissy's life, I'll elaborate on how, if you believe you *didn't* have a fairy godmother or you think she fell down on the job, how you might rectify this today.

Sure enough, for Chrissy, it was her grandmother, her father's mother, who knew her son was as she called him, *a real nutcase,* "but lovable just the same." Once in a while on a weekend and more especially in the summer, Chrissy spent time with Nana all by herself, because Sunny was too young and years later went to camp, and Robert wasn't interested. Her youngest brother, Norman, was a baby then, and Nana died before he had a chance to really know her. Chris's customary plastic smile softened when she recalled those summers and Nana's cooking lessons, fireside chats about Nana's botched acting career, and any other topic Chrissy or Nana introduced. This was the reprieve Chrissy needed, the sum of Nana's time minus the "insanity" she knew so well at home.

Later on, when Chrissy left home at age sixteen, never to return again, her investment of time with Nana who had died the previous summer helped her through many a tough spot. Chrissy, actually, "Chris" (because the day she left was the day she officially changed the way she would be identified) took her work money, which she had saved "forever," and rented a room in the next town. She continued her job as an administrative assistant and finished her G.E.D. at night. She earned enough to finally enter nursing school and obtain her degree.

In the meantime, she predictably ended up in very abusive and dysfunctional relationships with men who "needed her." She eventually married one of them, had three children, and then divorced "the loser." Presently, when she came to see me, she had been remarried for about five years to a somewhat better choice but not much improved from her earlier predilections.

Her mother had died, and her father, whom Mother had finally divorced about five years after Chris left home, now lived with her and her truck driver husband, Jack. Daddy, as she continued to call her father, held an unduly firm grip on her emotions similar to the tight physical clutches he used to have on her as a child in those late night encounters. She was constantly under the scrutiny of her husband, Jack, for including Daddy in everything and thereby not meeting Jack's needs. She was in a quandary as to how to muddle through all this, and due to not having the coping skills to deal with all this turmoil, she had developed what the doctor's called Chronic Fatigue Syndrome. In addition, she experienced anxiety attacks, where for hours at a time she felt as if she couldn't catch her breath.

Chris was still working as a nurse, as well as providing gourmet meals for her husband and father. Of course, all the holidays were celebrated by the extended family at her house and naturally, she was the gracious hostess. Among her female friendships, with a few exceptions, she was the arranger and support person for all the others.

No surprise this woman was tired! She was an overworked Wonder Woman.

You can see how Chris's past helped to shape who she is today, or at least who she was when she first entered my office. With Chris, as with all the patients I treat, even though they want to be out of pain, to make the past go away, they simultaneously are compelled to hold onto their past for dear life.

It's human nature to fight the change for which we are yearning. So it was for Chris. From the first day we met, Chris and I were preparing for battle: her fight to keep herself exactly the way she had been functioning as her miserable self, pitted against my job to help her overcome the fear to move ahead. I became her fairy godmother but, no, I couldn't, on day one, make some of the proclamations I just presented above. I had to help her find the fairy godmother within herself who, after the cobwebs were cleared, would come to know her own value, her right to breathe all the air she needed, her entitlement to live in this world as much as anyone else, yes, even if she didn't take care of the others around her. And if bad things happened, it wasn't because she had caused those catastrophes.

I'll be talking about Chris throughout the rest of these pages, but even though waiting for knowledge and insight isn't easy, you will have to gain understanding of her the way I did. We saw each other twice a week. When time was up in one session, I had to bide my time just as you will be doing until the next encounter to discover how the story would develop...

You ask: Why would people be reluctant to give up pain? Don't they want to feel better?

At a workshop entitled "Do I Have To Change the Past In Order To Take Charge of the Present?" I asked participants to address their natural resistance toward facing reality, the reticence that comes from fear of any kind of change. I asked them to complete the following phrases with one positive and one negative answer: If I change, I... If I take charge, I... If I take responsibility, I... If I forgive my parents. I...

The examples I gave were: If I change, I'll be independent, and then I'll lose my friends who want me to go along with their wishes. If I let go of a behavior that is dysfunctional for me, I'll feel free, but then I'll have no way to control my impulses. If I change, I'll get what I want, but I won't know how to handle being happy for a change and people will stop calling me to see how I am. If I take charge, I'm forgiving my parents, and they don't deserve to be forgiven. If I take charge, my parents will get what *they* wanted, a good girl, etc. If I take responsibility, then I have to stop blaming others. If I take responsibility, with what will I replace it (this behavior, habit, defensive stance)? How will I fill up the emptiness? If I take responsibility, then I have to give up being the child and become the adult. Then people will expect too much from me or won't take care of me anymore.

Hey, my conversation partner: how would *you* fill in the blanks? Later in the workshop, I read the following:

> When you were growing up, you came to believe certain things about yourself based on your experiences with your family, friends, and school. As time went on, you took these beliefs and turned them into facts about yourself without question. Today, a fairy godmother comes along to set the record straight. She wants you to understand that what you learned as a child about yourself is not necessarily the way you actually are.
>
> Here are examples of some of the specific things your fairy godmother might say: *Because you were given lots of rules to follow didn't mean you were an uncontrollable person. Because they were angry with you doesn't mean you were a bad person. Because you were unique and sometimes nonconforming does not mean you were incorrigible. Because your daddy left you, doesn't mean you are unlovable. Because*

> *you were called names by people who took out their problems on*
> *you doesn't mean those words were true about you.*

I, psychologist, Phyliss Shanken, am asking you, my new friend, what does your fairy godmother tell you?

Wouldn't it be grand if we would know all this good stuff from the start? Who are the people in our lives who will tell us we're not only okay, but we're wonderful and all we need to be is ourselves? Ultimately, in order to make change, it's not what others tell us but what we must end up believing about ourselves!

WHY "PERFECT" STRANGERS?

I love to talk to strangers. And every stranger starts out "perfect." When you don't know anything about people, there can be nothing wrong with them. They are perfect. At least that's how I feel about people in general. I have no preconceived notions about the human beings who walk into my office nor the ones I meet out on the street.

Have you ever gone on an airplane and sat next to a perfect stranger? You strike up a conversation, and you each spill out your life story. You wonder: what would behoove me to share all that information about myself with someone I don't even know?

You meet someone in a checkout line at the supermarket, and you both commiserate about the high price of lettuce. Sharing the same crisis, you feel close to this person. Now you're not so alone in your budgetary dilemma.

I savor the connections I enjoy with each new person I encounter and with many people I will never see again. Sometimes, I get in a little too deep. I forget that others don't view human contact the way I do. As I speak, warning bells begin chiming in my head, the ones that tell me I'm acting a bit too weird. I know this by the look on their dumbstruck faces. I feel as if I have walloped them, the way a hardball smacks a window and the batter says, "Oops!" My intensity overwhelms people. Often, there is a very long pause as the person's speechlessness becomes a companion to his or her sculptured posture. Then I admonish myself: don't I ever learn?

I think I barge in on people's psyches when I'm outside my office, because I have to be restrained in the office and in the real world. I'm finally permitted to totally be my usual curious self without having to be so responsible for the other person. Both in my practice as well as in the outside world, I want to grab onto human beings I "bump into" who start out as perfect strangers, and after having made a major impact on my life, eventually say good-bye to me. These new arrivals gradually become familiar to me, and in the same way I feel when I hug my children, I want to squeeze them to pieces. Okay, not really, but really. I fall in love with everyone who shows his inner workings to me.

With outside strangers or with my patients, I try to *squeeze the moment.* I am a vessel into which my patients pour their liquid secrets. Over time, I gradually replay what they have built up in me and give them back these confidences couched in an illuminating way so they can be enlightened by what they see. Together, we are making poetry in therapy. Within my core, I am a romantic. Without design, over and over, I somehow end up in a love place, finding ways to extrude a metaphor of heart. If my patients don't produce poetry, then I perform the deed by reflecting on their singular words and phrases with a literary spirit.

Speaking of poetry, here is a fragment of one of mine that reflects my intensity*: Like a vulture I eat life/ and leave broken bones/ so others will know/ I have lived.*

So much for the "stranger" part of the deal. How about the "perfect" part? I believe that people are perfect when they are born and manage to get messed up along the way. So they are perfect when they come to see me, and then gradually, as they share their history, the "imperfection" reveals itself. I don't really see it as imperfection, more as the stuff that gets in their way of functioning, but often they see their vulnerabilities or weaknesses as "failures" versus traits that were wrought from their early life experiences.

KEVIN

This is the question Kevin and I needed to explore. Kevin was another visitor who arrived in my office and generously shed his unfamiliar façade to become a "stranger no more" to me and to himself. We set out to remove the barriers in his way of allowing himself to develop into a grown-up version of the little baby in the bassinet who had been born "perfect."

Kevin had a vague memory of a man with gigantic hands and dirty fingernails who carried sleepy Kevin on his back after taking the little guy out of the car at the end of a long family trip. He even remembers feigning sleep so the big man would carry him; he liked the smell of his daddy's hair. It must have been the greasy hair tonic, because Mr. Herbert's hair was *shiiiiiiiny*, to be sure. Sometimes Kevin gingerly put his own tiny hands on Daddy's hair, tap, tap, tapping against the glossy black strands that stood erect like his toy soldiers did, all stuck together and standing at attention. Daddy's laugh was like a loud echo. He didn't mind when Kevin touched his well-combed hair. In fact, Kevin was the only one allowed to do it.

Daddy's friends busted on Daddy. They lightheartedly asked, "Is that shellac you use?" Then they would move toward him, lifting their hands toward his head as if to check on the answer.

And half joking, half serious in an affected voice, Steve Herbert would say, "Don't touch the hair!"

Kevin had confusing memories of loud grunts coming from his parents' room and sometimes scary shouts, but Kevin wasn't sure if he heard these before or after his father died.

After Daddy died, Mommy went to pieces. It seemed to Kevin that she grieved and grieved and cried and cried all the time. The first time he saw her do it, he said to her, "Mommies don't cry."

"Your daddy died, Kevvie boy. He's never coming back!"

Then Kevin cried too but still wouldn't accept the truth. He ran around the house touching everything in sight singing, "Daddy is sleeping. Daddy is sleeping." He might have said, "Daddy is on a business trip," and would have gotten himself to believe it, because his father traveled a lot, but Kevin had seen his father at the time of his death.

Kevin had been right there in the garage by the car. He had been watching his father work on the "jalopy," as Mommy called it, something Daddy did every weekend. Daddy loved that car, and Kevin watched his Daddy at work as often as he was permitted. His father made him sit on a big stool and promise not to get off unless he announced his exodus. Mr. Herbert was worried his son might get hurt on the equipment or one of the tools might fall on his foot.

Kevin loved it when his father finished up and washed his hands in the big laundry sink. He would rub with a nailbrush, using grainy gray soap that scratched his skin. Kevin knew all about the soap, because Daddy allowed him to try it. He remembered the warmth of Daddy's hands on his and how clean he felt after Daddy dried them. Then Kevin's eyes became transfixed as Daddy got a pointy thing to clean the grease from his nails, but his hands never really got spick and span, except maybe by the end of the week, but then as Daddy went back to work on the car, the dirt would start to build up again.

One Sunday morning, both father and son took their usual spots in the garage, Daddy under the car and Kevin on his stool. Suddenly, the jack that holds up the car gave way and crushed his father but only after his father had pushed back on the moveable metal bed, getting only his head out from under. It was a good thing. Otherwise, Kevin might have seen his father's head crushed in. In the end, all Kevin saw was his dad's face that looked like a person face-up toward the ceiling and taking a nap on the ice-cold floor.

As an adult, Kevin couldn't recall if he started to smell alcohol on his mother's breath before or after his father died. What he does know is that everything changed. Because he didn't remember much about life before the tragic day, he couldn't really say what the difference was.

There were long periods of time when his mother was away, "to get dried out," is what everyone used to say. During those times Kevin stayed with his mom's brother, Uncle Morton, and Aunt Mary, a childless couple who gave him lots of hugs, bedtime stories, milk and cookies, and plenty of books and toys. It wasn't too bad being without his mom at those times. However, at their house, he had nightmares:

> Thumping giants with black fingernails and toes marched around the outside of the house. They snuck into the bedroom where he slept at his aunt and uncle's house. They swept him into their bazooka arms as he tried to wriggle free. They tossed his now limp body into a black van made only for Goliath. There were no windows, but a bonfire burned inside.
>
> As Kevin's sweat poured out of him like a hose about to go dry, the giants bellowed: "You are a bad boy! We are taking you where bad boys go, boys who hurt their mothers!"

When he awoke screaming from these bad dreams, he could not be consoled for hours. Many a night of sleep was lost by his loving aunt and uncle. Eventually, his mom would come back, and Kevin's bellyaches would start up again. He had trouble eating. No wonder he was a skinny kid. Mom got angry with him, because whenever he came back from Aunt Mary and Uncle Morty's house, he had gained maybe ten pounds.

Mom would say, "Why don't you eat like that in *my* house?"

This awareness of his having thrived without her and his being uncooperative at the dinner table really drove her mad. "Kevin, you don't have a stomach ache. You just want to make me

43

mad, you stupid nudnik. You are a lazy, good-for-nothing sloth. You're gonna sit here until you clean the plate. I mean lick it clean, you dimwit."

Of course, she was drunk. Then she probably went to her room to sleep it off.

Kevin sat at the table in a quandary about what to do. If Mom was her usual drunk self, she would probably sleep it off and forget what happened, but could he chance it? He sat for hours at the table, or sometimes he found a way to get rid of the food (with no tell-tale signs—he was good at it and became more talented the older he grew.) Whenever his mom awoke, be it that evening or the next day, she presented herself to him as if nothing had happened. In her husky, hoarse voice, she would moan and whine about how sick she felt, but as soon as she had her coffee and the first cigarette, she put out her arms to Kevin, hugged him, and told him what a handsome young man he was turning out to be.

Eventually Mom stopped going on those long trips away. She gave up alcohol, she stopped being verbally abusive, and Kevin's nightmares ceased. The only problem was, by the time Kevin was in junior high school, Mom went out at night and sometimes didn't return until morning. There were days when he left for school and she still hadn't returned.

By high school age, he heard whispers about his mom, but he found a way to close his ears to them. His ability to not hear or see what was right there in front of him increased through high school and college. Kevin sensed it but didn't want to face reality: his mother had become what people referred to as *the town whore*. He had intuited this truth but was very protective of his mom. Not that he would fight to defend her, no, he used the "I didn't hear or see it" tactic, but in his mind, his mom was a good woman. She just had a few problems, that's all.

Kevin could have physically fought battles for her, because he grew into a large, athletic guy who worked out with weights and was the star first basemen on the school baseball team. His love of baseball helped to divert him from the truth, particularly about his mom. He memorized all kinds of baseball trivia, read magazines, and never missed a pro game on television or radio.

Kevin managed okay with women; he was actually a pushover because he tried so hard to please them. He was often caught up in lies he told to save himself from their demands. His passivity eventually drove women crazy, one by one, and he was out looking to get attached yet again. Finally, he found a woman to marry, or should I say, she found him. She latched on with the claws of an eagle, sunk them into Kevin's heartstrings, and they were married. He had been attracted to her, because she presented herself as very self-sufficient and ready to take care of him, not the kind who would ever leave him.

Unfortunately, she changed. Yep, the day after they were married, on the first day of their honeymoon, she got sick on something she ate at the restaurant in which they dined. After that, she contracted one sickness after another, and he basically became her nursemaid. Oh, how you try to get away from one thing and end up with the very thing you thought you escaped!

Despite her ailments, she did manage to give birth to a baby boy, but Kevin had to provide most of the care. He was the disciplinarian, which he hated to be, so his son, Dirk, grew up in an inconsistent atmosphere just as Kevin had in his own youth. (Yes, history does have a way of repeating itself.) If Kevin imposed a punishment, he invariably changed his mind after the pronouncement. Or, as Dirk grew older, Dirk fought to get his own way and won. All Dirk had to do was sulk, balk, or the best one of all was to accuse Kevin of not loving him.

Many things happened in between, which Kevin relayed to me as we went along, but ultimately, to be expected, Dirk left home and rarely made contact again except to call his mother now and then and never ask to speak to Kevin.

When fifty-year-old Kevin came to see me, he was angry and depressed. At work, he flew off the handle at the slightest provocation, and most of these incidents were exaggerated or imagined by him. He was having an affair with a single unmarried thirty-eight-year-old woman Diane, for whom he had babysat when he was a kid. She adored him and wanted him to divorce his wife so they could be married. She's the one who sent him to me, hoping for him to "get his head on straight" so he would make the right moves. Kevin's wife and he hadn't slept in the same room for years and lived in a silent household with blank walls with maybe a few pictures of Dirk on the end tables. Kevin's auto parts shop was profitable but just barely.

Diane actually made the appointment for him, and I didn't know who she was at the time, but she had said she worked for him and his schedule prevented him from making the appointment for himself.

When he arrived, Kevin didn't know why he was here, but Diane said it would help, so here he was. Fortunately, Kevin had good recall about his life and was pleasantly cooperative when I asked him for elaboration, so the first session went smoothly. His suspicious nature shone through, however, when I asked him about his marriage.

His eyes darted from right to left several times; he started to say something then stopped himself and asked, "Why do you want to know?" The words were straightforward, but this guy was not only angry; he was scared.

"I'm wanting to get to know about you and your life so we can identify the problem and see how I might be helpful."

His rising chest seemed to sink lower, and for a moment our eyes met almost in a fixed stare. It was as if he were deciding whether to go on the trust route or not.

I smiled slightly. "Is there something about my asking the question that troubles you?"

Chuckling, he said, "No, I was just checking."

Ready. Get set. Go. The journey had begun. We were on our way…

PARTNERS IN PAIN

So how do I feel after I've met for the first time someone like Chris or Kevin? Do I just turn off the lights, lock the door, and go home? I'm supposed to leave my patients at the office and not bring them home with me, right? Nay. Not I. Not I. Especially when people are new to me, more like strangers, I am likely to think about and look forward to seeing them again. It's exciting to unravel the spider web threads surrounding these new characters in our mutual play and to examine what makes it problematic for them to clearly discover their personal route to inner peace.

People often ask: "How can you stand listening to people's problems all day? Don't psychologists have to put up a wall so you're not affected by your patients?"

Here are some of my responses:

The most important ingredient in my training was that I entered into my own personal analysis with a doctor who specializes not only in treatment, but also in training others to conduct psychotherapy. Yep. I was what you call analyzed: four times a week, lying on a couch, crying my eyes out. Why not? I've been a crier from birth. Actually, I'm a laugher too. When I emerged from the womb, the doctor slapped me on the behind, and what did I do? I laughed. (I've already given myself permission to lie. Why not now? I like the image.)

My own therapy helped me to understand what it feels like to be a patient, to examine my conflicts and motivation, and to receive difficult and unwanted feedback, which, of course, I proudly resisted, as any good psychoanalytic patient will do, if she has any oomph to her.

I resolved many of my own hang-ups before I met face to face with someone who needed my help. So, when I began treating people, I felt assured I could separate myself from my patients.

CHRISSY

What do I mean by separation of self? In my work with Chris, I can provide an illustration. As we went along, there were times when I felt angry with her. Here she was pouring out her chronicle of how this one or that one was hurting her, and I'm imagining the joy I would feel if I could punch her in the mouth! Uh oh. A big no-no for a psychologist. I've learned enough about myself to know that I don't generally fantasize about hurting people. I'm a kind, gentle woman. If my compassion were a liquid, it would overflow from most containers. Loving feelings often ooze out of me. If most people could see the real me, they would probably get nauseous from my sappiness, which, by the way, is one reason I don't show it most of the time. Okay, I know all this about myself. It's for real. So why would I want to punch poor Chrissy in the mouth?

I know my aggressive impulses are coming from her. I also know and will definitely check it out with her that there must be others in her life who react in a similar fashion. Why is she in such an abusive relationship? Why do people use her the way they do? I also know that masochistic people often bring out the sadistic side of others. The fact that this sadistic part of me has been called forth from under my facade again and that I'm not using her to work out my own issues confirms my hypotheses about her.

The idea of punching Chris in the mouth rather than in the stomach is revealing as well. She maintained a fixed smile on her face, which was supposed to be a good camouflage for the grimace that I hypothesized was probably more true to her inner workings. She thought she was getting away with it: her fear that I might abandon her by "killing myself" as her mother attempted to do merely because I was detecting her unhappiness governed her need to smile in the face of misery. When I fantasized about punching her in the mouth, I was most likely wanting to say, "You are sad and lying about it. Wipe that smile off your face, young lady!" the way her mother, in essence, was telling her to put the smile on or lose mother.

Because I know who I am and am certain that my reaction has nothing to do with my hang-ups but rather has to do with Chris's impact on people, I can move ahead and feel confident I'm treating Chris, and not myself. Although I don't tell her my association about my urge to hurt her, I use this daydream of mine to help her see how she covers negative feelings with feigned happiness and how this brings out the aggressive counterpoint in those around her. (Later on, I'll talk more about how I make use of my personal associations, memories, feelings, and hunches, which are all stored in my unconscious mind.)

KEVIN

By understanding what makes me tick, I can ascertain, for instance, why I'm unexpectedly feeling overwhelmed. I'll take note: why am I all of a sudden doubting my ability to help Kevin? Am I in touch with his feeling of hopelessness, which is due to his insecurity about and fear of not knowing what will happen next and how others (his mom) will react to the same behavior he exhibited only yesterday? His reality testing was impaired. When he said or did something, he was never given confirmation that his actions could help or hinder a situation. What appeared positive turned out to be negative, and vice versa, depending on his mother's mood. Of course, I always have to ask myself: has our discussion of Dirk's, his grown son's, "dumping on" Kevin, triggered something in my memory or current life that is overwhelming to me but unrelated to him? In other words, do I feel "dumped on" in my life and feeling unable to control it and therefore overwhelmed about my ability to help Kevin? I must and do ask this question every time I experience emotions with my patients—which is just about always.

I make many of my interpretations from observing how the person relates to me. Since I don't take anything personally, the person can tell me how he or she is feeling about something I did or didn't do, and we can learn from it. I might ask: "When else in your life have you felt this way?" Or, "Why, if you say I'm so important in your life, do you treat me as if I'm a stranger?" so that we can explore a person's ambivalence about getting close to others.

The love cake is a good example of exploring the "I want you but stay away from me" stance. If you love someone and that person bakes all their love for you into a cake, wouldn't you want to eat it?

Suppose you said, "I don't need anything from you. You were rotten to me, and I feel powerless with you. If I ate your cake, you would have further power over me. No way!" That sure leaves you hungry, doesn't it?

Never mind. You go out and buy your own cake. Maybe you steal it. And you gobble up that cake as fast as you can say, "Take that! I hate you!" Well, you've retaliated against that bad person, but now you're getting mighty fat on your own anger and counter dependence. (Note: not independence, which can be healthy, but rather a fear reaction counter to or against the idea of being dependent.) You'd better start getting rid of the stuff with which you gorged yourself. It never sated your hunger anyway. You remain hungry, and the person who wants to give you her love is still there for the taking, taunting you and whetting your appetite again and again.

Just suppose at this point in your life, I become the baker of the love cake, and every time you come into a session, I present it to you in various forms of feedback, observations, affirmations, or questions to help you dig down into your gut for explanations of your pain, and you reject it because you are afraid if you succumb to me, I will devour or destroy the little bit of self you are clutching onto, and you will never be able to emerge from my control. You will be dependent on even the smallest "crumbs" with which I tease you.

I will confront you about this over and over, and you will hate me for it, but if you keep coming back, we might reach some understanding about why you use food as a way to say something totally unrelated to food but related to a close neighbor: love.

DICK

I have on occasion spontaneously experienced a grief reaction even when the person is relating a seemingly neutral topic. Often, I welled up in sessions with Dick, an elderly man whom I'll tell you more about later. In his case, this was a tip off that he was isolating his feelings. I would say, "Dick, how is it that you are smiling, and I feel like sobbing? I suspect I'm doing all the feeling for you!" (Remember the *internal camera method* where I match my feelings to what the person is saying and if these are out of synch, I might be onto something!) I revealed this contradiction while at the same time questioning him as to why he was afraid to look deeper. If I had tried to remain a detached "blank screen," I wouldn't have confronted Dick, and I would be an accomplice in his denial, his dismissal of emotion accompanying his uncomfortable thoughts, perhaps ones of which he is ashamed. It is from my engagement with him that we both learn together.

So, if I get this involved, how do I sleep at night? I do think about my patients when I'm "off duty," but I don't carry their pain with me as if it's my own. When I'm with them, I can feel their anguish, sometimes even more so than they feel it. Because I know where I end and the patient begins, I'm always aware their suffering does not belong to me.

Normally, believe it or not, I'm not actually analyzing people. I merely sit with them and see what happens. Yep, it's as simple as that. What astounds me is, you see, I don't say Dick has a problem expressing his anger toward his wife, so today we'll work on helping him with that. Instead, in essence, I say: "Hello, Dick, glad we have this time to spend together. I look forward to absorbing your anxiety, confusion, conflict, whatever comes my way as I open myself up to experience what it must feel like to be you."

Okay, I don't actually say this out loud, but it's essentially what is going on inside of me. We've having a conversation. That's all there is to it. Remember, you and I are in your living room by the fireplace having a nice chat. It's similar to what my patient and I are doing. In my kind of therapy, the only difference is that one of us has a trained way of looking at things. The one who is getting paid is good at active listening, researching, analyzing, and synthesizing. I was about to add to the list, "mesmerizing," but this can be a result, not the function of my job. One of us has a diverse set of experiences, has traveled the road not taken, and can give back a unique perspective to the other traveler on the journey to personal transformation.

Since we're on this journey together, I work hard to understand exactly what my patient is experiencing. I might have to "try on" or synchronize with him or her. This process has many advantages. First, for my patient, the mere overt expression of what ails him and what in his past haunts him is a cathartic process in and of itself. I've had people come to me for maybe two or three sessions, just long enough for us to imprint their histories on an imaginary tabloid equidistant between us. After which they say something like, "I'm feeling so much better. Do you think I need to come anymore?"

Imagine it this way: how many of you have anyone in your lives who really listens to you without being bowled over by your twisted stomach-wrenching tales of woe or who says, "Sure, sure. Now let me tell you what happened to *me*."

Then there are those who in disgust or fear turn their heads away like a doll with a twisty rubber head. It's as if your words and feelings made them avert their eyes, as if you had just struck them. But sitting with an authentic listener, their act of listening, or merely sitting with you as you release your distress, is a known antidote to solitary suffering.

Second, the idea is to help people go where they want to go and not to interject my goals for them. The places I want to go for myself are often much too deep for the preference of others. This reality of the disparity between most people and me is what often gets me into trouble in "real" life. I'm so curious; I want to find out more, incessantly wondering, "What do you really mean?"

You know something? I really do want to know. I take nothing for granted about how a person feels. I'm careful not to read into anyone's gestures or facial expressions. I always want to ask why. Fortunately, over the years, I've learned to exist without the answer.

I was saying that second of all, I have to go along with the patient's need and not treat him as if he were some alter ego of myself who always wants to know more, more, more about myself and about him, but delving further inside of himself is not necessarily what my patient wants for himself. It's not very sensible for me to say, "No, we've only scratched the surface. Don't leave yet."

EDNA

I remember a fifty-five-year-old woman, Edna, who came to me for depression. All I did was ask her what it was like for her growing up, and like a cloud burst, out poured a litany of sexual abuse experiences from age five to twelve that, of course, she had never told a soul about, and certainly was enough to make anyone depressed. We met two more times. Maybe I asked a few questions for clarification. I certainly mirrored in my posture and facial expression my sympathy for what I imagined she had endured, and I'm sure she got the message that I didn't consider what her father did to her to be her fault. Voila! At the third session, she said she was feeling better and didn't need to come back. She knew what she had needed. She called the shots. Despite my wish to provide her additional relief from other sources of stress in her life, her self-chosen decision was fine with me.

I guess we've established by now that I do feel my patients' pain. The extreme of my emotions has been viewed by some as ridiculous.

Yes, I've had great self-training in the art of learning to curb my emotions, but only to the outside world. In all my life, I never lost my wacky treasure chest of emotion. And once I came to accept myself as an offbeat, creative, compassionate person, I not only didn't discard my passions, I came to embrace them. How fortunate for my patients, many of whom came to me completely clueless as to what a feeling other than happy/sad is.

JANIE

At an all-night marathon group therapy retreat when I was exhausted and more vulnerable to blurt things out and less likely to think before I spoke, I urged Janie to reveal more about her struggle with anorexia. She had been active in the group but talked about everything except her disorder. After months of laying low and not pressuring her to open up on this topic, I said, "Tell the rest of the group how much you weighed when you first came to see me." My memory of those early months of therapy vividly and unexpectedly returned to me, and without warning, my tears gave way.

In the first months of treatment, she had been skin and bones and suicidal. The rest of the group sat in rapt silence. Janie had achieved so much in psychotherapy, but it had been touch-and-go for a while. I could have focused on her stick-thin legs, but most of all, I'll never forget her eyes. In all my years of working with eating-disorder patients, I had never seen anything like it. Around her eye sockets were giant blue circles. I had seen the hollow cheekbones before, the veiny hands with bulging knuckles and other characteristics that made many of my eating disorder patients resemble concentration camp victims. For a young woman who believed it was her job to keep her mother happy, the tears that erupted from me when I asked her to share her history were a real no-no.

I didn't apologize or make excuses for my behavior. There are times when I do express regret to a patient, but not for allowing her to see what I felt deep inside for her. What I did do was ask her and the group to share how they felt about my reaction. Thank goodness our marathon was an all-nighter. We could have used a few extra days to pursue the issues that were stimulated: feelings toward overly emotional mothers, love toward me because of my compassion, fear of my being vulnerable and then whose shoulder could they cry on, fear I'm not the strong person they thought I was. More. More. More.

I hold back most of the time, because even though some patients welcome my empathic expression of synchronicity with them, others would be distracted by my intense emotion and feel responsible for me.

We'll come back to all this later.

SHEILA

I'm reminded of Sheila. Whenever Sheila didn't do what her mother wanted her to do, her mother manipulated her to take care of mother's needs by sobbing loudly behind closed doors. If Mother were confronted by others about this behavior, she would deny the effect and say, "I didn't want you to see how upset I was, so that's why I closed the door," as if her loud sobs were inaudible. If she had been so concerned about how Sheila would receive her mother's display of misery, why wouldn't mother try to stifle the sound? Sheila learned to deny emotion even when it was readily visible: no, it didn't happen. I'm fine. Mother is fine. Why do I feel so empty?

In our mission for you to get some bennies from listening to my patients and me, let's pause for a second while I ask you to do something for yourself. We all need a break sometimes, especially from our Partners in Pain discussion just as I do when I've seen many people in a row.

Think of how many things you do because you *want* to do it and how many you do that aren't necessary for survival, those that originate merely from your *need to please others* or because, as Sheila did, you fear you might lose them. Ask yourself what it costs you to compromise your own self for the sake of getting some imagined goodies from others to whom you've given power. Make yourself a list, check it twice, and question each action or behavior.

Your paper should have five columns: *Action or Behavior*; *Rationale* (for performing the action); *Cost to Me* (for going through with it); *Benefit to Me* (by my making the choice to sacrifice my internal needs to be my own person); *Decision for Future Action*. Most of the items might be ones you would choose to do over again because even though there are costs, you decide the benefits are worth the sacrifice. But, at least after this exercise, you will have the choice and not just be on automatic!

With that little recess, dear Reader, we will follow the thread I had been interweaving into my introduction as to how I work.

Sometimes, even before the patient realizes it, I see change occurring, and I want to lift up my clenched hand and shout, "Yes!" but my expressing this would be premature.

VICTOR

On occasion, I've allowed my enthusiasm for people's progress to overtake me. Twenty-five-year-old Victor, a homosexual man I treated, needed a certain kind of support from me and was very responsive to my exuberant cheerleading:

"Victor, look how you were able to convey your feelings to me! Remember when I used to ask you how you felt and you would say over and over, 'I don't know. I don't know.'?" His eyebrows formed a wrinkled V shape, and I determined that if he were freer, he would have cried at those times.

"Today you told me you felt guilty about how you treated your brothers. You said the other night you were furious with your mom because she was so pushy about her wanting you to stay home and keep her company and how sad you felt when your mother took attention from you and gave it to your newborn brother, and you gleefully shared memories of your grandma, how much you loved and missed her." He always closed his eyes languorously and grinned like a child when he spoke of his grandma.

"You're really learning how to express yourself, Victor. You're finding out who you are. Bravo!"

CHERYL

Withholding my thoughts can be the name of the game for me. How many times did I want to say to Cheryl: "Don't you get it? You're okay. Your abusive mother doesn't live here anymore!" I wanted Cheryl to see how she was treating her husband as if he were her mother, when in reality, he was just trying to please her. Due to her over sensitivity to being "crushed" by misperceptions of criticism, I had to bide our time and internally slap my hand and say to myself, "Shut up, Phyliss!"

KEVIN

A difficult emotion for me to tolerate is what I call "I want to take you home to live at my house" feeling. Remember Kevin, the man who lost his father at an early age and whose mother was hospitalized many times for alcoholism? He brought out this maternal tenderness in me. But Kevin needed to work through his defense of personalizing any subsequent loss as an abandonment, about which he fantasized his having done something wrong to cause it.

We found clues in his early nightmares of giants (his dad was a large man) with black fingers and toes (his father's black grease under his fingernails) taking him away because he was bad for hurting his mother (he was convinced it was his fault his mother had to go to a hospital for treatment of alcoholism). This early belief was further reinforced by his mother's verbal abuse, particularly when she was drunk. My mothering him too much wouldn't have helped him; it would have been even more detrimental, because when his mother was sober, she was apologetic and loving but then turned on him again when drunk. Subsequently, he became more confused as to how to read people. Is Phyliss's loving expression an indication of her caring about me, or is it the love that comes before or after a tirade of battering declarations?

Whenever we met, I often thought, *If only I could bring him to my house and give him what he missed—a steady, consistent, honest depiction of love—it would be so much easier for him.* My eyes would moisten, and the old familiar lump in my throat from submerging my emotions would make itself known to me, the way my throat used to throb as a child when I exhibited my tears and others were saying I was making "too big a deal" over nothing.

I'm ordinarily an expressive person. It went against my grain to withhold my feelings. With Kevin, I often waited until he left my office, after which, I allowed my sentiments to come gushing out.

SARAH

I'm reminded of Sarah, a woman with whom I worked for about a year for treatment of anxiety. One day, she told me her doctor had called her to report her mammogram looked suspicious. She left my office, and I felt as if my good friend had just gotten kicked in the stomach. I thought about her and waited for her to call with the results of the biopsy she was to have. She never did. Instead, she returned for her regularly scheduled appointment as if this were just business as usual for me. I went out to the waiting room to see the answer on her gray-colored face, with newly formed wrinkles. Her eyes darted to and fro as she smiled politely and said, "Hi."

How is it people don't know how they impact me? (Duh! Phyliss, you're a psychologist. You know better than to ask that question!)

During that session, with her hands clasped over her knees and only moving them to reach for a tissue, she told me how devastated she was, because the doctors insisted she have a mastectomy ASAP. I remember that session vividly, because as soon as she left, I immediately rushed into the therapist meeting room in my group practice, grabbed a colleague of mine, blubbered out something or other, and fell into her arms sobbing.

DICK

I worked with a very sweet man named Dick, who I mentioned earlier, the guy who I said, "Dick, how is it that you are smiling, and I feel like sobbing? I suspect I'm doing all the feeling for you!"

Dick had a chronic heart disease and was always in danger of sudden death. In the meantime, a slow and progressive invalidism threatened his existence and frightened him terribly. It was as if he and I were companions, sitting on a bench, waiting for a tsunami to appear out of nowhere and gush over us, knocking us over. We kept each other company in the process.

At that time, we met in my home office, and my dog, Roxie, sat with us. Dick would come in and ask, "Where's Roxie?" and I would open the door to the residential part of my home and, of course, Roxie, having heard Dick come in, was right there waiting for the invitation. She would greet him and jump onto his lap as soon as he sat down.

What scared Dick more than dying and going to an unknown state of being was that due to his death, his very dependent wife would be left alone with no one to take care of her. I told him I would watch out for his wife, whom I also treated, and if he had to die, he needn't worry about her.

When I was told he had been rushed to the hospital and on life support, I called him and invited him to share his feelings. His first words had to do with his concerns for Alice. "Dick, I want you to know, when you die, I promise I will continue to help Alice become stronger and more self-reliant. She'll be okay."

He died two hours later. I've always wondered: *Was it because I basically gave him permission to die?*

I definitely want to tell you more about Dick later on, but for now I will tell you what happened when I learned of his death. The cold, cruel answering service phoned me at home and reported to me, "Mrs. Randell called to say that her husband, Richard, died this morning."

Nooooo. Aaaaaaah. A noise erupted from me I had never heard before. Was it a cry? A guffaw? I couldn't speak correctly. In a froglike croak, as if it really mattered (I think I was trying to turn this into a neutral and objective phone call), I asked, "What time did that call come in?"

Do you think I remember the answer? Who cares what time it was? I was all alone at home and desperately needing someone with whom I could talk and cry and grieve. But I'm not allowed to tell anyone. I called Mrs. Randall to express my condolences, and her brother answered. I had met him at a family session, so I was able to say who I was. I said I was so sorry to hear of the family's loss, and I wanted to leave a message for Mrs. Randall, because I didn't want to bother her on this difficult occasion.

I heard Mrs. Randall's inquisitive voice in the background. When she found out it was I on the phone, she requested to speak to me. She cried and told me the details of his passing. She asked me what he and I spoke about when I had called him at the hospital just the day before. Uh oh. This is always a difficult place for us psychologists. Even after a person dies, you must maintain confidentiality. I wanted to soothe her, but what could I say? I also didn't want to come across too therapisty (another one of my invented words) by being cold and in-your-face protective of the ethics, you know the deal. I said we had discussed his feelings about dying, and he reiterated to me what he had told the family: no extreme measures to keep him alive. This elucidation seemed to suffice.

Well, that was it. We got off the phone, and there I was again—alone. I started cursing and shouting, "You all have each other, and I'm not allowed to be with you." I was furious. Finally, I had a brainstorm: I would call the therapist who led the men's group, of which Dick was a member. Michael was a colleague, and Dick had signed a release saying the group therapist and I could consult with each other about his treatment. What a lucky break! I called Michael immediately, and fortunately, rather than my having to leave a message and pace the floor waiting, he picked up the phone. Due to his failing health, Dick had not attended Michael's group for the last few months, so Michael knew that Dick's death had been imminent.

"Thank goodness you're there, Michael," I exclaimed. "Dick Randall died this morning and—" I broke into sobs on the phone. Michael was silent while I collected myself. "I feel so alone, and the family is together, and it wouldn't be appropriate for me to go there, so I'm glad I can at least talk to you. You are the only other person who knew him."

"Phyliss, you're overreacting. You are too involved with him. You should take distance."

A thunderbolt hit me. Betrayal. Yes, that's what I felt: betrayed. Man, talk about laying yourself open to someone you think you can trust, someone in the field for God's sake, and what do you get? "You're overreacting." My stomach felt the punch, and I wanted to strike back, "For Christ's sake, Michael, I worked with the guy for three years, twice a week. I know his whole family. What do you think I am, a robot or something? He just died a few hours ago. Give me a break.'"

"Well, your reaction is beyond what a therapist should feel is all I was saying."

Whew. The whole interaction put a real cramp in my day. I did settle down, but only after I allowed myself to cry freely. In grief, if you don't empty the mourning bucket of tears completely, you are in danger of suffering depression, which is a sensation of a heavy, dark cloud encasing you. Sadness is distinguished from depression, because there is more of a focus. You know what it is that is making you sad. When you are depressed, you feel a pervasive, murky mountain of weight on you causing you to sigh a lot or well up and not know why. So I allowed myself to be sad, thereby forgoing the depression for another day...

A few days later, I went to the funeral. It was weird, because just a few relatives in the immediate family knew who I was, but no one else did and, of course, I didn't tell them. So, picture this: there I was, sitting in the back of the church, crying more so than one would expect from a casual acquaintance. I felt like a mystery woman dressed in black, all alone. Who knows what people fantasized about my relationship with Dick? Once again, I was in a position where I had all this emotion but felt it inappropriate to display. The lump in my throat and chest was throbbing. After the funeral, the family went to the cemetery and then back to a relative's house. Of course, I was left out again.

Rarely, but sometimes, I really do hate my profession.

JIMMY

Another time I got caught in a web of needing to be consoled and having virtually no outlet in which to debrief was after I met with the parents of a fifteen-year-old boy, Jimmy. I had been treating Jimmy for about a year, and I surmised that his father was physically abusing him. It was a sticky situation in that this was an everyday family with whom I had met for a number of times in family therapy. They were all likeable people and certainly stressed to their limit because this teenager, Jimmy, was very challenging to them. I could completely understand how he could bring them to the edge of violence, because he did seem to delight in pushing their buttons and maneuvering them to fly off the handle. It was clear he was fighting back because of their expecting more from him than he could produce, and the parents favored the younger brother who was, of course, the model kid. How many times had I seen this scenario? So comparisons were made often, sort of "why can't you be more like your brother" exclamations.

At isolated instances, there was accidental damage inflicted on Jimmy. I was sure the physical wounds were not intentionally administered. Jimmy often tested his parents, and at those times his father would come after him, mainly to stop him from doing something or to shut him up from a tirade. Then accidents would occur. For example, his father lunged to get Jimmy off of his younger brother whom Jimmy was brutalizing, and his father inadvertently pushed against Jimmy, who fell down the steps.

I usually got a call from Mother after these events. She wasn't complaining about Father. She merely wanted me to know that another incident had occurred in which they were at their wits end and also to ask me, "Is therapy really helping?"

Needless to say, as much as I felt I was helping Jimmy, I too felt exasperated.

After one of these phone calls from Mother, I considered it my professional responsibility to consult with a colleague. Number one, I was getting discouraged and losing some of my objectivity. Number two, I wondered what my obligation was to this boy in terms of his safety. But I knew if I confronted the father in any way, Father would pull Jimmy out of therapy just as Jimmy and I were really making headway. Could I take that risk?

My colleague told me I had to report this case and not take it upon myself to decide if this was an abuse case or not. I was obligated to report my suspicions to the Department of Children and Youth, and they would be the ones to decide. He said that if I didn't report the case, and if on one of these occasions this boy did get seriously hurt—such as falling down the steps, breaking his neck, and becoming a quadriplegic—I would be liable. The question would be asked: "You mean you knew of times when Jimmy's father caused him bodily harm, and you never reported it?"

My fellow advisor said also the Children and Youth Department would probably drop the case or suggest that father get therapy. The result wouldn't hurt much, because on occasion, Father was already in family therapy with me. I could tell the family the likelihood of no further legal or other drastic action, and you never know, all might turn out okay, especially if they understood my reporting the father was my ethical responsibility and that my hands were tied.

I agonized over the decision and to this day, I continue to believe it was the most excruciatingly difficult professional determination I ever had to make, even worse than committing someone against her will to a mental health hospital.

I asked to see the boy and his parents but didn't tell them why. I didn't have to do this. I could have reported Father, and all they would have been told is that someone reported them, but I felt it my duty to tell them to their faces what I was going to do. I believe that even if it's unbearably difficult, you must "face the music" and be true to yourself. You don't take the easy way out at the cost of your integrity. Otherwise, in the end, you pay for your deceit or attempts at distraction by suffering from stomach aches, headaches, depression, anxiety, and any other psychosomatic or psychological condition that happens to be the usual place where you are vulnerable. Also, if I had reported the father anonymously, Father would have certainly blamed Jimmy as the culprit. I had to tell the family everything.

They all greeted me in the waiting room in their customarily friendly style. I had always believed this family liked me. And I liked them. I was sympathetic to all of their perspectives. The father was gruff and quick to temper, but in the last few sessions, I had managed to get through some of his austerity and into the soft side of him. We had talked about how difficult his growing up had been. I linked some of his past to why he was now inordinately frustrated with his son even in instances when his son had done nothing wrong. He relaxed, and we even laughed together.

I know people write in books and songs about how they can hear their heart pounding—you know the drill—but I'm telling you, I truly felt as if my heart were bulging through my chest. Here I am smiling my usual greeting and almost wondering if they could see the bulbous blood vessels that were rhythmically beating. Tick tick. Tick tick, like a time bomb. Bong. Bong.

I asked Jimmy to come in first. He looked right at me, and I knew he could tell something was up. We had worked together too long for me to hide my disconcertion from him. He never took his eyes off me as he warily lowered himself into his seat.

"Jimmy, your mom told me about what happened on Sunday. We've talked before about these mishaps that occur between your father and you. You could have been badly hurt."

Jimmy fidgeted in his seat, brought his right leg over his left, and began playing with the shoelaces on his ripped sneakers. "Yeh, my dad really lost it that night." He switched and crossed his legs in reverse. "I couldn't help it. He was getting on me again because John had the phone and it was my turn. Mom had promised me I would get it at eight, and it was already eight fifteen, and I grabbed the phone from John, and he pushed me, so I hit him in the back with the phone, but it was only once, and I wasn't going to do it again, and Dad came in just as I was hitting John, and as usual, he didn't see my side of it, his precious Johnny boy, angel who can do no wrong. Man, I know he didn't mean to push me down the steps. He looked like he felt pretty bad about it. He didn't apologize, though, that would be too much for him, and you know him, what a jerk he can be—"

I put my hand up as a signal and interrupted him. "Jimmy, I'm going to have to do something I don't really want to do, but I feel it's my duty to protect you. And because of this action, I'm concerned your parents will pull you out of therapy, and we won't have the chance to complete our work together."

He took in a great amount of air and said, "Don't tell me you're going to report him?"

"Yes, I am, Jimmy."

I waited for the reality to sink in and continued, "Remember that time you casually said you were thinking about reporting your dad for child abuse?"

"I was just saying that. I was pissed. I would never do it. I know I do stuff to make him go off the deep end. Sometimes I even like it. But I never meant to do it. Don't tell me you think I want you to do this."

"No, I am totally responsible for reporting him. I will tell your parents so. You have nothing to do with it. You may not even agree with it, Jimmy, but I am thinking of your welfare. If your parents pull you from therapy, years from now, as you think about this experience, I want you to remember that I stood up for the reality that you are a human being who should not be permitted to be hurt by your father even if he is your father. Even if you provoke him, and we both agree you do inflame him deliberately sometimes, nevertheless, you are not to be manhandled, and someone has to take a stand in your behalf."

Jimmy's eyes were so watery, I momentarily wondered when the first tear would fall down his flushed cheeks. His bottom eyelid served as a glass shelf, balancing a massive puddle of water. I was reminded of a science class when the professor says, "We'll keep adding one drop of water to the beaker and measure how many drops it takes before it overflows. With fascination, the students watch the dome of water above the top of the rim. It's like gambling, always exciting to adolescents who are most ready to deny reality and take the risks thereof. So it was with me now while I bided my time, as I had many sessions before, awaiting Jimmy's expected avalanche of tears, which never came. How was he able to hold on so tightly?

His lips curved in. "My father will never let me stay here. You know he'll say what he's said lots of times: 'Why pay her all that money? What is she doing for him anyway?' I know. I've heard them argue in their bedroom, Mom always saying, 'Give her a chance, Joe. Please give her a chance. Jimmy's grades have improved,' and stuff like that."

Jimmy and I talked a bit more, mainly to help him deal with his suddenly realized fear that Father would take all this out on him and blame him for the problem in the first place. Dad always told Jimmy it was Jimmy who drove him to do things he didn't mean to do.

I knew that everyone in this family had been through so much turmoil. I was causing this family further trouble, but it couldn't be helped. I figured I would lose Jimmy, and he would be deprived of therapy, and this is why it was so important for him to understand that he was a worthwhile person who deserved to be treated with respect. Even though he would miss the opportunity to work with me again, hopefully, he would maintain the memory that there was one person in this world who was willing to put herself out for him and safeguard him.

Next, I called in Jimmy's parents. Oh boy. Here we go. I took a deep breath and launched in. I started by saying in my clinical experience this is the most difficult thing I've ever had to do. I told Father I was reporting him to Children and Youth, which didn't necessarily mean I was accusing him, but I had to leave it up to them to determine if he was a threat to his child or not. I told him the rest too. You know, it's just too painful to go into detail about it right now. Suffice to say, it didn't go well.

Father's face reddened, and he was so angry I actually feared he might have a heart attack right in my office. Fortunately he stayed in his seat, but the longer he sat there, the larger he appeared. After badgering me with questions, he yelled, "Oh, so you're accusing me not because I'm guilty of doing this ridiculous thing. You are doing it to protect yourself!"

At one point, I admitted there was some truth to that notion but also the law says I am not allowed to be the person who makes the determination.

Later he said, "You keep saying they will probably investigate and drop the case or maybe recommend I get therapy, but I can keep coming in to see you, and they will probably accept that. So why do you need to do it at all? Do you realize this won't help us? It will make things worse. I have a reputation to uphold.

We're upstanding people in the community. Who do you think you are anyway?"

I assured him that the report was totally confidential, and no one would know unless he told someone. As we went along, I also clarified that Jimmy had nothing to do with my decision. In fact, Jimmy was against it, and I hoped he wouldn't take it out on Jimmy. He completely lost it when I said I thought Jimmy had gotten a lot out of therapy and he should continue. Since they might not be comfortable with his seeing me, then certainly with someone else.

His cadence was accelerating as his volume increased: "You've got to be kidding. And do you expect to be paid for this session?"

I nodded. (I didn't say what I was thinking: *You don't just pay me for sessions where you like what you got out of it. You pay me for my time as a consultant even if you don't like what I said. To offer for him not to pay today could have been kind of like payola—my trying to pay him off, so to speak, for something I thought I was doing wrong.*)

He guffawed. "Yeh, right, that will be the day you see my money." He stood up, looked at his wife, and said, "Let's go. We're getting out of here."

After the family left, I was conscious only of the silence in my office, I stood there, stunned and numb. Like a robot, I was acting as if nothing had happened. I walked around the office, closing the lights, putting away my files, and getting ready to leave. It was such a weird reaction. The emptiness I felt inside was peculiar too. After about fifteen minutes, I called home and told my husband I would be home at seven. Then I started to shake. That was more like it.

It took me the whole weekend and then some to get back to myself again. I assumed the Children and Youth Department would investigate and determine there was no "official" abuse. I thought it would not be in the investigative equation for me to find out nor were they obligated to report back to me. I made the dreaded call, and lo and behold, then and there, they informed me they would not be pursuing any investigation of suspected child abuse. Since Father was in family therapy, he could work it out there. They were not as concerned as I thought they should be, but I think deep down I was relieved.

As it turned out, if I had made the call anonymously and had not told the family I was planning to do so, the Children and Youth Department would have informed me of the result beforehand, and therefore, I would not have found it necessary to tell the family of my anticipated action. What a catch twenty-two and how really pissed off I was at the "system." I kicked myself for insisting on the "honest" route of being up front with them when it really wasn't in their best interests to be so diligent. The most important thing was to assure the safety of this child and the well being of his family. My needs should be secondary. At least based on the outcome, and on hindsight, even though it went against my personal credo to always tell the truth, it might have been better to be devious about reporting Jimmy's father. I remonstrated myself after the fact.

I spent the first part of the week composing a letter to each person in the saga: Jimmy, his dad, and his mom. I told them each that as I had suspected, the Children and Youth Department informed me they would not be pursuing an investigation, and we should work out the inappropriate discipline or temper outbursts in therapy. This had been my recommendation all along.

I put a great deal of effort into these letters for each one, summing up our work together, reflecting on their positive strengths, and ending with my wish for them to find further assistance in their quest. I also told them how much I had enjoyed working with them. Each letter was two or three single-spaced pages. If we were never going to see each other again, I wanted them to at least have some keepsake to feel good about, and maybe when the anger and confusion cleared, they would have something on which to cogitate. I especially wanted this for Jimmy to have something to carry with him into adulthood, to covet in a secretly cloaked desk drawer and retrieved whenever he felt bad, wrong, or unlovable.

Contrary to the family's having closure with me by my providing letters of good-bye to them, it was predetermined that I was to have no closure. The worst part about my having executed my obligation was that I was going to lose the opportunity to complete my work with Jimmy. The law, which had bound me to do something better achieved by problem solving and insight, ultimately cost Jimmy his right to a wholesome self-esteem and a peaceful life. I was convinced of this, because I knew this father well enough to know he would never allow Jimmy to see another clinician.

And how would Jimmy interpret what had happened? Would he now feel responsible for the family strife and believe that when you confide in someone you thought trustworthy, somehow you are betrayed and you were dumb to have trusted that person in the first place? Did he think it was stupid of me to cause such a ruckus which was all for naught?

But there was one major contribution I felt I had proffered: Father would have to think twice before blindly lunging toward his vulnerable son.

I grieved the loss of Jimmy, for he was essentially dead to me. He existed out in the real world and in my memory, but I would never see him again. However, as fate would have it, a few years later, I "bumped" into Jimmy, who was working behind a counter in a department store. My how he had grown. I knew by now he was driving and look at him: he held a responsible job! Proudly, like a gloating mom, I eyed him from afar. I felt like a spy as I hid behind one of the aisles.

He was relating to a customer, taking the money and producing change. I even managed to hear him say, "Have a nice day." Jimmy was living in the world as a responsible citizen.

Of course, I was making up stories about him in my head, because I had no idea what was going on at home. I had always believed Jimmy was a good kid with a winning smile and a cute sense of humor. He would make it in the world. With no further therapy, he probably wouldn't feel very good about himself, but from anyone else's point of view, he could function independently.

No, I didn't go over to him and say hello. My intuition told me to leave well enough alone. Hopefully, he had continued therapy with someone else or had adjusted to the family dysfunction. I didn't think it fair of me to barge in on his newly remolded life. It took a lot for me to hold back, though. I felt as if I were standing at the back of a colossal waterfall, holding up the mountain over which the water flowed. It was not for me to change the nature of things.

I had one other redeeming experience to expiate some of my regret over what I had been "forced" to do. Shortly after the infamous day of my announcement to the family, I bumped into the physician with whom I had exchanged information at the time I was treating Jimmy (Jimmy and his mom had signed a release permitting us to do so). She mentioned to me that at one office visit Jimmy's mom told her she and her son had wanted to come back to me for therapy, but Father had nixed it. I felt better knowing this, because I worried about Mom. I knew she felt guilty for having called me, thinking she was accomplishing one thing but inadvertently "betraying" her husband. I'm sure she got in trouble for it too. Nevertheless, she was trying to find a way for her son to get back into therapy. Hearing about Mom's and Jimmy's consideration about returning to therapy helped to soothe the oozing wound buried deep within my heart.

What is the moral of this story I have just told you? Obviously, it's 100 percent true. Psychologists can and sometimes do take their patients home with them.

FIRST ENCOUNTERS

I am always energized when I'm about to meet a new person in my waiting room. A fresh challenge confronts me, and I don't know with whom I'll be working, how his or her life will unfold, what troublesome issues will be presented, or how I can help.

At the same time, my patient is going through a process: who is this woman to whom I'll be telling my secrets? Will I ever feel better? How can I do a good job of telling her about myself and my problem? Is she trustworthy? Suppose I cry. It will be so embarrassing. Whatever I do, I mustn't tell her about... What do I say first?

VICTOR

When I was talking about my sometimes being a cheerleader for my patients, I told you a little about the twenty-five-year-old homosexual man Victor. I described how in one session I pronounced, "Bravo," in response to his directly expressing his feelings.

Our first phone conversation foreshadowed how the beginning of our adventure was to proceed. As soon as I answered the phone and said, "Hello, this is Phyliss Shanken speaking," he asked nervously, "Do you treat homosexuals?"

Initial phone contacts with patients are sensitive beginnings. There is so much a therapist learns about someone in those first few minutes. "You seem concerned about how I will accept you, about whether or not your sexual orientation would affect my decision to treat you?"

He laughed uneasily. "I guess so."

Strongly sensing his vulnerability, I gently responded, "I'd be glad to talk with you."

That phone call marked the inauguration of our journey. Victor's initial fear of my rejection and my subsequent acceptance of him laid the groundwork for a bond that was to mature over time.

At the appointed hour, I opened the waiting room door to find a very flushed Victor. He peered up at me from his chair, finding it difficult to look directly into my eyes. After I said hello, he allowed himself to study me. He stood up, transfixing his gaze on me, and penetrating me with his eyes as if he were searching for something. He didn't shake my outstretched hand. Perhaps he didn't notice it. His eyes quickly swerved to the left of me in the direction of the doorway from which I had just emerged.

I gestured for him to walk in front of me toward my office at the end of a long corridor. As we walked, I had to glance upward at him, because he was tall, about six feet one. This slender, blond haired, blue-eyed man moved gracefully, with ease, almost cheerfully, despite his blatant anxiety.

His physical attractiveness didn't come through until years later. There was something in the way he carried himself which sent a message, "Don't bother with me. I'm a nothing." It's only because of my experience as a therapist that I didn't allow the initial impression to take me over. I believe deep inside everyone there is a one-of-a-kind person. The challenge is to find a way to get through each person's many layers of protection and into his core.

As soon as Victor entered my office, he looked at me, smiling anxiously. He quickly glanced at the empty chair. Clearly, he wanted someone else to lead the way. I wondered who the invisible person in his life might be who if called on, would be there for him. He looked much younger than his twenty-five years. Strange sounds came from his throat, a seemingly muffled giggle. His jeans, sneakers, and polo fit as if a tailor had sewn them onto his body.

Each time he smiled, I felt as if I wanted to know him, to discover his uniqueness. His smirk was very warming yet childlike and innocent. In later sessions when we joked a bit, his laugh was distinctive. It was loud and throaty, sounding like a series of guffaws. Although something in me didn't want to admit it, on the first day and on each occasion Victor emitted one of those uproarious laughs, I was forced to acknowledge his effeminate self, because there was something uninhibited, little girly about that giggle.

Once he got started, Victor, an uneducated, blue-collar worker, was open, revealing the details of his sad, painful life. We talked about what had triggered his coming to see me.

He had just broken up with a lover of three years. It had been his first long-term relationship. Until now, Victor had dated many men, primarily engaging in one-night stands. He now knew he wanted to find one man with whom he would spend his life, and he had thought this man, Tom, was going to be the one.

Unfortunately, the more he felt himself getting closer to Tom, the more he had the urge to run away from Tom. It wasn't as if he planned it that way. It just happened. At first he was loyal, but as soon as his lover went on sales trips out of town, Victor would roam the streets, usually drunk or high on drugs, looking for a one-night thrill, telling himself what he really wanted was to find "Mr. Right."

Then there was another problem: he'd get drunk and not remember what had happened. One incident spurred his eventual coming to see me. When he was on vacation with his lover, they had had a fight, and Victor left the motel in a huff. He got drunk and "tricked" on Tom. (He told me that tricking meant having sex with someone other than one's established partner.) Victor had no memory of the incident, because he was inebriated at the time. In his own way, Victor was apologetic, but we later learned how incapable Victor was of saying, "I'm sorry." This semblance of an apology was not satisfying to Tom, who had all he could take from Victor's unfaithfulness, drunkenness, and distancing.

Everyone knew Victor became oblivious when he was drunk. He talked in his sleep, and lovers often had conversations with him; previous lovers even fought with him, beat him up. He'd wake up battered and not know why. Once he woke up punching Tom and then asked, "What were we fighting about?" Tom knew Victor had a problem. Tom wasn't the first man who said, "You need help. You better do something, or you're going to end up dead in some gutter!"

The combination of the fight, Tom's statement, and Victor's realization that something was terribly wrong (we later identified the something wrong as his being depressed), caused him to casually mention to Dr. Watkins, at a recent appointment for treatment of the flu, that he was not feeling well mentally. Fortunately, Dr. Watkins, a doctor who had worked with me in the past, was astute enough to recommend Victor to me for consultation.

Victor wanted to find out why he couldn't be happy, why he found himself in painful situations, why it seemed he could never find someone with whom he could commit himself. As is so often the case with people who come to see me, he wanted me to "fix" him, maybe give him medicine to change his way of thinking. He was unfamiliar with the process of psychotherapy, but he knew if he didn't do something to help himself, he was headed for even worse times. He had a difficult time telling me what was on his mind. It was as if his mind slept. While we talked about recent events that brought him to see me, I knew I would need to accept reality: I was going to learn about Victor in bits and pieces and at his pace. We were in for a long process.

The first session and during subsequent sessions, I learned a lot about him: Victor's life consisted of going to work on the weekdays, carousing on the weekends, and hanging around with other gay friends on the weeknights, sometimes taking drugs and alcohol, and sometimes just sitting around talking about their various escapades. Much of the time, during these weeknights, the mission was to "kill time" until work the next day, then get through the week so he could come alive on the weekends. When it got too boring, he'd go to a bar and pick someone up, although he tried to avoid that during the week, because when he succumbed to his reckless impulses, he often missed work the next day. He was responsible about his job, which is why he was able to keep the same assembly line position for so many years.

Victor was afraid of growing up and being mature. It meant being sedentary, which translated into having to go along with the boredom of daily living, so he'd protest by constantly being on the move, bar hopping, drinking, dancing, trying to cajole his lovers, but never stopping to experience himself. Victor needed to keep moving in any direction, no matter what the consequences, in order to remain alive, for if he stopped, he'd be confronted with how empty he felt. I imagined his floating away, finding out he was a separate human being, alone in the world, completely unattached. His flighty defense had served him well, and he just couldn't relinquish his playboy life for the stability of adult life.

He had difficulty identifying his feelings. "How do you feel, Victor?"

"Feel?" he would answer in a questioning tone. "Feel?" How do I feel?"

Whenever he answered himself, of course the answer was: "I don't know." He could have asked, "Feeling? Feeling? What's a feeling?"

He had trouble seeing himself as a separate human being with his own identity. He couldn't use words such as "thank you" or "I'm sorry" or "I made a mistake" or "I love you." He would almost gag on the words if asked by a lover to recite them. There was too much "I" in them.

During our sessions, Victor answered questions when asked but never initiated a topic. After my repetitive interpretations of Victor's need to remain distant, he endeavored to elaborate his feelings and thoughts. But before those attempts, his responses were short two-or-three-word phrases, the most popular being, "I don't know."

That's why whenever I thought of Victor, I pictured him with clouds surrounding his body. I imagined his brain: all I saw was fog. This man lived in a dream. He floated through life. In fact, I pictured him, as Santa's reindeer, gracefully leaping through the air into oblivion.

Yet, even on the first day, I could feel something likable in him, something very sensitive beneath the murkiness emanating from him. Maybe it was his vulnerability. He appeared defenseless and childlike in his scrutiny of me as he stole glances toward my face. Maybe it was his almost immediate trust, which loomed out beyond his terror of me. I later understood how much he longed to be able to love someone. His hopelessness competed with his wish for deeper connections. Victor saw himself as a misfit. Of course, he didn't verbalize these ideas, but somehow he managed to convey those sentiments to me. I'm sure he sensed my sincere concern, and maybe that's what kept him coming back week after week, even though sometimes very little was said beyond quick answers to my painstakingly phrased questions. I persisted in providing him with hypothetical feelings that I imagined he might feel or I might feel if I were in that situation.

If I presented three options, he would choose one and then try it on for size. "Yes, that's it. I was mad that Tom didn't pay attention to me. Yes!" His eyes shone like spotlighted clear marbles, and the smile creases revealed themselves in his joy and pride at picking out the "right" answer.

I'm sorry I'll have to reluctantly defer my discussion of Victor's therapeutic process for now. There is so much to say about him.

Even though I'm postponing an in-depth analysis of Victor's journey in therapy, I will tell you now about some of his therapeutic gains. After years of visits with me, the fog around him miraculously lifted. He was now able to relate to me how he felt and what he was thinking, and through this exploration, he was released from the prison, which for years had bound him. He attended college and majored in restaurant management. He began cooking feasts for his friends as they encouraged him to open his own restaurant someday.

He accepted his homosexuality, came "out of the closet," and was no longer ashamed of his body, which as a child had been chubby enough for the neighborhood kids to torment him, calling him "Victoria." He came to terms with his belief that he was a defective male, expressed himself in a more masculine way, overcame his fear of women, began to go out with women as friends, and one day found himself in bed with a beautiful woman who had been interested in him for several years.

He and his girlfriend and subsequent wife, Aimee, had to deal with reactions from the gay community, who rejected Victor, and the reaction from the straight community, who suspected Victor. They were similar to an interracial couple, not accepted by either side, gay or straight. Victor, as well as Aimee, had to deal with his newly masculine self, especially when he found that women were suddenly "coming onto him" and that he was indeed a most handsome man.

We'll get back to him periodically so he won't be totally lost to you.

ROBERT

For now, we'll resume our discussion of first encounters and how these impact the rest of the therapy. I've had some wacky kind of initial phone calls or sessions with people whom other psychologists probably would have referred on to other therapists. Oh no. Not I. It's as if I go out looking for these challenges when in actuality the dilemmas find me, and I just don't have the sense to turn them away. Well, that wasn't very nice to say about myself. The real truth is on occasion I can be a mulish little bugger. This trait or should I say, fate, has been with me since birth.

When a man named Robert called me on the phone and asked, "Do you treat sexual problems?" of course I said yes. Then he said he had a particular problem where he allowed women to sit on him and hold him in a scissors grip, which caused him to have difficulty breathing. He often passed out. He really needed help. Without blinking, I gave him an appointment.

After hanging up the phone, I wondered if I might be getting into something a bit heavy and maybe even dangerous. I looked for the mace I keep in my drawer "just in case" someone ever gets violent, which until then, no one ever had. I set aside the defensive "weapon" to have on hand. I called a number of male therapists in the building, one of whom had a black belt in karate, and I worked out a means of signaling them if I needed help.

Robert came bouncing into my office on that first visit, plopped himself down on my sofa, and immediately launched into his tale of woe. His curly hair resembled a mop, and his at least one-day-old beard made him look sinister—or was that just my anxious imagination? His puny frame helped me to relax. If the worst happened, I think I could overtake this guy or at least put up a good fight in time for someone to hear my screams. I had so many people on the lookout, a brave soul would rescue me; I was sure now.

I listened intently and accepted the photograph he wanted me to view, which displayed a woman in lacy lingerie sitting on top of his face in a scissors hold. I repeatedly asked him what kind of help he wanted from me. I don't normally ask this, but his vagueness and evasiveness confounded me. It wasn't as if he were saying he needed help to stop engaging in this behavior. He wanted to know how to continue this practice without fainting from lack of oxygen.

I began to get a glimmer of what he was really after, and finally he popped the question: "Will you help me by sitting on my head and help me learn how to hold my breath longer?"

I remained serious and respectful. "That is not how I help people. I believe in trying to understand what is in your way of achieving your goals and trying to help you get there. I don't help through action. I help through talking," I said.

"Oh," he said, without emotion.

"I think you may want to go elsewhere for what you are looking for," I continued.

He rose up from the sofa. "I was hoping you would practice this with me." His flushed face was looming larger as he moved toward me.

Now I was thinking about that mace. Where did I put it in the drawer so it wouldn't show but I could reach it easily? When would be the best time to reach for it without further provoking him?

He put out his hand, and I almost grabbed the phone to intercom my back-up protectors. Then I realized he was advancing closer because he wanted his photo back. I gladly gave it to him, almost tossing it so as not to get too close.

He walked toward the door. "I wish you could have helped me," he said and walked out.

"Phew," is all I said after I closed the door, locked it, and checked the door to be sure it was really in fact, in actuality, in truth, locked.

You ask: "Was that the most bizarre interview you ever had?" (Knowing that you understand that in order to protect my patients' identities, what I present here as true is really a lie, I'll have to say yes.)

ROSE

I had another unusual experience on a first interview that wasn't as wild and crazy as the one I just related but another memorable one-time meeting with a woman whose husband had left her. Very depressed and overwrought, she wanted me to do whatever I could to help her get him back.

As soon as I saw her in the waiting room, I recognized her immediately. She was an old friend of my parents. I hadn't seen her since I was a child. All I could remember was how she and the other friends, who had grown up together from early childhood, used to have so much fun together. I would be in my nightgown, the one with the little flowers on it, upstairs on the landing of the second floor, peering down at the grown-ups who were having a rollicking good time. I loved to see the people, as well as my parents, loosened up and really free. They would slap each other on the back or move toward one another saying, "You gotta hear this one!" or "Remember in fifth grade when Joe rode his bike into the creek?" When I grew up, I pledged to have fun like this.

So here was this woman, Rose, one of the adult crowd coming to me for help. She had known I was the same kid from our early days, but she hadn't mentioned it to me on the phone. I needed time to get my bearings. I couldn't imagine how someone who saw me running around in diapers could bring herself to ask me for full-fledged adult help. It was weird.

She didn't mind at all. She was desperate for help. After listening to her story, commiserating with her (after all, I had known her husband also), and looking over the realities of her insurance benefits and travel time, I referred her to someone I thought would be better suited to help her. If it weren't for the practical issues, given my "never say never" attitude, I probably would have treated her.

Rose wasn't the first of those who consulted me who have relationships with people around me. My husband, who is a psychiatrist, and I are very steadfast in our resolve to not reveal anything about anyone whom either of us knows. So, a mutual friend, co-worker, or aunt or uncle on either side of our families could call one of us for a referral or just for advice, and we won't reveal this information to the other one. People are always so surprised about this. I've had friends call and say, "You know Will referred me to Dr. So and So, and it worked out well for my depression." I will say I didn't know anything about it, and they will say, "Well, I figured he would have told you. I never said to keep it a secret."

This credo to which we both adhere makes the situation that happened with Rose even more difficult. Obviously we would never reveal any details, but to not even disclose that someone asked for a referral or not being able to go to the other one for help on the emotions engendered in ourselves where we might want support from each other is tough to take sometimes.

ANNA

Another very "sticky" situation occurred on the first meeting of a thirty-something-year-old woman, Anna, who was so anxious she looked as though she were "jumping out of her skin." She spent the major part of the session protesting that she had a secret she couldn't tell because she feared discovery. I reiterated to her my ethical constraints: all is confidential unless I believed she was going to harm herself or someone else, if I suspected child abuse or dependent adult abuse, or if the court ordered me to testify. She asked me questions using hypothetical situations to test me.

"What if I had already done something unlawful but was not going to do anything wrong in the future," she asked as she rose from her chair and started pacing back and forth.

"I would hold it in confidence," I assured her.

Anna posed many of these questions, and like a student who is being tested in an oral exam, I obediently answered all of them. Finally, toward the end of the session, she spilled the beans: "I used to be part of the underground. It was in the sixties. I was a hippie, completely opposed to the war. I thought I was doing right by my country. I dropped out of the resistance movement, oh, about twenty years ago, but I know my name is on a list somewhere. No one else knows, not even my husband. If anyone finds out, I will probably be arrested."

I really felt for this woman. Haunted by her past, Anna lived in constant fear of unearthing her identity, and also, she harbored enough guilt for ten people. She never divulged what she had done while in the movement, and I don't think she had any plans to do so. She was plagued with regret and had no place to go with it. I had read a book about a woman in this exact dilemma. She had to move from town to town, changing aliases every six months or so, and only had contact with other fugitives every once in a while. Apparently, many of these people remain at large, and there is a whole internal society within our environment that has networks for communicating escape plans, fake identity paper work, and the like. These are not designed to do harm nor to engage in political activities but purely to help each other remain incognito and provide safe harbor from police.

I had also read in the newspaper about a woman who was involved in planting an explosive that killed a number of people. After twenty years, she turned herself in even though no one was actually hot on her trail at the time. She just couldn't take the guilt. She wanted to pay her dues.

Anna was a tortured soul who was quite depressed. Nevertheless, despite our very engaging interview, she never returned.

ANTOINETTE

I had a similar reaction to a very petite woman, Antoinette, who in her croaky voice, hinted that the reason her husband wouldn't allow her to go to therapy is because he was concerned about what I would find out about his affiliations "with some really bad people." In the middle of the interview, she blurted out, "If John knew I was here, he would kill me!"

Based on my hunches as to who these bad people in her life were, I feared she might have been referring to a threat, which was meant literally rather than as a figure of speech. (And this incident occurred well before the *Sopranos* began airing on TV!)

If her husband would kill her when he found out she was seeing me, what, pray tell, would he do to *me*? My imagination began to distract me from what she was saying. However, she wasn't articulating much other than she was in pain and felt trapped to continue with me in treatment. I saw her as a fragile little spider in a cobweb whom, with one swat, I could knock unconscious. I was in touch with my capacity to hurt her; imagine what he could do to her.

I didn't learn much about Antoinette other than ascertaining that she was never coming back to see me. At the end, instead of asking when she could see me again and scheduling our next appointment then and there, she said, "I'll call you to make another appointment." Dem words aren't courageous words, to be sure. Those are avoidance words. I never saw Antoinette again, but over the years, I sure have thought about her a lot.

NAMELESS

One day, I was sitting in my office going over some notes for a talk I was giving the next day. Rather than seeing a patient, I had specifically blocked out this hour for preparation. I heard a knock at my door. Rarely do people rap on the door, because they assume I'm in conference with someone. Startled, I went to the door, and there appeared a bewildered man whom I assumed to be in his early thirties scowling at me. I asked if I could help him, whereupon he barged into the room and took one of the seats close to the doorway. I stood by the doorway, continuing to grasp the doorknob and wondering what to do next. I told him he could make an appointment on a day when I would be available, but right now I was not able to talk with him.

He didn't move. He planted himself deeper into the cushions of the stuffed chair. He demanded, "I have to talk to you now. I was passing by your office and saw you were a psychologist, and I knew I had to see you."

I reiterated my denial of service to him now, and of course, I didn't make a move to settle into a conversation with him.

He said, "I can see you are afraid of me. They all are. I was seeing a therapist down the street, and all I did was get up from my chair, and she called security. I'm not going to hurt you. Why don't you close the door?"

Certainly this man was pushing the boundaries of appropriateness. I was concerned if I showed too much alarm I would make him more anxious, and this could provoke him, whereas if I treated his behavior as an ordinary, everyday interaction, he might settle down. What he said next confirmed my hunch.

He beseeched me: "Please sit down. I don't know why people think I'm dangerous. All I want to do is talk. I have a bad problem." There were no tears in his eyes, but his face looked as if her were sobbing minus the sound effects.

Softly, I said, "I will sit down for a few minutes with you to determine the problem, and then we can set up an appointment for the future, but I will have to keep the door open." I made sure to sit so that I would be the first one out the door, and he wouldn't be able to entrap me in the room.

Suspiciously staring straight into my eyes, he asked, "Are you afraid of me?"

I'm always honest with the people I treat, and my values with my friends and family compel me to tell the truth. If I don't want the person to know the truth, then I say something like, "I'd rather not say," or "I'm not comfortable discussing that right now," or

"I'm not sure if you really want to hear what I'm thinking." To this gloomy looking man, I responded, "Yes, I am uneasy with you."

He blurted, "Why, why should it be? I bet it has to do with my nose being so big." His large brown eyes darted to and fro.

Without bias and in a monotone, I retorted, "You come barging into my office, take a seat without being invited, and demand that I talk to you now. This kind of behavior doesn't make people feel safe. Take responsibility for causing a reaction in other people. The other therapist had every reason to call security."

"She never gave me a chance." He shifted in his seat.

"I understand, but think about the impact your behavior has on other people." I didn't even know his name yet, but I parented him just the same. He composed himself and gradually settled down. His arrhythmic breathing became more uniform, and I knew we were about to embark on something new.

"I have this problem with my nose. It's so big. People can't stand to look at me. I saw you staring at it when you opened the door."

"What makes you think it's big?" I asked, truly perplexed by his unwarranted and severely disparaging self-assessment. His nose appeared within the normal range of size and shape. Uh oh. Was I dealing with a psychotic man? I knew now I'd never get him out of my office.

"Come on. Don't try to deny it. That's my whole problem."

"Has anyone ever told you you had a big nose?"

"No, no one has to. I know it. It's all I think about. If only I could get a nose job, but I don't have the money. I could be a happy person, but I'm so grotesque!"

I looked at him sympathetically. He was an average-looking guy with dark skin, dark hair that was too greasy, nice clear brown eyes. If he cleaned up a bit, he might look decent. Certainly, his nose was not his problem. I really felt for him. My intuition told me he probably wasn't psychotic. I believed he was suffering from

Body Dysmorphic Disorder, which is a preoccupation with an imagined defect in appearance.

This fixation on his nose and constant verbal reference to it had probably frightened away potential friends or coworkers. The alternative of not talking about it could be just as detrimental to him, because without someone with whom he could talk, he would then ruminate about the imagined flaw. In addition, he must avoid contact with others for fear he would turn them away. How humiliating to believe so wholeheartedly that you are misshapen and grotesque.

I told him I would like to help him, but he would have to make an appointment. I gave him my card and suggested he think it over. He thanked me for spending these few minutes with him. Everyone else always retreated when he was near; he was such a turn off.

I never did hear from him again, but he made an impact on me. For some reason, I imagined him as a sculptor molding clay faces and caressing their noses as he contoured them into perfect shapes. I would have liked to help him get to the bottom of his obsession. Obsessions are useful as a defense. They serve the purpose of distracting you from what really ails you. But you have to suffer so much to divert your attention from something even more painful. It's another case of the cure—the obsession, being worse than the disease—the painful thoughts you're trying to avoid.

What did he feel was so deficient about himself as a person that he put all the anxiety onto his concern about his nose? He reminded me of a child who sneezes and runs to his parents saying, "I sneezed and nobody said God bless you." With his scary behavior, he would never get the help he needed. He would just turn people away and then blame it on physical unattractiveness as the cause of his isolation and abandonment.

Other initial sessions that come to mind have to do with adolescents who are sent into treatment for me to "fix them." Sometimes these youths present themselves as incorrigible, or at least this is the way their parents describe them, but most of these kids are really good kids who somehow got caught in the discord of the generation gap, and the family needs help in conflict resolution.

Despite my compassion for the children and their parents, on any given day, one of these teens walks into my office like a caged animal just released into the jungle for which he is not prepared. The best thing he can do is—you said it—shut up. Shutting up serves many valuable purposes: it puts me in my place immediately; it establishes to the parents that you can lead a teen to a therapist but you can't make him talk; and it kills time until the session is over, thank goodness for both of us.

I've had first sessions like this dozens of times throughout my career, so although it's challenging, I'm not afraid of it. And I've developed some nice ways to deal with the electively mute young patient. I talk my brains out. That's it: the sum total of my technique. I talk about my life, my reaction to her parents, the reason I think he is here in my office, my sympathy because she is forced to be here. I start listening to myself talk and make comments on what I'm saying. I usually laugh when I do that, because I sure do appear silly. I also relate the one-way rule: anything said here is confidential. Anything parents say to me goes right back to patient: unfair to parents, really cool for their kids. What do parents know anyway, right?

Very often, in fact just about always, the melt-down process begins usually when we start talking about what a bummer it is to be forced to come in here to talk to a total stranger about things that have nothing to do with anyone and are perfectly fine. It's just that parents are completely unreasonable and overprotective and make too much out of nothing. Why don't they just leave me alone? How can anyone resist this kind of understanding and compassion? And, by the way, these empathic remarks are real on my part. I am very sympathetic to adolescents and their plight to get out from under the bondage of parents.

After I see the teenager, I then call in the parents to discuss my recommendation. The parents, the teen, and I had met at the beginning of the appointed time, so we have already established a mini relationship. Then I see their child and report back but only what the teen and I have agreed to impart or what I tell the teen I'm going to say to the parent in terms of the recommendation.

JIMMY'S FATHER, FRANCO

Remember Jimmy, whose father I reported to Children and Youth for suspected child abuse? Well, our first session consisted of Franco's saying, "Listen, my wife said I had to be here or you wouldn't treat my son, but I want you to know from here on in, leave me out of this. I'm here today, but that's it."

And I retorted silently within, *Yeah, and gone tomorrow.*

So much for first visits. We will now move on to the next stages in our adventure. The people who visit with me for our "conversations" are pilgrims in a voyage to the land of self-acceptance, personal integration, and peace of mind.

THE HELPING PROCESS

Over the past forty-plus years, I've gleaned a few pointers about the helping process. Certain helping behaviors, which I utilize in my therapy practice, are just as beneficial for you to use in everyday life, be it with a friend, child, spouse, or boss.

Most of us can tell when people aren't listening, can't we? They avert their eyes to something else of interest. They get a glazed look in their face, and we're thinking: *Oh yeah, you're hearing me all right. I wonder what daydream you're into right now.* Or they ask a question you answered only a minute ago.

Therapists, as well as everyday people like you and me, find that we maintain a better connection with people by asking open-ended questions, which are questions that can't be answered in a yes-or-no response, questions that require the person to deliberate on the answer. By going for more elaborate information than just a confirmation of what we already know, you invite the other person to share more than he or she might have originally felt comfortable expressing. You, dear Reader, can practice these investigative questions before, during and after you are with someone as you try to deepen the relationship. In fact, I charge you with the task of making yourself a list of good conversation starters. Use these when you really want to hear from the other person not when you could care less. Otherwise, you might get an earful!

Examples of open-ended questions include: "What was your initial reaction when you heard the diagnosis from the doctor?" "What came to your mind when you…?" "If you could have said something at that time, what might you have said?"

A closed question would be more like the kind some of the not-so-great sportscasters ask such as: "Were you excited when you realized you had broken the record?" Well, duh! Yeah! The guys in the camera booth at the other end of the TV interviewer's earpieces are screaming: "We need more! Get us more!"

But sometimes, with clients such as Jimmy, Melanie (you'll hear from her in a few minutes), and most definitely the I-don't-know king, Victor, I had to ask more closed-ended questions but gave options for the answers so he wouldn't just give me a rote, "Probably," or "I don't know," or "What do you think?"

VICTOR

I would never ask Victor, "Were you glad your mother encouraged you to try on her dresses?" Rather, I might ask, "How did you feel when you wore those clothes?" But better yet, given Victor's difficulty in articulating his feelings, I probably would make a statement first and then pop the question: "Maybe you were afraid or angry or resented your mother's insistence, or maybe you felt more loved by your mom when you paraded around in her clothes. Maybe you felt something was wrong with you. Sometimes you could feel more than one emotion. What feelings did you have?"

Yes, these interventions may seem tedious and in some ways more like a close-ended question, but Victor required coaching, or as I used to think of it, he needed me to "feed" him multiple-choice answers. After he cited an answer, I would help him delve into the derivations of the thought or feeling. For example, if he said, "I was embarrassed," I might ask, "What about being dressed as a girl by your mother embarrassed you?" If he gave me the "I don't know" response, I would likely ask, "Were you afraid of being laughed at?" or "Did you enjoy her pride and admiration over your being in girls' clothes rather than how she looked at you when you wore boy's clothes?"

If I hit upon an answer that fit, Victor's face would light up. I think his grin was partly from relief at being able to provide an answer to me and partly from finally filling in the pieces of the puzzle for himself.

Back to our guidelines for everyday tête-à-têtes. *Clarify what you hear.* "I hear you saying that…" You are testing reality to ascertain whether what you hear is actually the message he intends you to receive. "Do you want me to give you my advice, or are you wanting me just to listen?"

CINDY

Very early in my career, I really put my foot in my mouth when a relatively new patient, Cindy, having had only a few sessions, told me she was pregnant.

With a wide smile, I said, "That's wonderful, Cindy. Congratulations!"

She broke down sobbing. "It's not wonderful. It's the worst thing that could ever happen. I find out I'm pregnant right after John said he's leaving me. This is a disaster."

The reason I had been remiss as the listener was in not clarifying what I was hearing. I made assumptions she was as happy as I might be (I love babies) and didn't wait to see where what she said actually took her. I should have asked in the traditional shrink manner, "How do you feel about being pregnant?" Can you see now why I need to ask so many questions?

Yet, sometimes asking questions is a premature endeavor. I could have waited also and not asked anything. She brought up the topic for a reason. The natural flow of things would probably dictate where she was to take the topic of her pregnancy. But this requires keeping one's mouth shut. Patience. Trust. Cindy will get where she is going, and you can tag along, being there for her and not for your own needs.

So, you can probably add my gem advice, "*Shut up!*" as a good one to cherish. At least it can keep you out of hot water. But don't just shut up. That could be rude or reflect your lack of interest. No. *Shut up as a form of listening.* You can't hear someone else if you're doing all the talking.

If you think you might consider following these rules, then maybe you better first figure out if you actually want to hear what the other person is saying. If not, then keep talking!

Relate personally to what the person is saying to show you understand. (Be careful not to abuse this by spending all of the time telling your life story and forgetting about the person you are helping.) Psychologists must be wary of a natural proclivity to share their own stories. I probably share more personal anecdotes than most therapists. When I do it, my tales are short, to the point, and relevant to the discussion at hand.

Here's an example of how I share personal data:

KEVIN

Remember Kevin, the man who lost his dad at age four and was rejected as an adult by his grown son and who married a woman who appeared self-sufficient but turned out to be a semi-invalid, the man whom I wanted to take home to my house to live? One day, he was in a perspiring tirade about his wife, Darlene, and her incessant demands on him. In one long exhale of breath, he said, "I finish one thing, and she's directing me on to the next chore. I say, 'Yes, Captain!' Boy, how she hates that. On Saturday, I was cleaning out the garage, and just as I went to take out the trash, she says, 'Kevin, don't forget to take out the trash!'" He sucked in a massive amount of air to catch his breath.

I, his therapist, slammed my hand down on the sofa cushion next to me and emphatically blurted out, "I hate when that happens! I remember as a kid, just as I was going upstairs to clean my room, my mom would say, 'Clean your room.' And I'd say to myself or to her, 'Can't you let me have this? Why does it have to become yours?' I couldn't even have the satisfaction of knowing I had thought of it and chose to do it. It came from inside of me. Kevin, how did *you* feel when Darlene said what she did to you?"

Notice how I very personally and emotionally related to his feeling, then to a similar situation where I had to deal with the same type of issue, and then *brought it back to him*. After all, it's his story, not mine, but I have demonstrated that my empathy toward him is more than mere lip service.

Keep in mind, though, that I wouldn't do this with all my patients. Kevin needed extra reassurance from me that what he felt was real and couldn't be taken away as his mom used to do by being abusive one minute and then all sweet and loving the next as if his feeling of rejection had been a figment of his imagination.

There's an old Chinese proverb: "When you have a disease, do not try to cure it. Find your center and allow for healing." Therefore, when people are suffering, don't try to cure them. Instead, *keep them company while they heal*. Understand. Listen. Commiserate. This is all you can do.

When you go into the center of pain, when you relax and allow the sensations to take you over, it doesn't hurt as much. Once, I asked my dentist, "When I hold on tighter to the hand rails, does it help you to do your work?" We had a good laugh as he said he was doing fine without my help, thank you. Pain is actually resistance. Bracing yourself merely magnifies the pain. Therefore, as a comforter of someone in physical pain, you might ask the sufferer to *investigate the pain rather than to try to eliminate it.* Is the pain sharp or dull? Cold or hot? Suppose you could draw the pain? What colors would you use? You need to encourage the person to flow with, rather than to oppose his or her feelings.

Don't make assumptions about how to make the person feel better. If you talk to someone in pain, ask him or her, "What do you need?" You may offer your help and then ask, "Is this what you really asked for? Did I come through as you wished, or is there more I can do?"

PREGNANT COUPLE

I'm thinking about a couple who came to see me because they were pregnant with their third child and were having difficulty deciding on whether or not to have an abortion. So much of our first session had to do with my continually asking them what part they wanted me to play. The wife kept saying, "I don't want this child, but how will I feel if we really go through with the abortion?"

We had only two sessions. They went on their way without having made this life-changing decision, and I was destined to never find out. But really it wasn't my concern whether they aborted the child or not. My interest was more in helping them clarify their conflicts and find a way to be together in the decision.

I learned later from the gynecologist who referred the tormented couple they did decide to keep the child. I often think about their family, because by now the baby would be in his or her thirties. My fantasy is that they wonder every once in a while, "Look at our beautiful daughter. To think we might never have had her in our lives. What a loss it would have been."

I combine that fantasy with memories of other babies born into this world who might not exist had one or the other or both of their parents not gone into therapy. I can think of a number of women who started out convinced they didn't want children, but as they explored their early life issues or problems over body image, femininity, control, fears of abusing the child the way they were abused, and more, they retracted their steadfast belief that their life should be devoid of children.

Here's a big no-no. *Don't jump in and give advice. Don't tell the person how he should feel.* ("You should be happy you're still alive!" or "Look how much you have to be thankful for!") *Don't tell the person he* shouldn't *feel that way.* "Dry your tears," are not necessarily comforting words. Heed the Mexican saying: "Cry, child, for those without tears have a grief that never ends."

Be careful about telling someone he or she is making too big a deal out of it. I remember how I felt as a child being called Sarah Bernhart whenever I expressed strong emotion? Respect people's feelings, especially your children's.

Don't tell the person everything will be okay. You are not a deity. You don't know that things will turn out all right.

Don't make jokes to lighten the situation. The person may politely laugh, but the hidden message is, " Please stop talking about it. I'm too uncomfortable to deal with this serious thing that happened to you. I'd rather pretend it's no big deal. Who cares if it's painful to you! I need to take care of *me*!"

Parents too often do this with children.

"Daddy, I fell down and cut my knee!" exclaims little Johnny.

"Did the ground get hurt?" says Daddy.

Johnny hesitates for a minute, and depending on his age, smiles in an approval-seeking manner, then resumes crying even louder. Why? Because he hasn't gotten what he needed yet, which is something like this: "There. There. Come on my lap. Getting cut really does hurt. I'm sorry you got hurt... You're handling it so well. What can I do to help?"

SUZANNE

Sometimes I kind of go crazy. I get the wacky notion that I'm funny. Well, I am hilarious to an audience of *moi*. So sometimes, when people are talking and especially since I try to help people use humor as a coping strategy, I see situation comedies in my mind. (I'll talk more about this later when we get to the discussion of funny stuff.) As Steve Allen says, "Comedy equals tragedy plus time." So all you need is a little bit of pain, mix in some creative juices, and voila! You've got a new weird slant on an old catastrophe. If appropriate, I help people find a new version of an old story.

Suzanne described a very calamitous event in her family. An unmarried sister shamefacedly told her parents she was pregnant. Her parents went berserk. Then her seventeen-year-old sister blurted out, "Yeah, me too."

Rather than replicate with her parents what had happened with her two sisters, as an adult, Suzanne terminated her unwanted pregnancy by having an abortion and suffered terribly as she couldn't shake the belief that all her current physical problems (arthritis, diabetes, and chronic fatigue syndrome) were her penance for this transgression from years ago. During many of our sessions, we reviewed her early life history as well as the impact her abortion had on her current, everyday functioning.

One day, I said, "The scene in your parents' living room would make an amazing situation comedy. Just picture your parents settling down from the reality of one daughter's devastating news. They take a breath, and the next daughter pipes up, 'Oh yeh, by the way, I don't know how this slipped my mind, but I forgot to tell you—me too. I'm pregnant too.' It's too unbelievable, yet it would make for a lot of laughs as the audience would see their faces. Imagine if the parents are people like Archie and Edith Bunker!"

Suzanne got right into it. "Yeah, I think it would be great on a show like *Roseanne*." She laughed from deep below her throat into her diaphragm, so much heartier than when I had first met her.

We kept expanding on the scene and making it more and more absurd. We even arrived at a point in our scenario where Suzanne also joins the crowd to announce her pregnancy. This was a sore topic, because Suzanne never faced the music as her sisters had done. She elected to have an abortion, and forever after she punished herself for it. By the time we broached this tender topic, we were really giggling. We both had tears running down our faces because we were laughing so hard.

When Suzanne first consulted me, she presented herself as a vulnerable, overly serious, woe-is-me woman who revealed virtually no sense of humor. Of course, I didn't make jokes in our beginning sessions. Over time, I helped her lighten up a bit but never by minimizing her pain, more by helping her use her visual mind to "see" things with a new perspective. Obviously, her early life choice and subsequent regrets were not funny, but the pain she suffered as a result of her decision needed a place to go. All that pent-up tension was causing her to beat herself up from the inside out, and it was slowly doing a number on her body.

(Remember Maya Angelou's "history, despite its wrenching pain, cannot be undone" statement?)

But now I'm getting ahead of myself. Later, I'll tell you about using humor in therapy. I merely wanted to give you an example of how careful you need to be about irresponsibly and selfishly attempting to lighten people up for the purpose of getting them not to experience their emotions. When I use humor, it's only after a long period of serious retrieval of past aches, acknowledging the severity of their pain, melancholy or grieving. (I just can't wait till we get to our conversation of "Funny Things Can Happen on the Road to Inner Peace!")

If you want to be helpful to people, *always tell the truth*. If you are uncomfortable, admit it and ask to be excused. Feel free to explain why, such as, "This is too close to home."

You ask: "Is honesty always the best policy?" I've devoted my life to the study of truth.

My love affair with candor began at age four when the cashier asked my mother my age, and my mother responded, "Three," and I said, "No, I'm not, I'm four." The scowl on my mother's face in reaction to my pronouncement of truth imprinted indelibly on my mind as I asked myself what I had done wrong.

Now, as a psychologist, I search for truth and help people deal with the guilt and pain they experience when they distort, minimize, and deny reality in the same way their parents taught them to do. Their parents believed they were being loving and protective when they said to their children, "Don't worry. It'll be okay." (When it wasn't okay, didn't their children feel betrayed?) The children were told their pain didn't exist: "Come on. It doesn't hurt that much!" Parents tried to fix the pain: "The kids are picking on you because they like you!" When their children asked, "Mommy, are you mad at me?" their mothers shook their heads no. But during bath time, why was Mommy rubbing the washcloth so harshly over their tender skin?

I've learned that telling "white" lies is merely the coward's way to protect your own hide. Deep inside, you feel small and weak since you don't have the courage to face the music. Because you fear your girlfriend will be angry if you decline her offer to go out to dinner, you kid yourself that telling her you have a meeting will make her feel less rejected. Isn't it kinder to say, "I enjoy your company, and I'd understand if you were upset, but after my busy week, I need time alone this evening."

Truth and trust go hand in hand. I have never knowingly lied to my children. If I had, why would they have believed me when I declared, "There are no monsters in the closet." I want my friends and family to tell *me* the truth. Otherwise, how can I trust their assurance that they will always be there for me?

Asserting the truth is an act of kindness. It's a loving promise: I care about your thoughts and feelings, but I attend to my own needs as well. In my desire to preserve our relationship, I will not take manipulative shortcuts to modify the truth. Because I respect you, I'll make every effort to tread lightly on your vulnerable heart. You may feel hurt by what I say, but it is not my intention to hurt you.

Each time you are faced with a truth-telling dilemma, you pace the floor of your brain and ponder: *To lie or not to lie?* This exercise is draining. Far better it is to maintain a consistent personal creed: you never lie to yourself, and you are willing to face the consequences of your actions. With these convictions, you are able to sleep well at night, maybe even with a smile on your face! But best of all, if you are needed to be supportive to another person, you can be confident you will really do a credible job.

CHRISSY

What if a patient asks me a question, and I don't think it's appropriate to answer? Chrissy, who was so unsure of herself, used to say something and then ask, "Do you think I'm right, Phyliss?"

After many of these tries on Chris's part where I explained how I treat questions as statements, I would answer, "Chris, I know you want me to confirm what you are thinking or direct you and tell you not to think this way, but my satisfying your wish will not help you. Therefore, I'm not going to answer your question." I didn't hedge here. I just stated it as it is.

Sometimes, to save time, I said, "No comment." When I uttered this succinct statement of truth, she laughed out loud. Like a teacher in school, I had caught her trying to squeeze out personal reactions from me yet again. Had I complied with her wish, I would have been confirming her belief that only my impressions are correct, whereas her ideas, perceptions, and emotions are not the right ones.

You may feel inadequate, uncomfortable, helpless, and angry that your loved one has to suffer. The experience of pain is so lonely. Merely sitting beside the distressed person or holding his or her hand may provide a precious gift. In any case, the very best thing to say in these critical situations is: "I'm sorry!"

I'm thinking about what people often say when, for example, a woman's new baby turns out to have birth defects. Many a patient of mine has expressed the hurt she feels when well-wishers say, "This happened to you for a reason. It's because you are strong enough to handle it." *Then, excuse me! I'd rather be weak if strength means I get hit with all the bad stuff!*

KATIE

What do people say to a woman who suffers a miscarriage? Katie was mourning the loss of her precious unborn child. Her aunt, who was trying to comfort Katie, espoused the following: "This was for the best. If the baby had gone to term, it wouldn't have been right. You would have had to deal with a sick or retarded child."

Katie smiled politely while gulping down her true reaction. What did she tell me, her therapist? "I didn't want the miscarriage in the first place! I don't care that my baby would have been deformed. Why should I have an abnormal baby at all? I wanted a healthy baby that got a chance to be born! Period. I wish everyone would stop telling me what not to feel. They act like I didn't lose anything. This was my baby!"

My previously courteous, obedient, approval-seeking patient suddenly broke out of her shell. She threw my accent pillows across the room. This refreshing tantrum was the beginning of her healing.

So don't tell me I'm stronger than you or things that happen to me were meant to be. Tell me you understand my pain, and you admire my ability to cope. Tell me that in your life you've been in this same scary, excruciating, depressing, frustrating place, and I'm not alone in my agony. Give me your ear and listen to me discharge my tension through tears and tantrums.

CHRISSY

Frequently, I refer to the idea of "offering someone your tears" as giving the other person a gift. Chrissy always laughed when I espoused this point of view. "Phyliss, you keep saying this, but I just can't fathom the idea of crying being a good thing, that having someone else actually want my tears like it's a gift. Come on! That's so ridiculous." But then as expected, Chris would recant her exclamation for fear she might have injured me. No matter how much I told her I was trained not to take anything personally, she still didn't buy it.

I would say, "Chris, I know it's hard for you to see your tears this way. Based on how you were raised, it must be such a foreign idea. It's darn hard to reverse an old learning. And it wasn't like something you are taught in school, just factual stuff. You learned it within the emotional atmosphere of some very traumatic stuff. It's even harder to shake beliefs you learned when you had no choice to believe otherwise. You were at the mercy of people who could abandon you if you didn't adopt their views. For you it was life and death. If you cried, your mother decided it meant she wasn't a good mother. And that meant she would kill herself and abandon you. That's a high price to pay to have the luxury of the healing power of tears."

We therapists pay attention to those basic rules I've just outlined, and then we go further. How do you get to know and help a perfect stranger? You embark on an adventure with him or her. What questions do you ask? And then how do you put it all together?

The first question has to be: "Why do therapists answer a question with a question?" My answer to you has to be: "Why do you ask?" (Sorry, I couldn't resist.)

Behind every question is a statement a person is making. I take nothing for granted as to a person's motivation. Another reason I ask why is because we're separate people, each with our own reasons for doing things. I don't make up stories about them or try to get these imaginary treatises to fit into my preconceived notions. I have to ask, "What do you mean by that?" Okay, there I go being a shrink again, but I refuse to "kill you off," by arrogantly deciding I know more about you than you know about yourself.

If you tell me, "I'm upset because my boss said after I complete my report, I should show it to him," what do I assume? You don't want him looking over your shoulder? With his red pen, he's going to change around your words, and it won't feel like your report any more? He will show it to others and make fun of you? You think he is treating you like a child the way your parents did who over-babied you? Is it because you just don't like him?

Should I have assumed you're upset for any of those reasons, skip the request for clarification, and continue our investigation without knowing the veritable answer as to why you hurt so much inside? By deciding *my* own plot to your story, I have essentially killed you off. You don't exist; only *I* do. Everyone's life is my life. No one else in the world exists but me. Also, the stories I would make up about you have more to do with *my* experience and background. If I have an issue about people's breathing down my neck, but you have an issue over people's correcting your work, how will I ever find out unless you elaborate on what it means for you to be "upset" with your boss?

It's narcissistic to shape the world and make up stories according to your own needs rather than to accept what's real.

Darn right. You got it. And this confusion over who's who is not just something therapists deal with by asking questions. I see people in my office every day who make up stories about other people as if these were not fairy tales but 100 percent true accounts. Then they shout, cry, or laugh based on the "fake" reality they personally imagined rather than reacting to the "real" reality of what the recipient is sincerely imparting. The recipient retorts, "Wah, where did that reaction come from? All I said was…"

Here's a corollary to what I've just said. Did you know that *feelings are not facts*? If you feel angry with someone, it doesn't mean he was trying to make you angry or deliberately trying to hurt you. Just because you feel afraid of someone doesn't mean the person is trying to scare you. For that matter, because you are afraid doesn't mean there is anything of which to *be* afraid. You feel the usual sensations that accompany fear—rapid heartbeat, sweaty palms, maybe even light-headedness, but you don't know why you are shaking like this. There's no danger to behold. You attach a meaning to this experience of invisible danger, because it's too uncomfortable to feel the nebulous emotion without being able to say, "I know what ails me." Maybe you decide that if your insides are jumpy, it's because someone else is going to hurt you or someone else is being unfair. The reason doesn't matter as long as you can put your anxiety onto someone or something.

KATIE

I told Katie, the woman I described a few minutes ago who had lost her baby to miscarriage, "If today, you are having a feeling of a bad hair day, it doesn't mean your hair really looks bad. Maybe you think you are ugly because when you get angry, you feel like a monster. In the mirror you see an atrocious-looking person. Then you act as if what your eyes see is the truth. Your eyes are merely obeying your fury and internal agitation."

Eventually, we concluded, "If you feel guilty that you lost your baby, it doesn't mean you are actually guilty or have committed a crime."

DICK

I remember getting into this with Dick, the man with the terminal illness who died and left me grieving all by myself. "Dick, you are worried your wife won't make it on her own. Just because you believe it, doesn't necessarily make it so."

Dick was gracious in receiving my feedback. His smile always reflected an invitation for me to continue giving him my observations as well as gratitude that I cared enough to offer them. He said, "I know, you keep telling me—what is it again? Yeah, feelings are not facts. Okay. Good. Yeah, Alice can get along without me."

"Dick, the issue is not that Alice can get along without you. We have yet to determine that. The issue is, you are basing your perceptions of her on your feelings as if your feelings are indicators of absolute truth. All they signify is that you are worried."

CHRISSY

Chrissy made up stories about her husband. (Even though she was called Chris, I always thought of her as Chrissy, because the hurt little girl came through to me like a television character darting out of the screen and running to sit on my lap.) If her husband, Jack, showed any emotion whatsoever, she immediately assumed he was trying to manipulate her to do something for him. Her tirades baffled him. "Hey, all I said was I was stressed out at work, and now suddenly it's like I'm trying to get you to fix me chicken soup or something. Jeez, get a life, Chris!"

Then he would go off pouting and withdraw from her for days, all because she confused him with her mother, who exhibited distress as a way to manipulate her, and she didn't check out what he meant when communicating his displeasure.

When Chris brought this anecdote to me, it was very hard for her to see that her husband had done nothing underhanded. I had to drum it into her head very dramatically. I told her the lawn mower story, which tells of a man who, assuming his neighbor would begrudge him the use of the man's lawnmower, worked himself up on his way to his neighbor's house. By the time he got there, when the neighbor opened the door, the guy shouted, "You can keep your darn lawn mower!" She saw how she had caused the problem with her husband, but yet, she didn't see it. She resisted considering it, because in her mind her going along with it would make Chris wrong and her husband right.

We acknowledged that as a child, Chris was compelled to raise herself. Her parents lived in a haze. I pointed out that her mother pressured her through fear of religious retribution ("If you don't rake the leaves for the neighbor, it will be a mortal sin!"). Her mother virtually molded Chris to become the end all and be all for anyone who could make use of her talents. Chris resented having to take care of other people, but she took care of them anyway in order to be taken care of herself. She never experienced the joy of giving for it's own sake, and it's hard to receive when you had to give something away in order to get something in return.

Rather than Chris's using this information to help her reduce some of the strife in her marital relationship, she used it against herself, saying, "I really can be dumb sometimes."

Turning feedback given to you onto yourself and hurting yourself with it is a tactic many people use to stunt the therapeutic process. Personal reactions to feedback are important issues to explore as well as the actual insights themselves. Chris's specific reaction was typical for her. I was "giving" her information, and she couldn't take it in. She spewed it out at me, but she had to be nice in the process. For her, being "nice" translated into shouting to the world, "Look what a bad girl I am!"

The way people resist new learning is as important as the fact that they resist seeing the truth in the first place. It's just another hump we need to get through and a reaction from which we learn. In Chrissy's case, she was behaving toward me the way her mother had behaved toward her with the "see how you hurt me" stance. Of course, I pointed this out to Chris, and we strolled deeper into her psyche, slowly, patiently (on my part) and optimistically (on my part as well). Being optimistic on Chris's part was a big turn off. She couldn't give up her misery just yet. As a child, she had lived with her mother's pathetic locution, and by now, suffering for its own sake had a life of its own. Chris would feel naked without her gloomy despair.

MELANIE

We're still talking about therapists and our incessant, exasperating inquiries. I help people identify their feelings by questions, questions, and you guessed it, more questions. The investigation sometimes takes the form of hypothetical statements.

"Hi, Melanie, how's it going?

She sighs.

"You look like you have something on your mind," I gently query her with this statement of what I observe.

"I'm kind of down."

"Because?"

"My mother made me clean the kitchen, so I was late for Danny's party."

"What a bummer. Is this a frequent demand from your mom?

"No."

"But this time you were down about it. Could you give me another feeling word to describe your emotional reaction so I can understand better?"

"I was sad."

"Why sad?"

"I didn't want to miss the party. She didn't care."

"Then you're sad because you felt she didn't care about you?"

"Yeah. She always comes first."

"Do you ever get angry about that?"

"Well, yeah, but if I yell at her, she grounds me, and then I really can't go out with my friends."

"So you're not only sad because you feel she doesn't care about you but also angry because you feel she deliberately puts obstacles in your path to having fun."

"Yeah, and she's got all the power."

"She not only has the power, but you have to submerge your feelings about it."

Silence.

"What do you do with your anger?"

"That's a dumb question. I don't know."

"You feel the anger, right?"

"Sometimes. I've kind of worked out a way to get rid of it. When she looks at me with that mean face and says, 'Melanie, you're not going out until you clean the kitchen'—sometimes I even see her smirking—I distract myself by imagining my father and how he used to really put her in her place, oh yeah."

"What kind of thoughts?"

"I want to kill her."

"How do you feel when you realize you want to kill your mother?"

"Sometimes I feel guilty but...I don't know."

"Melanie, what were you going to say?"

"I wish she had died instead of him!"

Here it comes: the outbreak, the downpour. Torrents of tears come gushing out. (Melanie was referring to the car accident the family had on vacation when Mother was driving. Father was killed instantly when a van hit their car. Melanie's mother, who was driving, Melanie, and her brother were just scratched up a bit, but that's all.)

To think, Melanie was sobbing now, and it all started with a sigh, which I didn't take for granted, and then an exploration of, "I'm kind of down." These four words on the surface evolved into anger and grief heretofore unknown and unexpressed. And there was a lot more to come.

With gentle probing, we both learned about her feelings of responsibility for her father's death (she had been jibing at her vexed mother just before the crash), her promiscuity to assuage the emptiness inside, and her sneakiness as a way to undermine her mother.

More. More. More. Squeeze, squeeze, squeeze until we scrape the bottom of the data bank and begin to build it back up again. We get the information, but the facts alone won't do it. We need the emotion that swarms alongside the pearls of wisdom we have presently gained.

Naturally, people aren't always prepared to feel things. Many of us spend our whole lives trying to shed the ugly, repugnant, unmanageable feelings we were told make us bad, bad, bad human beings.

With Victor, Chrissy, Kevin—heck, with myself—I glean that we are persons who would rather not feel anything today, thank you! Yep. I, too, the human being that I am, have fashioned external ways to avoid the aches of life. The problem is, it's the evasive methods themselves that develop a life of their own and cause the harm. Therefore, I work hard to discover what's underground by being alert to my characteristic way of disguising my internal truth.

Patients and fellow human beings who don't want to feel often ask or rather declare: "What good is it to get in touch with uncomfortable feelings? It doesn't change anything."

Good question.

MELANIE

So now Melanie knows that if one of her parents had to die, she wishes her mother dead and her father resurrected. Now she can feel even worse!

Well, maybe we can ask Melanie for the answer to the question: "To feel or not to feel? What do you have to say, Melanie, dear?"

After traveling deeper into the caverns underlying her wish that her mother had died instead of her father, over time, Melanie began to change. We talked about how wonderful Father was, but then we got into what a hard time Father sometimes gave Mother by not taking her seriously, by countermanding Mother's discipline, by passively "forgetting" promises made, and by allowing Mother to take the fall for the unfavorable joint parental decisions. The more we went along, the more Melanie began to appreciate the challenges her mother faced.

She and I imagined how guilty her mother must be feeling, because Mother had been the driver of the vehicle of his demise. What a lonely place to be. Gradually, Melanie confided more in her mom. This helped her fill the empty place inside where she missed her dad, the vacant spot which would never completely go away, but hopefully would get smaller and smaller. Having assumed Father was the only one who could fill the void and now realizing that she could allow Mom in, Melanie diminished her promiscuous behavior and drug abuse.

It all sounds so simple now. But this took months of digging, resisting, insight, more resisting, and more digging. So maybe getting in touch with a horrifying feeling of wanting to kill off your mother so you can resurrect your father paid off in the end.

KATIE

There's a whole other side to the discussion of blocking your feelings to save yourself pain. There are lots of us in this world who, the more we feel and express our feelings, the more we want company. As we went along in treatment, Katie, the woman I described earlier who suffered a miscarriage, lamented because she was bursting with enthusiasm but surrounded by people who were very adept at neutralizing emotions. She was left feeling isolated and lonely. Except for the session after her miscarriage, she hadn't really shown me much emotion, yet we both agreed she was loaded with it.

Early in one session, I asked Katie if she ever gets excited. She said yes. I asked, "Have I ever seen you excited?"

She said, "Probably."

I heard what she said, but I'm in a quandary. I think maybe she feels everything thumping in her body but is so accustomed to squelching herself and reigning herself in, she is restrained. In actuality, she wants to burst out of her tight body and dance, jump, sing, and break free. Whether she knew it or not, given my intense passion for life, we were in sync.

At the end of the session, Katie and I set up the next appointment, and she said, "That's a good time slot. I'll be able to stop at the health food store on the way."

I took in a great deal of air. My eyes widened. I smiled broadly. With exuberance, I said, "Great! That's wonderful."

She asked, "Why did you say that?"

"Because I'm a weird person."

She laughed. "That's what I love about you." This spontaneous declaration of love for me was new for Katie.

I was modeling what it looks like to be excited on the outside and taking the risk to show it to others. She knew I was kidding around, but I think it made an impact. At least, she got into the groove, and as evidenced by her pronouncement of love for me, maybe even forgot her commitment to lock herself up at all costs. Sometimes actions do speak louder than words!

People ask me how I can remember so much about them. My good memory derives partly from my faculty of concentration.

Also, I'm an unrelenting detective, and my visual memory is acute. If I don't remember something by visual memory, I discover it by good investigative work. I'm the finder of lost objects in my house. For people close to me, I put myself into their brains and walk through the places they've been. Knowing a lot about how they process thoughts and feelings, I muster an educated guess as to where they would go next and how they could have inadvertently misplaced the item.

Same with psychotherapy: the things you learn as a child get "misplaced" or become connected to the wrong beliefs. Together, we must retrace our steps and work through the confusion.

My determination is to solve mysteries— that's what the therapeutic process is all about: gathering information, searching for clues, trying to make sense of how the clues fit together, understanding what makes you tick, using this new awareness to reexamine old scenarios, getting shook up because you don't want to see what you are seeing, knowing you need to change in order to feel better, fighting it all the way, looking at why you're fighting change for the better, overcoming your fears about changing, and then ta da! Finally—you change, and there's no turning back.

You really need someone with you who first of all knows how to dig for more, more, more information, or as I frequently say to my patients, "I need data. Give me daaaaaaaaata!" I usually do this in a lighthearted way but with exaggerated drama.

Next you need this same person to be a good detective in terms of putting the clues together, helping you stick with it while you're in the fighting stage, and partner with you throughout the whole process. Through it all, you need someone with persistence, who is cocky enough to think if she tries hard enough, she's bound to get to solution.

Why. Why. Why. Tell me why. Yes, this is important but not at the expense of the person's need to take it slowly and maintain control. Kevin's difficulty with trust, Chrissy's readiness to be abused, Dick's passivity, Victor's scarcity of descriptive feeling words, Katie's isolation because she couldn't be herself around others, Melanie's fear of aggressive feelings toward her mother, Jimmy's poor self-esteem and consequent acting out as a way to feel more powerful—all had to be worked through, each person at his or her own pace.

I want you to know I do not poach on people in a ghoulish way. All will be clear to my partner in pain as well as to me in good time—assuming we have the time, of course.

Here is an example of how my patient, Natalie, and I, through good detective work, solved the mystery of her symptoms.

NATALIE

Natalie was a twenty-something-year-old woman who in some ways was more mature than her age, and in others she still carried her adolescent rebellion into adulthood. She had already been married and divorced from a motorcycle gang member who had swept her off her feet and promised to rescue her from her bad stepmother, who of course, wasn't bad at all, just not a replacement for Natalie's biological mother who had died when Natalie was four.

When Natalie first consulted me, she was depressed and feared she would never find a man who would be good to her. She knew she deliberately looked for men who didn't give a care about her but who used her for their own needs. Even if she tried to find a first-rate guy, initially he would appear to be refined, but as soon as she fell for him, he would turn on her somehow.

Now she had come back from Utah to live with her two younger brothers and stepmother who had legally adopted Natalie when she married Natalie's father. Her father had died the year before.

We spent many of our beginning sessions trying to understand Natalie's anger toward her stepmother, whom as a young child, she had welcomed as a replacement for her deceased mother. The problem was that except for a few dreamy sketches, Natalie couldn't remember her mommy. Finally, I asked Natalie to bring in her father's photo album. In a very unique way, we were able to move on.

We huddled together, side-by-side, viewing the pages of her parents' courtship, her mother's pregnancy, and Natalie's subsequent birth and growing up. As is often true with first children, there were numerous photos of her: in the bath, in the carriage, on the swings, being tossed in the air by her daddy, and other pictures like these. The photographs to which we paid the most attention, however, were the ones where her mother appeared in the picture as well.

For hours, we reminisced, making up stories about how her mother must have felt:

"Look at her arm over your shoulder in this one. She appears so relaxed."

"Look how she's smiling in this one. She seems proud of her little girl."

"I wonder if your mom was a little harried here. Was she the hostess for the Easter dinner? Maybe she was overwhelmed? Or maybe she just didn't want her picture taken just then?"

Natalie added her observations:

"She seems tired in this one."

"This is my favorite. She looks so serene, and I remember when this one was taken. She had just brought me home from my cousin's wedding." Natalie beamed. "I was the flower girl."

We pieced together a story about her mommy using information her father had provided her while she was growing up. When we had exhausted our exploration and summed up a complete story of her mother's and her life together over the four years before her mommy died, we both felt somewhat satisfied.

Then it was time to bring in other family members. We decided on a great aunt and her mom's best friend. We had one session with each. We learned how ecstatic her mother had been to discover she was pregnant, her thrill at giving birth to a girl, and how her mother had fretted and cried when she realized that due to her terminal illness, she would be leaving her precious little girl. We gained knowledge about her mom as a child and teenager and how much Natalie resembled her physically as well as personality-wise. Finally, twenty-two years after the most devastating loss of Natalie's life, she was able to grieve.

Through our detective work, we ascertained that Natalie's father, in his attempt to keep his own emotions in check, hadn't allowed little Natalie to cry. He kept telling her, "Mommy will be back someday, you never know when." He kept this up until he couldn't take Natalie's pestering any more, so he admitted, "Mommy is in heaven, and you'll see her one day when you go there, but stop asking me. She's not coming back."

Even then, Natalie was told to get over it. Her daddy was very loving to her. He just didn't have the coping skills to deal with his own grief as well as his little daughter's. Somehow, Natalie realized this, and to save her father the hurt of which he was so afraid, from an early age, she stopped bringing up the topic.

As an adult, she was looking for her mother in the men she met, but at the same time, she chose men who had no sophistication particularly in the emotional arena. Just like her father, she had learned to keep her emotions deep inside and therefore sought a cold, emotionless he-man who would take her in his big hairy arms and keep her safe from disaster, something her father had failed to do. This was the kind of man who would never ask her how she felt. By being with him, she protected herself from getting in touch with forbidden feelings herself.

After Natalie had many good cries in my office (and I had many a lump in my throat, which accompanied reluctant and dripping tears), she began to rebuild her life. By our conjuring up a history—which wasn't real but was close enough to the truth, an internal truth—Natalie was open to meeting and falling in love with a sweet, maternal, and emotional man. She got engaged and bade me good-bye. On the last day, after we said good-bye, she closed the office door, and as I looked out the window to watch her get in to her car, I freely cried for joy and allowed myself the fantasy that she lived happily ever after.

We psychologists have our pet ways of imparting certain concepts. I use stories, visualizations, jokes, recounting of embarrassing moments, and linking book, television, or movie scenes to something the person is saying. I use my free associations, the things I imagine while talking with the unique person who sits across from me. The question to myself is: "Why did I think of this or that at this specific time with this particular person? What I'm remembering or fantasizing about must be connected to this person's way of relating to me or to others, or to his or her history." The detective rides again!

The idea is to link the patient's unique situation to the concepts exemplified in the story or memory or thought I articulate. The "love cake" is one of these shortcuts, as I call them, to broader ideas, which might take many more words to impart than the actual image we conjure up in the session.

When my patient speaks, he is saying things that are abridged; the words shrink the meaning of the whole thing. We as therapists, counselors, listeners, or teachers take the phrases and "unshrink" them, or unzip them in our minds and hearts just as we do with an unzip program on the computer that reverses the original condensation that was used to save memory or energy. Inside the listener, the thoughts become broad and comprehensive again, with full magnitude, but now we listeners need to communicate our understanding to the other person.

Words diminish the transmission of what we are thinking in relation to what the person just imparted. We wish to reflect something back, but our expression would also be a shrunken version. We hope these words are not shrunken too much so the person will know we have an understanding ear.

SUZANNE

Suzanne—the woman with all the physical problems and who in her twenties had an abortion—and I enjoyed many a session where I used my unconscious free-associative mind. With her, I provided zipped images to convey concepts that would have required too many words to get across. Suzanne was saying that in her mind, she revs up to do something. For example, she imagines people being so happy for her and giving her positive regard for the amazing feat she hopes to accomplish. Then, in real life, as soon as she takes a first step toward her goal, she gets discouraged and retreats.

I asked her if she had ever seen a specific Steve Martin routine on *Saturday Night Live.* She affirmed that she had. (For those of you who don't know what it is, I will oblige with my own twist on it. Exuberantly, Steve Martin spews forth a litany of all the things he will do. "I'm going to do this, this, and this." After he delineates all his grandiose ideas, he stops and looks at the audience. A sudden realization takes over him, as you can see by the expression on his face. He says, "Nahhhhhh!" denoting a never-mind attitude.) Suzanne said, "Yes, that's it! Exactly how I feel when I think up these things I'm attempting to do!"

Suzanne got the biggest kick out of my reference to Steve Martin's comedy. The therapeutic use of my association made our chances for progress a shoo-in. The first time she saw this routine, she most likely laughed with gusto. I linked her relaxed viewing of the comedy sketch and all the mirth that goes with it to the present day not-so-pleasant conflict she experienced whenever she imagined herself doing great things. Her laughter from the first event then became attached to the second, more painful one, causing the perception of pain to diminish. This kind of intervention works as a helping tool only when the person has familiarity with the event or if I can depict it so it's as if she had actually viewed it herself.

Also, there was an added benefit. She knew instantly when she brought up the whole topic in the first place that I understood exactly what she meant without my having to use a lot of words.

Also Suzanne imagined people looking down on her for not doing the something or other she had first believed she could and wanted to do. I told her this made me think of Julius Irving, the great 76ers basketball star, who when asked the secret of his success, responded, "I dare to be great!"

We talked about the courage it takes to be great. I suggested, "Suzanne, when you exercise each day, why not recite a mantra, telling yourself over and over each time you breathe in, 'I dare to be great.'"

I recommended she use affirmations to try to "drum it into her head" that she could be great if it weren't for her fear of what people would think if she attempted a difficult feat. I don't always suggest the use of affirmations for people as an antidote to an internal conflict. I usually prefer to go to the detective place and search for where the destructive self-message originated, but Suzanne had difficulty utilizing her recent and long-ago memory. I was hoping that through the use of affirmations, as she cognitively challenged her old ideas, she would unlock some of her earlier feelings and thoughts.

KEVIN

I often use sports situations to convey a point. It works well with most people but has the most pizzazz with sports enthusiasts like Kevin. (Remember, he was the boy who lost his dad and dealt with his mom's alcoholism, but as he got older, he diverted his energy and became the star of his high school baseball team.)

At the end of the 1990-91 Philadelphia Eagles football season, I was able to use a current sports example when I confronted Kevin about his not trusting me: "Kevin, most of your life, you were like Randall Cunningham. You have all this talent, but no receivers to catch the ball. This leaves you hungry, empty, angry.

You turn the anger on yourself, but you are the one with the talent. To take better care of yourself, you need to open yourself up to capable receivers, people who can take you in. For now, I'm your logical choice. I am ready, willing, and able to catch the ball, but you keep throwing it in the opposite direction. And because of your talent, just like Randall Cunningham, you do throw the ball well! Only in the wrong direction! Then you are out of my reach!"

The problem for Kevin is he wanted so much to trust a woman, in particular, just as he had entrusted his wife with his heartstrings, but she had turned on him. Or was Darlene just being her usual self but due to his wish to be taken care of, he had blinded himself to what she really was? In any case, why would he trust me now?

When I used the football illustration, Kevin smiled at me as if I were his football buddy, one of the guys. I know I earned some points that day.

As a therapist, I'm not necessarily trying to get people to *do* things; I am trying to get them to examine issues that are painful, but when worked through, will relieve their distress. I am always a coach. I'm asking people to move full throttle ahead toward the pain they have been avoiding all their lives. And like a coach, I sometimes give pep rallies in my office.

"Yes, it hurts. Yes, it is easier to eat away your troubles. Yes, you miss me too much when you are out there alone and you have to leave my office knowing that. But, you are making it. You are handling this pain without abusing food more than you used to. Now, get out there, team, and stretch yourself even further to achieve even more! Take me with you. Take me in today, and then you can think of me and know that I'm with you even when you're not in the office. Yes, it's hard to connect with me because you feel the pain of not having me when you want me, but you are learning how to take me in when we are together. Then you can carry me around with you forever. Then I'm always part of your team. This is what love is all about."

As you sit across from me in the warmth of the fireplace in your living room, which you have so graciously offered me, we will continue talking about my use of associations and stories as a way to convey hypotheses or points of confrontation to patients.

CHRISSY

I related what I call The Train Theory to Chrissy. This is my dilemma about whether or not to drive across train tracks even though the red light kept blinking but no train was in sight and the drivers behind me kept honking and I had to deal with defying the law or making those people unhappy. Chrissy made use of my *train theory* when it came to everyone's expecting she would be the chief cook, hostess, and bottle washer for every holiday. With the *train theory*, I made a decision that rather than fret about what to do every single time I came to the tracks each morning on my way to work, I would determine my choice of action once and for all and be consistent no matter what. Who needs the stress, right? Otherwise, it's like you are reinventing the wheel every day.

Chrissy decided not to cross the tracks—even though people around her were blinking red warning signs for her to be a good girl—by not going along with what everyone else (oops, I mean her mom) expected her to do, and she would just sit there even if everyone got angry at her (just as I had resolved to do so as not to have to agonize over the decision each time I approached the track!). Congratulations, Chrissy!

Here's another one of the ideas I use a lot—the this-versus-that dilemma. It has to do with scales. You identify a conflict.

121

Put one opposing thought or idea on each side. Address the conflict by weighing which side would feel less uncomfortable to do (or think or try on for size, whatever). You know what? I'll demonstrate with Kevin:

KEVIN

Kevin says he hates it so much when people brag. We establish that Kevin holds himself back for fear that if he is competent, he will necessarily have to sing his own praises about it.

I say, "Kevin, you have it set up to not feel good about yourself because if you do, you are in danger of tooting your own horn. It's as if you have a choice: to be conceited versus feeling like a nobody because you won't let yourself succeed! But as a nobody, at least you don't have a swelled head. Good for you. You have chosen being unconceitedly miserable over feeling obnoxiously successful."

"Yep," he agrees.

"Do you want to expand your business and become rich?"

"Well, yeah," he concedes.

"First, I need to know. Did you ever watch *Cheers* on TV?"

He nods.

"Do you remember the episode where obnoxious Cliff is shocked by a psychologist every time he does something stupid or annoying?"

"Yeah," he says hesitantly.

"Okay, let's try this, Kevin. You pretend to brag, and I'll shock you every time you show off. Sooner or later, you'll have had enough zapping until you get down on your hands and knees and swear you will never brag again. Then maybe you can become a rich man."

I told Kevin that I'm writing a book, and when I read over what I've written, I have to be satisfied, or why would I want to show it to others? We can assume if a painter allows his work to be displayed in a gallery, the painter is saying to the world, I am satisfied with this. I like it! If that painter had to worry about looking as if he were bragging, then he will not paint on the canvas in the first place and/or he won't display it. Since part of art is sharing your work, if everyone were afraid to brag, there would be no art.

All this came from the this-versus-that dilemma. I have proposed this formula to others, especially to creative people who are blocked.

My kind of therapy usually requires many sessions. This is why I have chosen not to be on any of the managed care insurance lists. It would just put a cramp in my style. Can you imagine my trying to treat someone like Chrissy in just twenty sessions? That kind of therapy just wouldn't cut it.

I do whatever it takes to help someone reach his or her personal growth goals, and I need the time to do it. When someone is drowning, it doesn't matter what you do to save the person. You do whatever you must to keep him or her from drowning...

I've made some unusual interventions in my day, all for the purpose of helping to prevent someone from drowning. Many of my colleagues might find these too way out, but I kind of like them.

For instance, I've had a few pillow fights with patients. However, I learned my lesson from engaging in these rollicks. The bottom line is simple. I'm just plain too old. Although I exercise regularly, pillow fight muscles aren't the everyday kind. The last time I engaged in such a battle, I could hardly move the next day. I hope those who were fortunate to catch me doing this with them, before I realized my body determined it to be a dumb idea, were able to get in touch with their anger, break through some barriers to spontaneity, and generally find the whole endeavor worthwhile, because no one's ever going to join me in that again!

I've gone out to lunch with patients, which is another ordinarily professional no-no. These were not social events. These were part of the therapeutic plan and were considered actual sessions. When we get to the eating disorder section, you'll learn more about occasions where I treated others to lunch and times when they paid for mine.

DICK

When I called the hospital and talked to Dick, the man whose death had caused me such lonely and isolated feelings, he said he knew he was never getting out of the hospital and was disappointed because as soon as their new kitchen set was delivered, he had wanted to have me to his home for lunch one day. It was the first time he told me about this wish. I was touched by his intention and would have been happy to oblige him. Given all the issues my visit would have engendered, we could have had enough data (remember: I need data. Give me daaaaata!) to discuss for months. Sadly, his aspiration never came to fruition.

KATIE

There was a point in Katie's therapy where she spent most of her time crying. I sat next to her on the sofa and offered her my shoulder. She was self-conscious about having her mascara stain my clothes, so I produced a terry cloth hand towel to cover my clothing. When I went away on vacation and she began grieving my absence, we decided she should keep the towel at home so she could have something of mine in her possession to help her through our separation. Katie had lost her mom at age twelve and had to grow up so fast; she never had time to grieve. It happened at a time in her life when she hadn't yet become a full-fledged teenager, so moving into adolescence was especially rough.

Then in her early twenties, she had a miscarriage, which brought back so much of what she missed with her mom. I temporarily took over the role for her, but she didn't want me to be hurt in any way by the overpowering emotion that erupted from her each session. We determined some of her concern about hurting me related to the formerly unconscious belief that her intense love, perhaps devouring her mother, had caused her mother's demise. The crying towel, as we called it, served as a transitional object for her, sort of like a teddy bear is for a young child when her mother is away. When Katie ended her therapy, she took the towel with her. I assume, years later, and hopefully many babies later, she still has it.

I've attended weddings (Natalie's would be among those you would recognize), funerals (I told you about Dick's), theatre productions, dance recitals, and school play productions (I did attend Melanie's senior play. Melanie was the teen whose father died in an accident while her mother was driving.). I've attended a Bris or two. A Bris is an ancient traditional Jewish ceremony commemorating a newborn boy's circumcision. Most significant in my memory is at a couple's house who, when they had first consulted me, in response to my question as to whether or not they had children, proudly announced, "Oh no, we choose to remain child-free!" which was the new buzz phrase of the era and designed to counteract and aggrandize the more negative sounding, "We are childless."

When I attend these functions, we discuss how I will be presented to the other guests: I either announce myself as a friend, or I attend incognito and only the person who invited me knows who I am.

I visited Kevin's auto parts store to admire his "empire," just as his father would have done. For weeks, Victor brought me some of his culinary treats. Each week I provided the tea, and he brought me one of his delicacies. We then discussed his feelings about feeding me and squeezed out as much therapeutic juice as possible.

I've given gifts and received gifts; I've also refused gifts from patients who unconsciously or consciously believe their paying my fee isn't enough. Somehow, they felt unworthy of my attention, support, and love and feel compelled to give me a little something extra.

I've brought in people's adult families for family therapy. In addition, we've arranged these meetings to deal with specific matters such as inviting a woman's extended family to attend so she could finally confront the reality that she and others siblings had been sexually abused, but it had never been said out loud. By speaking with the family in a formal session with my being present, we could avert the possibility of a violent reaction, at least in the office.

In one person's case, it was too late for me to serve as mediator, because the deed had already been done. A young woman who finally broke the ice of silence in her family suffered brutal repercussions. In her parents' living room, she spilled the beans. In response, her adult sister, brother, and mother wrestled her onto the plush-white carpet, and as they screamed obscenities and denunciations, they literally beat her up.

JUDY

Another non-traditional intervention I made was when I referred a patient of mine who had a dental phobia to a dentist. I treated not only my patient but also the dentist, who was extremely anxious that he couldn't do the work in his usual perfectionistic manner because my patient was so frightened and kept putting up her hand, signaling for him to stop the work, just as he had assured her she should do.

For me, this experience challenged my ingenuity. Other than behavioral techniques such as hypnosis, desensitization, and other methods, which had all been tried by other therapists prior to her seeing me, I was in a total quandary as to how to proceed. I'll describe the first visit to the dentist. The main characters are:

my patient, Judy; Judy's husband, Rick; the dentist, Dr. Oglesby; and I.

Nervously, she entered the office to which I had referred her and to which on other occasions she had already completed three or four harrowing, fragmented attempts by the dentist to get some decent work done on her teeth. This time was to be different, since I had suggested I come along. I could see her shaking from the inside, and beads of perspiration were forming on her upper lip. She introduced me to her husband. She and Dr. Oglesby had a good rapport. I had spoken to him after each visit she had with him, and he expressed his fond feelings for Judy that collided with his frustration over the poor care she had received in the past. He felt so inadequate to do right by her.

Judy didn't have problems with the pain. She had a great tolerance for it. Her difficulties arose from any instrument having to be left in her mouth for more than a second or two. You see, her fear was that she would choke to death, and if she had to swallow and there were things draped in her mouth, she might swallow them and/or choke on them.

Each time she raised her hand, signaling her need for him to remove the devices or so she could sit up and swallow a few times, just to be sure she still could do so, Dr. Oglesby became unmistakably agitated.

He explained, "Judy, it will help if while the things are in your mouth and we wait for the enamel to harden, you clench you teeth, because when you put your teeth together, you can swallow more easily." This advice seemed to help.

At one point, Judy put a tissue up to her mouth to absorb the excess saliva and in the process, she obviously ruined some of the work the dentist had done.

Seemingly ready to lose his cool, he blurted out, "Don't do me any favors please!"

As Dr. Oglesby continued working, he kept shaking his head, muttering almost inaudibly, "I'll have to redo this. It didn't come out right."

In the meantime, I kept reiterating to Judy, "It looks great. You're going to be happy with this."

The ball was back in the distressed dentist's court: "It's not right." I could hear his breathing, which sounded like a wind instrument of some kind. I was hoping we weren't going to lose him on our team. His internal motor was running fast enough for him to take off.

I quietly and unobtrusively put my hand on his shoulder. A few minutes later, I joked, "Dr. Oglesby, wouldn't it be nice if you could do dentistry on just teeth and not people?"

He looked up at me from his concentrated work and smiled. "Oral surgeons do it."

Supporting his newfound calm, I said, "Yes, they can do it perfectly."

Throughout the procedure, I continued to ask Judy how she was feeling. Her main concern was whether she could "handle it or not." She beseeched me, "How am I going to get through this?"

Soothingly, I assured her, "Judy, your fear is actually a fear of becoming afraid. You are afraid of being afraid. If you could distract yourself from worrying about your panic, you would be less anxious."

At this moment, Dr. Oglesby placed a band around the tooth to be filled. She abruptly sat up, shouting, "Get it out! Get it out!" Now she was sobbing. "What's the matter with me?"

I came closer to her, put my arms around her, patted her on the back, and said, "Okay, Judy, let it out. Make noise. Go ahead, cry it out. It's okay."

Before this first dental visit where I accompanied Judy to the dentist, we had discussed her associations to her teeth. In high school, she used to be known as the girl with the pearly white teeth. The tooth that the dentist was to work on had a temporary filling for five years, because she had never allowed her former dentist to work on it. This was the same tooth her father had told her should have been pulled. She described how angry he was at the dentist when he sent her with instructions to have the dentist pull it. The dentist felt the tooth should not be removed. She had already had another tooth removed when she was in sixth grade, which created a space, and her teeth spread out. If this present tooth were extracted, her mouth would be further misaligned. Obviously, Judy, herself, hadn't wanted the tooth removed.

I interpreted, "Then what you are doing by going to the dentist and having this tooth worked on is doing something wrong. It's going against your father's wishes."

She agreed.

"And whenever you do something wrong, you fear you'll be punished, and the way to be punished is to be choked or to smother."

At one point, I asked her how she was feeling about Dr. Oglesby. She said, "He's God. He doesn't make me feel embarrassed as all the other dentists did."

I said, "The Lord can give and the Lord can take away. You may be feeling loving toward him but angry at the same time." My provocative statement related to her telling me that at the last visit he put the band in, and she had assumed it would be a minute or two, but it turned out to be for twenty minutes. When she related this to me in my office, she appeared very angry about it. I had asked her then if she might be angry with him, and she had denied it.

When Dr. Oglesby left the office for a few minutes, I again brought up the possibility of her anger. "Even though you know he never said otherwise and it was your assumption, you could still be angry at him for not telling you the band would be left in for that long."

She nodded.

I suggested that Judy try a method of distraction so she wouldn't be worrying about panicking and therefore choking. "Judy, try this: use your right hand [the one the dentist had said she could raise whenever he was to stop], and count from one to five. Rick, you count out loud in correspondence with the amount of fingers Judy puts out." They were to perform this ritual during the five or ten minutes the dentist had the band on her tooth.

At first, Judy just put her hand up, but I said, "No, that's too many fingers. You're supposed to put up one finger at a time." She then performed the exercise correctly.

Later she told me that when the dentist began to work on her again, and I didn't ask her to count, she started to panic but began counting in her mind and that seemed to help.

Sometime in the middle of all this, another patient in the next office began coughing loudly and making choking sounds. Dr. Oglesby called out to the next room, "Are you all right?"

I almost started to panic then. I looked at Judy, Rick, Dr. Oglesby, and his assistant and spouted out, "Oh great! This is just what we need!"

It was like a dam burst. Shrieks of laughter filled the tiny dental office.

During the time Judy waited for the filling to harden, she and I walked around the waiting room, to kind of work off anxiety, and I learned more of Judy's history. In sixth grade she had a tooth pulled for which she was put to sleep. She remembered being afraid, because they took her from her mother, and she didn't know what was to happen. Then they put something over her nose. When she woke up, her mother wasn't there.

Later on, the children in her class were supposed to go to the nurse for inspections of hands, ears, and teeth. The nurse looked in twelve-year-old Judy's mouth, and in front of all the other children said, "Look at this. You've had a tooth pulled. This is a disgrace."

Judy told the nurse she had gone to the dental clinic, and the dentist said it had to be pulled. At the time, although Judy didn't know why, she felt as if she had done something very wrong, because the nurse said she was a disgrace.

I said, "Once again, you felt you had done something wrong, and it had to do with your teeth."

"Yep, I thought maybe I didn't brush good enough."

At the end of the dental visit, I asked Dr. Oglesby if he thought I should come back again, or if next time she should try it alone.

He said, "No, I think you should come again, not for her sake, but for mine. I need you. When I was starting to lose it, you sensed it and put your arm on my shoulder. I immediately settled down. Our talk yesterday helped too. Now I realize I just can't do everything I want to do for her. Your being here helped her cry it out, or else she never would have made it. She probably would have cried the whole rest of the time she was here."

This was a situation where Judy was "drowning," and I had to do whatever it took to help her even though I didn't rightly know what I was going to do. I learned that to express logic to her didn't help. It merely seemed to make her feel more embarrassed and childish. More importantly, when I asked her how she was feeling and to what these feelings related and also of what the experience reminded her, she experienced some relief.

We all met together in Dr. Oglesby's office on at least three other occasions. We relieved Rick of his duty as coach and on-deck supporter. He remained in the waiting room while I treated Judy and Dr. Oglesby alternately. I realized that the dentist's plight was equivalent to a hypothetical situation where I would be trying to understand my client's problem while someone else shouted in my ears. Here I would be attempting to do my job while at the same time having to blot out the clattering in my brain. If I were in this predicament, I would undoubtedly come undone as Dr. Oglesby had.

I was on the lookout for Dr. Oglesby's reactions as much as I was for the effect on Judy. The reality was, I was holding all three of us together. What an amazing adventure this was, and I'd have to say, given my advice to the dentist as well as to myself that we couldn't do a perfect job, we had a therapeutic as well as a dental victory.

How do I think up some of the stuff I do to help people out of the depths of despair? Do I have the answers or the remedies tucked away in my hip pocket and pull them out when the textbook tells me to do so? The reality is I'm a slow thinker and not as glib as Judd Hirsh was in the movie *Ordinary People*. He said some of the coolest stuff, didn't he?

Many questions my patients ask have never been asked of me before. I'm trying to link their words today with something they might have said a year ago. Or when they bring this topic before me, I recall one of the dreams they reported three weeks ago to which I now associate. I am slowed down to a dull and painstaking (as felt by my patient) pause. Whatever comes up, it's coming from this person, this unique history and our novel therapeutic relationship. It's a first for both of us. I don't use formulas, but if I did, they sure would help to provide shortcuts to my protracted, methodical processing of the material they present to me.

When patients are particularly appreciative of an interpretation I make or of my recall of a very minuscule fact about their early life or when I bring up something from many sessions ago, they tell me I'm extraordinary. They're often surprised when I respond, "Thank you, but I would say quite the contrary. I'm very ordinary."

When they protest and I say, "It's the idea I can be ordinary that makes me extraordinary." You see, I accept myself and my slow on-the-uptake brain, which works in my favor, because I make no assumptions about people and have to keep excavating for more data. It's not a technique. It's really because I'm a measured thinker. Not kidding. True. True. True. My sluggishness has made me into a good therapist by default.

Nevertheless, when you help people through their pain, it's hard for them to believe you are ordinary. I remember in one of my group therapy meetings, in response to the topic at hand, sharing my free association once again, I said to the group that I just had this fantasy that a gunman walks in and tells us all we are his hostages. Someone said, "Oh, that's okay, you would save us, Phyliss."

I sure hated to disappoint them (back to the "nothing bad ever happens to a therapist" theme), but I said, "If that happened, I would be as scared as everyone else. I'd be on the same page as you guys. How would we mobilize ourselves as a group to deal with the crisis?"

This gave us hours of further discussion, but for me, as I told them later, the idea of my rescuing everyone from the armed gunman: "All bets are off!"

What a reality blast to these people who thought me extraordinary and who were forced to look inside themselves for their own fortitude, resourcefulness, and ability to cooperate in order to survive in our feigned heist or in the outside world— they were one and the same.

When it comes to patients' appreciating my having helped them, even though I'm ordinary, I graciously accept their displays of love and gratitude. After all, I was once in their shoes. I know how it feels to transform with the aid of a smart and caring partner. When I was ending my analysis, as I lay on his couch and he sat behind me—a scene we had both shared for years—I sang the praises of this man whom I regarded as mother, father, and darn good friend. With love and admiration, I also saw him as a surgeon, because during many therapeutic hours, I felt as if he were cutting me up into pieces.

He said, "You did the changing. I was just a catalyst in the process." We both knew a catalyst is an agent that by its presence changes something, but it doesn't actually get mixed up in it. He was implying that anyone could have helped me; the healer almost didn't matter except that he is competent to do so.

At first, I tried to go along with his message. That's what we all tend to do when the authority speaks. Over those last few weeks of four sessions per week, I gradually began disputing his protestations of "you did it, I'm a catalyst" stance. As I professed love for him, I even teased him, "Oh yes, that's right. You're a catalyst, I know."

On another occasion, I said, "I know you'd like to believe that all you were was a catalyst, but sorry to disappoint you. You didn't do a good job of making it so. Therefore, you are a failure as a psychoanalyst. What would Freud say about all this?" I had such fun chiding him and thoroughly enjoyed hearing his laugh. (Remember, in traditional psychoanalysis, because the doctor sits behind the patient, the analyst can't be seen.)

A few years later, when I visited him, with a tender-yet-smart-aleck tone, I again referenced our catalyst controversy. He was just plain wrong. Yes, he was a catalyst in some ways, but he was more than that. Therapists can't help but rub off on their patients. I assume he had aspired to be a psychoanalyst clone of Freud's, a proponent of the idea that the analyst remains neutral and the patient projects all kinds of stuff onto the analyst. Then these imagined pronouncements by the patient are examined and related to the person's present and past life. In reality, Freud was known to be more than a blank screen. He once fed a starving patient, which is one example of his insinuating himself into the therapeutic relationship. But that's neither here nor there. The point is this man made a giant impact on my life and was denying the fact because of his style of conducting therapy.

My experience in my own intensive therapy taught me to graciously receive my patients' love, admiration, and gratitude. Also, part of my being the loving therapist is being able to not just give love, but to receive it as well. It can be such a put-off when someone doesn't take in the gestures of adoration from a person who feels so strongly toward him.

We have arrived for now at the end of our discussion of the helping process. There's so much more to it, but perhaps you have had enough for now and want to embark on some other really cool topics. At least, I do. The helping process will be embellished as we go along anyway, so you don't mind, do you, if we shuffle on?

In any case, we're going to get back to some concepts and to some of the people you've met so far. Each time we repeat something or talk about Chrissy or Kevin or Dick or Katie or Melanie or Suzanne or Victor or any of the others, just as it happens in therapy, we will end up where we started, back to their roots, but each time we will be traveling to the depths of the truth and be re-experiencing their lives on a more meaningful level.

I often imagine our sessions like a metal carving, the kind where you take a chisel and keep pressing in deeper so lines are formed, which get more entrenched, so the foreground gets more prominent. Each time I ask a question or a person gets in touch with something about which we've talked before, our etching becomes more of a masterpiece.

I'm glad we got most of the theoretical and technical stuff out of the way. Let's get back to the people who help to vivify my life. Let's move on to love.

IT'S EASY TO FALL IN LOVE: IT'S STAYING IN LOVE THAT'S THE CHALLENGE

JIM AND PATTY FIELDING

Mr. and Mrs. Fielding smiled in unison and followed me into my office. The timing of their grins was uncanny, sort of like a chorus of cartoon happy faces. There was the usual scurry of activity as they decided where to sit and the best place to set down her handbag and his briefcase. I arranged myself in my chair, put my feet up on my footstool, and gazed with interest at them. We were all in a state of readiness.

After a short pause, as if they both understood a clandestine dialect, she glared at him and shrieked, "F— you!"

So began our first session.

Over several months, my office became a battleground. During the period Mr. and Mrs. Fielding came to me for couple therapy, I worked in a commercial office building. My psychiatrist husband, Will, and I each had our own office, and we shared a common waiting room.

After a few weeks of warlike sessions similar to the initial one, Will started getting on my case. "Can't you keep them down? They're so loud. It's distracting me and my patient."

Normally, the common wall between our offices was soundproofed well enough to keep out reasonable noise, but we had never tested it for protection against shouting matches. Of course, Will knew better than to ask me to hush up my patients, but he was appropriately frustrated. How do you shut people up when this is an atmosphere of freedom: "Say anything that's on your mind."

Other than the concern I had for my husband, his patient, and their work together, I rather enjoyed the war zone that was recreated every week in my office. Most other couples I treat are often on their best behavior. This twosome was in essence allowing me right into their private bedroom. I felt privileged to be one of the family.

Jim's first wife had showered him with affection. It sickened him the way she catered to his every need without solicitation as if he were her prisoner and she the guard who rang the bell at chow time. Betty Boop: she treated him as a sonny boy. Many things she did to please him were incorrect estimates of what he desired and turned out to infuriate him instead. Arlene divorced him after she discovered he was having an affair with another woman, who lacked his wife's sweetness and innocence.

This second wife, Patty, turned out to be a shrew, like a dog who shakes off excessive moisture and sprays everyone around her. From the first day on, I expected her to come clattering into my office, which she did as if she owned the place.

So it is with many couples who are in second and third marriages. People make a mistake and marry for the "wrong reasons," or so they say, and then set out to find someone who is opposite the first mate ("jerk," "asshole," or "idiot" as these bad guys have been so named). To get as far away as possible from their ex's worst trait, they find themselves plopped right in the middle of a different kind of hell. In fact, they themselves become what the former spouse was to them. In order to get away from his first wife, Arlene, Jim became Arlene and was now married to Patty.

Allow me to clear up the confusion. Presently, Jim unctuously catered to Patty's every whim in the same manner his former wife had done in an attempt to please him. Of course, according to Patty, his attempts to make her happy were all wrong. He could never gratify her, and she let him know it. Nevertheless, he kept trying. The more he prostrated himself to strive even harder, the more she turned on him. The unanswered question that I asked myself but Jim never even considered was: "Would he rather marry a sappy woman or become one himself?"

Each week, her hair seemed to be pulled tighter into a bun than the week before. Without a hair out of place, she blasted him. He was like a little boy pleading and fawning and hoping, *This time she'll like my answer.* He didn't have a clue and looked at me to offer him the multiple-choice answers for which there was only one. Many patients hold the misconception that I'm holding an answer but waiting for them to discover it. Although this hypothesis is rarely correct, in this case, I *was* holding the solution: *Put this woman in her place. Stop her in her tracks. Send her to her room. Stand up to her. She'll love you for it.*

Women don't necessarily want to take over and allow their aggression to go out of control. Women want a man who is not afraid of them. Contrary to popular belief, they don't want a man to dominate them either, which is what can happen when a passive man tries to reverse his wimpyness by overcompensating and becoming a bully. Women want acceptance, but they want their man to respect *himself* as well. (Okay, I know I'm generalizing, so don't get on my case. It's just too cumbersome to put in a bunch of disqualifiers every time I say something about women or men. Give me the benefit of the doubt please.)

So, in addition to the objectives of helping a couple more effectively communicate, problem solve, and resolve conflict, my goals with Mr. and Mrs. Fielding were quite simple: help him discover his backbone; help her find the little girl deep within herself who feels vulnerable, empty, and unloved. She desperately wanted a mother couched in her husband's body, but he was trying too hard to please his own mommy substitute of a wife to be able to be a mother to Patty. She would never allow him to see her neediness, because she feared he might use it against her as her mother had. Ultimately, he would abandon her; deep down, she was sure of it.

Therefore, I "fed" her and I "beefed" him up.

"Patty, you must feel so lonely."

"Patty, when he re-created another dinner because you dumped the first dinner he had prepared into the garbage, I think what you really wanted was for him to take you in his arms and say, 'I love you. You deserve a better dinner.'"

When I made this interpretation, the almost imperceptible tremor on either corner of her mouth indicated to me that I had struck a sympathetic chord within her aching heart.

To Jim, I said, "I don't think Patty feels good about herself when she verbally abuses you. You are strong enough to help her by asserting yourself," or, "Jim, you need to take better care of yourself. Don't allow her to hurt you."

You might ask, "If in front of his wife, I was telling Jim to remind Patty to be more respectful to him, since Patty wanted to be boss, wouldn't she refuse to come back to couple therapy?" Funny thing how diagnostic it can be when people seemingly resist unpopular interventions yet still return for more sessions! Just as a three-year-old emerges peacefully from her room to which she was sent for "time out," so Patty wanted to be rescued; she sorely yearned to give up her wretched bossiness. It's no fun being a witch, especially when it emanates from rage over feeling irrevocably empty inside. The entire racket she creates never gets her what she wants anyway. I pictured Patty as if at her core there were a thunderstorm constantly erupting, causing her to be out of breath from desperation. In reality, whenever she went on one of her tirades, her red face loomed large, and she wheezed and coughed.

After months and months of my sounding like a robot who spouts out preprogrammed messages, I noticed that Patty began to soften and allow Jim to please her. Each one of her minuscule changes toward her acknowledgment of what he did for her and each time she exhibited her pleasure over some slight behavior of his, Jim went into covert raptures. All he wanted was to do right by her. Strange as it may seem to an outsider, he really did love Patty.

As he felt more competent to be "her man," and as he learned to assert his right to receive courteous and considerate conduct, he stood up for himself more frequently. He wasn't bossy as she had been, which would have been tit for tat, his turning the tables. No, he uttered such phrases as, "Come on, Patty. It hurts my feelings when you talk to me like that!"

She would immediately exhale, pause, and then meekly say, "I'm sorry."

Wow! The *I'm sorry* was the hardest for her, but I believe my being there with her in the office as if I were her protective mother helped her to unearth her soft side.

When this couple ended treatment, they literally walked out of the office holding hands. As I reminisced, recalling their first session, I must say, I did feel a bit puffed up and impressed with myself. It had seemed such an impossible feat to bring these two embattled creatures together. Not only were they reunited, but they were now lovebirds. What a joy to behold!

DIANE AND RICH

Here's a description of another couple with similar issues as Jim's and Patty's but not as "loud." Diane was constantly complaining about her husband, Rich. "He never does anything right. If only he would listen to me and do as I say, he wouldn't get into problems. If he tries it his way and fails, I always say, 'You should have just done what I told you!'"

One day, in our individual session, Diane was reciting her usual list of Rich's incompetence. "Why is he so clueless? If we're getting ready to leave the house and I'm busy, he shouldn't just be sitting around. He should find something to do. Wouldn't you think he'd get the diaper bag and fill it up with what we need that day?"

Knowing that one of the contributors to Diane's depression and anxiety had to do with her overwhelming need to be in control, I said, "Perhaps he doesn't know what you want him to put in the bag."

"But he should know."

When he's done it in the past, has he done it right?"

"No way!" she griped,. "He's so stupid, he forgets the important things and throws in stuff I don't even need."

I wanted Diane to put herself in Rich's shoes. I said, "Perhaps he's afraid that you'll scold him if he does it wrong, so out of nervousness, he either can't think straight, or he doesn't attempt it at all. I wonder if he feels that he can never please you."

"That's possible." Even though Diane could sound very harsh, given support, she had the capacity to soften and open herself to new ways of looking at things.

I suggested, "You could write down a list of what to pack and leave it in the bag for him."

It was hard for her to stay in that open place. "I don't want to do that. He should know what to do. Why doesn't he just use his head and figure out what belongs in the bag?"

I retorted, "Suppose people had genes for each type of survival skill they needed? There could be a letter-writing gene, a math gene, a reading gene, a going-shopping gene, a giving-the-kids-a-bath gene. [I knew Diane thought Rich did a good job of bathing the children.] Now, let's consider the idea of a diaper-bag gene. Whenever the issue comes up, you could say: 'Rich, you know, you have a missing gene. You don't have a diaper bag gene. I'm going to give you a report card. You get an F in Diaper Bag."

We both chuckled at the absurdity of this potential dialogue with Rich. Diane left that session laughing. Of course, she told her husband about it, and they both roared and playfully added their own preposterous notions. From then on, every time the issue of the diaper bag came up, Diane and Rich would look at each other and laugh, thereby discharging the pain that surrounded it. They were connected in the laughter. And, by the way, eventually Diane, on her own, made a packing list and put it in the bag.

The toxicity contained in the bag disappeared and was replaced with a list and a laugh, with space left over for more love between Diane and Rich.

LINDA AND TIM

Another couple I treated revealed the opposite picture from Mr. and Mrs. Fielding and from Diane and Rich. In this case, the wife, Linda, definitely didn't overplay the shrew role. In fact, her husband, Tim, treated her as if she didn't exist at all. She had a medical condition, which I never quite understood. Linda had some kind of mini-strokes and periodically passed out on the spot. One time in my office, without warning, she dropped to the floor.

He literally didn't miss a beat. He interrupted himself and casually mentioned, "You see her on the floor. There she is. That's what happens."

Then with Linda collapsed on the floor like a rag doll in a most unflattering pose, Tim continued what he had been saying before she so rudely distracted him by fainting on my carpet.

Finally, restraining my expression of disbelief that anyone would mistreat a person this way, I said, "Tim, how do you feel about Linda's being passed out on the floor while we continue our conversation?"

I must say, my usual neutral tone had a bit of value judgment in it. His nonchalant, unruffled, and dispassionate stance stunned me at first (even though it's hard to shock me) and caught me off guard.

By the time he answered, I had composed myself. He sputtered, "What? Oh yeah, I know it looks bad when I act like this, but she always comes around. The truth of the matter is you know what? She talks so much, I never get a word in edgewise, except when she's out cold. She even talks in her sleep, would you believe?"

You see how initial judgments can be so off base, how things don't always appear as they really are? While his wife was laid out dead center on my multi-colored tapestry area rug, with the specks on her mottled face matching some of the spots on her dress, Tim shared the thoughts that interested *him* for a change. It was then I learned how Linda's garrulousness might be more than just her being a chatty person. Perhaps it was a symptom of immense anxiety similar to the kind I see with women, and sometimes men, who virtually have a phone attached to their heads as well as a television or radio on in the background. Quite often, people like this are petrified to be alone. They might not even know it, because for so long they have survived by incessant chattering and/or making sure someone, be it real or a television character, is always with them.

I must say, as if I were looking at both of us from somewhere on the ceiling, I noted that Tim's and my conversation was much more interesting and substantive than usual. I was actually becoming accustomed to engaging in this conversation while his unconscious wife slept on. Oh my, what was happening to me? I was evolving into a hardened woman, or so it seemed in this case. However, by going along with Tim's way of relating to his wife's momentary verbal absence, he and I were developing a nice rapport, which served well for our future visits.

What a fortunate break for me to have witnessed this example of his suddenly disappearing wife; I never would have understood its impact nor would I have gotten to know Tim so well. I had wondered about Linda's rapid fire talk devoid of much meaning behind her words and had suspected she might be using unremitting language to cope with this anxiety, but Tim really straightened out the mystery, and I was much better able to help Linda because of it.

When Linda came to, as they say, we had to catch her up on the details of our experience. Rather than relying on (or rather counting on) Linda's losing consciousness in order to give Tim an opportunity to speak, we directly addressed the issue of her monopolizing the airtime between the two of them.

As it turned out, after further deliberation, she agreed her anxiety dictated her loquaciousness. Deep down, she feared silence, which she experienced as abandonment or as an indication that she was stupid and not worthy of any attention. In her attempt to cope with the anxiety, her fear actually came true, because the behavior assigned to deal with the anxiety resulted in pushing Tim away. So in the end, he was abandoning her as she had feared, not because she was unworthy or stupid, but because the things she did to countermand the anxiety were quite difficult to tolerate on his part.

Sometimes I think women (there I go again generalizing) take too much credit for being such experts on men. I'm thinking of the countless women whom I've treated in individual therapy who tried to convince me their husbands would never be willing to join them in therapy because their husbands don't care, are against therapy, think it's women's stuff and not related to them, or because they are just plain *tough guys*. In my experience with couples, despite what their wives tell me, I often find that many men are lambs dressed in wolves' clothing. All they want is to please their wives and just can't figure women out to ascertain what women want in the first place.

I usually say, "If you want your husband to join us in our therapy session, you have the power to get him to come in."

Sure they protest, but I insist I'm right, and if unconsciously they don't want him in, maybe they would ask him to join them in their session, but he'll get the message it's okay not to attend, and in fact, it would be best for their wives if they didn't barge in on her therapy. Then I ask the women to think of all the reasons they *wouldn't* want him here. Quite often, one of their worst fears is that I'll see their husband's side of it, and they will lose my high regard.

Based on the history of so many women who, along with their mothers, have been treated as less than men, it's understandable they fear losing my regard to their more coveted male partner. Don't women often remain silent in mixed company and turn to the women in the room to express themselves? Their behavior is based on previous experience of being cut off or ignored if they do venture an opinion to a man or to a group of men and women.

The truth is I always see the husband's side of the struggle. It's never failed to happen. However, I understand and respect their wives' viewpoint as well, and they would never lose me in the process. By searching for and acknowledging their husband's perspective, I can help the wife change behaviors, which she thinks are doing the trick but are, in fact, producing more harm than good. And obviously, I can help her man by facilitating his understanding of his wife's discontent, of his own hang-ups, and how these collide with his wife's.

You've observed a little bit of how I work with a woman who might, out of self-protection, push her husband away and not realize it. Even so, I must remind you and my patients that I truly make no judgments. When couples present their cases to me, I view it as two people passing in the night, two people in pain who each feel neglected and misjudged in some way and who are misreading their partners' behavior and motivation.

Their spouses are behaving in defense of early hurts in their lives, which has nothing to do with the other person in the dyad but can easily be misconstrued as being a personal affront by either partner. Neither has given the other the benefit of being an individual person with his or her own motivation for doing things. Remember when we talked about making assumptions or stories about why people do what they do or appear to be something they are not? Couples need to test reality and ask shrink-like questions such as "What do you mean by that?"

JANICE AND BOB

I'm thinking of Janice and Bob, who were moving along quite nicely in learning how to communicate more effectively. They had practiced some of the feedback skills I had taught them. For instance, Janice used to say something like, "You are so negative!" whereas now she described his behavior rather than evaluating it: "When you roll your eyes, I feel scared!" She was following the rule I had repeated so often: *describe* behavior rather than *evaluate* the other person's behavior.

At first, Bob took this feedback personally, but then we discussed Janice's fear of her father, whose facial expressions served sometimes as a warning that at any moment, he might soon be beating her up. Before long, Bob became Janice's greatest supporter. Here she was giving him the gift of telling him how he impacted her, and instead of his usual accusatory tone, he reached out to hold her hand. Once, to capture the stream of tears flowing down her cheeks, he actually took out his handkerchief and tenderly dabbed it to absorb the rivulets of salty moisture. (I nearly melted inside!)

Bob was also transforming in his own right. Rather than generalizing about her behavior, "You're always mothering me!" he reworded his feedback to be as specific as possible. He said, "When I say I don't need any help and you continue to push your point, I feel pressured." Bob had internalized another rule I had espoused: when offering feedback, it helps the receiver if you are specific rather than general.

Janice and Bob behaved as if they were my star pupils. However, in their daily life, they continued to make up stories about each other. You see, in our sessions, when I was present, I could redirect them and remind them of effective communication guidelines.

Like a little girl who tattle tales on the bad boy to the teacher, Janice complained, "He's always trying to control me."

Of course, I questioned her, "What makes you say that?"

Janice sat up tall in her chair as if she were on a throne and spelling out edicts for her subjects to follow. "I asked him for advice on whether or not I should tell my boss about Susie's starting rumors about me. He says maybe I should look for another job!"

"Did you ask him why he said that?"

"No." Her inflection made her "no," sound more like "*noooooo*."

"Then what makes you so convinced he wanted to control you?"

She grimaced. "Come on, Phyliss. You know how he acts like he knows what I should do all the time."

I turned to Bob. "Bob, what do you say?"

Bob squirmed in his seat and moved his chair so it more directly faced his wife. "I was feeling bad for her having to deal with those sassy women. She should work somewhere where they appreciate her."

There we were again with Janice making assumptions, not performing a perception check, and not being open to Bob's point of view, believing he was the same old Bob he used to be.

I told them the cute little story about the middle-aged man and woman who are driving in a car. They have been married for twenty-five years. The woman who is sitting in the front passenger seat says, "You know, it seems that every year, we sit further and further apart."

The man, who was driving, says, "Well, *I* haven't moved!"

This couple worked hard and bravely to open themselves up to self-examination and were rewarded for their efforts: Janice and Bob eventually accepted the newfound changes in their spouse, and ultimately, their mutual perceptions were more in sync with each other. They were now able to have more fun! Isn't that what it's all about: playing together, amusing each other, and having a ball?

Imagine a man has expressed his frustration over his disgruntled wife's seemingly whacky and meandering expectations countered by her complaints that her husband is clueless to know how to make her happy. The embittered man, whose main thrust has been trying desperately to be able to please his wife, and when unable to accomplish the task, depicts her as insatiable. In accord with his sentiments, I often reflect a man's frustration by putting my arms in front of me, palms up in a what-me-worry pose, and almost sing the words, "Women! You can't please them no-how!"

For the most part, both the man and woman respond positively. The guy sees it as my understanding his plight. The woman gets the point—*Give the guy a break already! He can't read your mind. You may want a mother in your man who knows how to nourish you, but you ain't gonna find one of those on this planet!*

But maybe you can come close by educating him as to how you think, what you need, and who you are.

I'm not going to elaborate on all the pointers that cause men their troubles. That would be reason for yet another book. But I would like to tell you some of the more salient concepts I've learned about men and women after all my years of working with lost relationships. In particular, I'd like to tell you what I believe men need to know about women.

Rule #1: Husbands and lovers, take heed: when your woman is being serious about something, she doesn't appreciate your jokes. Maybe that's what you do with the guys, but females hate it. And guess what? At moments like these, they don't find you as funny as you find yourself.

HARRY AND SALLY

Sally asked her husband, "Harry, my mother and I have been getting along a little better, don't you think?"

With a huge grin on his face, Harry responded, "That's because your mom's away on vacation!"

Sally was looking for confirmation, and instead, Harry responded with a wisecrack.

Upon my observing his wife's sunken face, I asked Harry, "I bet you're pretty funny with your friends when you tailgate before the Eagles game, aren't you?"

Grinning, he says, "I can hold my own."

"I can tell. You really are witty a lot of the time in here. When you joke around, Sally laughs at your jokes. It seems as if the two of you have fun together doing that."

"Yes, you should have seen her on Saturday when we were with Edith and Bill and I told them what happened to me the last time I flew to Chicago. She was torn up with laughter. Tears were running down her cheeks."

"Sally, how did you feel when Harry responded to your question about getting along better with your mother?"

Sally ran her hands over her shirt as if to iron out the wrinkles. She put her arms around her knees. "I hate it when he does that."

We determined that Harry often responded in this manner, yet Sally's neediness compelled her to keep coming back for more by asking these self-affirming questions. Eventually, her hurt over his whimsical put-downs built up inside of her. Without realizing her resultant behavior was the outcome of his chronic and questionably comical dismissal of her feelings, he was baffled as to why she picked on him for little things he did or didn't do around the house.

I asked Harry, "What do you think about Sally's reaction to your statement about her relationship with her mother?"

"I was just kidding. I don't know why she has to take things so seriously."

Sally piped in, "Hey, it's not serious to *you* maybe, but it is to me. You act like the progress I've made with my mother means nothing!"

Sally felt belittled by him, and from his point of view, what's the big deal over a lighthearted comment he made? I know it makes no sense to some of you guys, but you'd save yourself so many backlashes if you just took my word for it.

Rule #2: Another tidbit I pass on to fathers of teenage girls as well as husbands about their wives is to *be aware of her "thin skin."* During the time when your daughter is taking liberties to ridicule you, she is simultaneously super sensitive to every comment uttered by *you*! She's not so sure it's that great to be a woman. Even if you make a light joke about her, it will have an intense negative impact. She will feel "crushed" by the man who used to be her hero.

Adult women tell stories of irrevocable memories of their fathers' making comments about their bodies. These memories seem to be even more devastating than the lunchroom scenes of discrimination I talked about many hours ago.

Sandy remembers dancing at a family wedding with her dad. He was such a great dancer, and under the swirling lights, he made her look like the most graceful female in the room. As they spun around the room, they smiled into each other's eyes. Daddy laughed self-consciously as he said, "Sandy, when are you going to lose weight?"

Need I tell you how crushed Sandy was? The comment seemed to come out of nowhere just at the time she was feeling so adored by her dad. Sandy never forgot this dreadful moment in her life and referenced the experience at least once every other time we met.

Lucy primped and fussed over herself as she prepared to go to the prom. When she paraded into the living room, beaming with pride, her father said, "That dress is too low. You look like a whore!" She ran to her room, and when her date arrived, she refused to go to the prom.

Mary's father told her she looked matronly in her taffeta dress. She was only twenty-five at the time, unmarried, and despondent. She sunk lower into depression and eventually sought psychotherapy.

Katie's dad said she resembled his sister, Aunt Rose. Aunt Rose was fat! Katie didn't stay around to find out what he meant by that remark.

Karen's father said she looked like her mom, which made her feel good, because she knew he thought Mom was gorgeous. Then he followed it up with, "But you're so skinny!" Dad doth giveth and Dad doth taketh away!

All of these women plus scores more tell these stories with tears in their eyes, quivers in their lips, and big wads of tissues in their wringing hands.

Some teens develop eating disorders shortly after Father utters a seemingly casual, lighthearted remark such as, "Getting chunky, aren't you?"

My advice when it comes to comments about her body, is to take no chances. It's best to say nothing. Keep up the admiration, though, about how pretty she looks or how nicely she dresses. Anything that comes close to criticism is better left unsaid.

The same goes for your wives, particularly if you are married to middle-aged women. This is the time of life a woman's body is changing in the reverse way it transformed when she was a teenager. If you are married to a younger woman, very often, she can do something to change her body shape or size: go on a diet, exercise, and buy more flattering clothing; you can figure it out. But menopausal and post-menopausal women often have no options to prevent the formation of their sagging breasts, widening waistlines, and wrinkling skin.

The same advice I give to fathers of teens applies here: men have to learn to button their lips and to accept their sexual partners as mature women and stop pining away for the little skinny teeny boppers they married in their youth. Men need to decide: do I want a mature woman, companion, sharer of our common marital history, or do I want a concubine who spends her day prettying herself up to be a movie star for her husband?

Women are devastated by even casual and seemingly innocent comments about their bodies. This woman whom they just critiqued is the same one to whom they wish to make love in bed that night. Do they really expect her to feel loose and fancy free in bed after they've told her to lose weight or, "That dress doesn't look the same on you as it used to before you gave birth?"

Feedback is always much better received when it is *solicited* rather than *imposed* on someone without their asking. Is there any woman alive and in her right mind who would ask her husband to give her a treatise on her irreversibly sagging body?

Lest some of you men suspect your wives are secretly meeting with me and that I am passing their message personally onto you and you alone, I have this to say, If the shoe fits, *shut up about her body*! (The same goes for your comments about your daughters' bodies.)

She spent her whole teen life praying, parading before a mirror, preening before the prom, fretting over her fat thighs, gossiping on the phone for hours with her girlfriends, and hiding her body in shame in gym class, all so she could find a man—you! Now she is on the opposite end; her body is withering away as rapidly as when she first blossomed. Wake up, guys. She's scared to death of your offhanded comments about the things she thinks are the only things you care about—her now expendable body.

ROCHELLE

Forty-nine-year-old Rochelle sobbed in my office one day because her husband told her he didn't like the way she looked in a gown she had worn just last year, but she could see for herself it didn't look right any more. She hadn't even gained weight, but her body had changed, and she looked like someone trying to deny her age. The more we talked, I finally said to Rochelle, "I hope you do get wrinkles some day and your organs sag, because that will mean you have lived a long life and are still alive. Do you hope to get to age ninety and look like a movie star? Do you or your husband actually believe you'll be ninety someday and not *look* like ninety?"

I had told her about a new book I was writing. She looked straight at me. "Please write about that in your book!" she said, half hoping her husband would read it.

I know it sounds as if I'm picking on men right now. Since the purpose of our conversation is for me to tell you what I've gleaned from the people I treat, I felt compelled to elaborate on my forewarning to men who could save themselves a whole lot of heartache if they just kept the few most significant no-no's I treasure in my library of experience. Obviously, I just mentioned two. I won't even go into the one about *don't try to fix her; just listen to her*! Or all the other little tricks of the trade.

For both men and women, if you love each other, *always assume good intentions on each other's parts*. Then you give each other the benefit of the doubt; you don't assign the person false motivation. You believe your partner meant well but was either misinterpreting your behavior or having some problem that doesn't relate to you anyway!

Guess what? I have some pointers to espouse regarding women's most prominent fallacies about men. Again, I can't go into detail or list all the areas of which to be cognizant. I'm trying to skim the surface of this topic.

Okay ladies, here it is: *he's not out to rape you and use your body as an object.* Sexual intimacy is one of the ways he loves you. I think you get caught off guard because when you overhear him talking to his buddies, he joins in on the raunchy joke telling. You figure you're one of the women at which they are poking fun. In any event you think all those men are scheming to get into someone's pants. Men often struggle over their lust versus their love, but as they mature, most men have found a way to keep you and their fantasies in perspective. While they are reconciling their conflicting fantasies, they also have an image to uphold with other men.

So, when he embraces you in his arms just as you are about to finish preparing dinner, try to trust that he really, really wants you. He's not just using you for his personal pleasure. In fact, many men are most gratified when they feel competent to give you pleasure. They take it as their job, even more so, as the defining responsibility of their manhood.

Many a man has complained to me that he wants affection just as much as women do. His wife doesn't hold all the dibs on foreplay and/or pure affection sans sex, but when she misinterprets his gestures, rejects his attempts at reaching out, and does so angrily, he feels rebuffed.

One of the ways we've resolved this dilemma in my office is like this: we agree that when the man affectionately reaches out for the woman, he will assure her, "All I want is to hug you. I'm not asking for anything else." Or when he comes toward her, and her muscles start tensing from concern over his intentions, she kindly asks, "Can we just hug and not go further?" In this way, without fear of consequences, each party gets what he or she wants and needs.

Ladies, *if he offers you help, take it as it is, and don't try to belittle him or assume he deliberately did a poor job.* His brain is wired differently from yours. He truly believes he is doing exactly what you asked him to do. Remember: good intentions. Why would he want to participate in household chores if he thinks he will get "yelled at" merely for trying?

You see, both boy and girl desire the same thing: to love and be loved. Why should a woman deprive herself of his caressing and adoring her, something she desperately craves, because she is afraid he'll insist on going all the way, and she's either not interested in committing to a full-fledged lovemaking session, or she has conditioned herself to resist him because of a fantasy that he doesn't really love her; he merely wants to use her for her body. He wants to convey his love and have it reciprocated, and one of his most satisfying ways to express his love is through physical intimacy.

Suffice to say, women, in terms of their intentions with you, don't be so hard on your guys. Men, be aware that if you pay attention to your women, if you take them seriously and don't criticize their physical appearance, and compliment them on how attractive they do look, and if you listen and don't try to fix them, you've got a pretty good chance they won't store up past hurts and unconsciously take it out on you by "not being in the mood." No doubt, women are like large storage containers with sponges inside that absorb all your sleights, mismanaged jokes, and "how can you be so stupid" misdeeds. And all you want to do is love your woman. You never planned for it all to be so complicated.

And, of course, it's not as simplistic as I've reduced it to be.

Just about everything in life gets down to *love*: what you do because you want it, and when you finally get it, how you try to keep from losing it. I'm talking here about all kinds of love, not just the romantic kind. Many of my patients have questioned, "Is it possible to love too much?" Of course, in my traditional style of asking a question with a question, I ask them, you, and myself: "How can love be wonderful and painful at the same time? Why are romantic relationships often mysteriously terminated? Lifelong friendships are sometimes ended because of an insignificant conflict. Why? How does an emotion as manifestly pleasant as love transform into a frustrating and threatening experience?"

With love, there is always a risk: you might lose him through death, relocation, or change of heart. Suppose you love the person more than she loves you? The loved one might hurt you, make a fool of you, mislead or betray you. You give up your precious time, career, or money just to be with him or her. Because of these and other risks, you might try to protect yourself from loving someone. Even though you cherish the relationship, by withholding love or by sabotaging a successful union, you deprive yourself of pleasure and may experience loneliness, emptiness, and grief. As I did with Patty Fielding, Jim's bossy wife in psychotherapy, I help people identify the fears of loss and the early life defenses that used to protect themselves from the imagined pain.

I'll ask you this question as I do my patients: how do you ascertain if you are a person who is unfulfilled, frustrated, or depressed because your fear of loving too much prohibits you from "connecting" with other people? Do you exhibit a pattern of reaching out, pulling back, and then almost frantically reaching out again? Do you distance yourself from friends without realizing it?

Here is a scale I designed from my work with children, adults, families, and couples. I often give this to each partner in the dyad to be filled out independently and brought into our next session for mutual discussion. This scale delineates and describes some of the protective "survival" mechanisms anyone might use to protect himself from the "pain" of loving.

HOW I PROTECT MYSELF FROM LOVING YOU

Check one or more of the behaviors that you use in varying degrees to protect yourself from the risks of loving someone.

1. Counter Dependency

   I feel dependent on you, but I won't let you see it. I act unyieldingly self-sufficient, which is the opposite of how I feel, I don't need anyone; I have myself! If you compliment me, I shrug it off as not important. If you offer help, I may even resent it. Therefore, I won't have any problem taking care of myself when you leave, because I never gave over any control or power to you in the first place.

2. Excessive Dependency

   I do little or nothing for myself so that I become "attached" to you, have no "mind of my own," and am very dependent on you for my esteem, decision-making, etc. In this way, I treat myself as an appendage of you, because if I'm a separate person, I'd be in touch with the fact that you could leave me, and I can't tolerate being alone.

3. Possessive and Demanding

   I pressure you and watch your every move to ensure that you don't betray me or do "your own thing." Then maybe I'll be able to control for the possibility of your leaving me.

4. Withdrawal

   I'd rather have nothing than deal with the pain of not being in control, possibly losing you, giving more than I get, etc. Therefore, I pull back as soon as you respond to my love. It appears to you that I'm saying, "I don't care."

5. Irresponsibility

   I'll push you away by showing you that I can't be trusted in this relationship. You won't be able to count on me for anything. I'll always be late and not come through with anything I promised. My response to your complaints: "I can't help it. It's just the way I am." Sooner or later, you'll get the point and go away.

6. Becoming Aggressive

   I take every opportunity to remind you of all your negative traits. I try to convince myself and you that you are not worthy of my love. My overt behavior implies that I feel superior to you, but inside I feel inadequate and undeserving of your love.

7. Prove My Lack of Worth

   I am not worthy of receiving your love, and sooner or later, you'll figure it out. I'll speed the process by alerting you to my weaknesses and rebuffing your compliments and positive gestures. Now I don't have to suffer the loss of you. I'll encourage you to get rid of me by demeaning myself. I'll convince you that you are stupid to love me. Anyone who loves a loser like me can't be much good!

8. Taking Over

   I'll show you that if you love me, I'll take control of you and will not allow you to be yourself. It has to be "my way or no way."

9. Compliance

   I allow you to control the relationship. I am afraid if I speak my desires, you will find me unacceptable and reject me. My rule is: when in doubt, agree at all costs.

10. Keep You on a String

Since I'm afraid that as soon as I commit to you, you'll hurt me, I'll never completely agree to our relationship. By keeping you (and me) hanging, I assure that you can't make a move!

11. I-Don't-Care Attitude

I adopt this attitude to convince you that you are not that important to me. "There are other fish in the sea."

12. Be Receptive to Your Love

I'll enjoy "submitting" to you as you love me. I'll actively decide to receive you as you are, while at the same time, I know who I am. Sometimes I'll give over control to you and enjoy it. Sometimes, I'll take the lead and appreciate your allowing me to do so. This is a healthy way to love you, and I can tolerate these positive feelings.

13. Other Self-Protective Behaviors that I Use:

_____

_____

_____

_____

Using many of the self-protective behaviors, you achieve an emotional isolation so that you are prevented from being close to the important people in your life. In therapy, we explore the ways people cause their own pain when they run from love. The challenge is for my patients to examine their fears and protective behaviors in order to determine how these fears were born. What once worked to help them defend themselves from "real" danger in their early interactions with their families-of-origin is no longer necessary to adopt as an adult.

We look at each person's "favorite" protective behaviors and see how they complement and/or conflict with each other.

GEORGIANA AND JAMES

For example, Georgiana and James completed these forms and brought them into the session as I had instructed. James checked off *becoming aggressive* as his way of protecting himself from his fear that Georgiana could never love his unlovable self. James had been adopted at an early age and harbored the belief that he had been "dumped" by his mother onto the doorstep of a couple who couldn't have children because something was wrong with them. If his original parents didn't want him, and his surrogate parents were defective because they couldn't bear their own children, what did that make him? (Of course, we uncovered and discussed all this later.)

On the chart, Georgiana checked off *compliance* along with *excessive dependency*. By using these protective mechanisms, she thought she was guaranteed permanent love and commitment from James. But James's aggression toward her and his constant criticism of her increased. The more he screamed at her, the more Georgina tried harder to comply with his demands and allow him to control the relationship. If she continued to be a "good girl,' maybe he would finally love her.

Yep, you're right. The more she went along with his aggression, the further he pushed his agenda.

I urged James and Georgiana to delve into these defense mechanisms to see where and how they developed them. I helped them try on new behaviors so as to refrain from "feeding" their partners' protective trait. They each worked on finding more effective and love-enhancing ways to shield themselves from potential loss of love, as well as helping the other guy to feel more secure. The safer each one felt, the more likely he or she would be willing to give up the dysfunctional behavior. I know you can see the vicious cycle this couple developed. It helped all three of us to use the "How I Protect Myself From Loving You" chart.

VICTOR AND TOM

Victor's partner, Tom, was excessively jealous. If Tom had joined us in our session, he probably would have checked off *possessive and demanding* on the protective mechanism scale. Victor, feeling as unlovable as he did, adopted an I-don't-care attitude and one of irresponsibility. Victor's I-don't-care-attitude certainly reinforced Tom's reasons to be jealous. You see how each person protects himself and the behavior he uses to do so turns out to stimulate the other partner's dysfunctional behavior. I call it dysfunctional because, for example, Tom's excessive jealousy, which was an attempt to control Victor so Tom wouldn't lose Victor, didn't work to control Victor. Instead, Tom was essentially egging Victor on to continue acting as if he didn't care about Tom.

Isn't this stuff fascinating? (I guess my fervor over these examples is why I'm a psychologist!)

MARGARET AND DON

After years of showing marginal interest in Margaret, Don totally withdrew. Self-sufficient Margaret didn't know it, but Don had been having an extra-marital affair. It finally came out in the open, and they consulted me. Don couldn't decide which woman he wanted. Although he appeared cold and distant, he was also in severe distress over the predicament. He couldn't sleep at night, was missing work, and looked like a disheveled scarecrow. Margaret, in the mean time, was waiting around for the outcome of Don's dire decision.

Margaret, who had checked off counter dependency on her protective scale, was a busy lady who would never show Don how much she wanted to be the chosen one. In fact, her super-strong stance was one of the features that had encouraged Don to withdraw in the first place.

I'll leave you with that little sketch, because you're probably saying to yourself, "So what else is new?" Anyway, I'm sure you've gotten the drift by now.

The goal is to strengthen your sense of self so you are confident: "I reach out to you, and if you leave me or don't reciprocate, I will not assume that I am unlovable. What you are or what you do does not change who I am."

With this kind of attitude, you never have to worry about loving *too* much. The more you love, the more joy you experience, and the more positive responses you receive from those around you. You must "submit" to the love process rather than try to control it. As Kahlil Gibran says, "And think not that you can direct the course of love, for love, if it finds you worthy directs your course."

Now the question changes from, "Is it possible to love too much?" to a more accurate inquiry: "Am I afraid to love at all?"

MIKE AND NANCY

Most couples' hidden agenda is to have me serve as their judge and jury. When I really want to get my point across that this is not my role, and if the couple and I have a rapport appropriate to my lighthearted humor, I might respond similar to the way I did with Mike and Nancy.

At the end of our first few sessions, I recognized both Mike and Nancy were stumped. They were having trouble hearing each other, or me, for that matter. Each week they presented their case to me, which was designed to discredit their partner. They never looked at each other, just at me.

Very dramatically, I said, "Okay, after hearing both sides of the story, I now have the answer."

I paused. Knowing I had their undivided, wide-eyed attention, I resumed, "Mike—you are right."

Mike beamed with self-satisfaction, and for the first time, he looked straight at Nancy.

To the flushed-faced, crestfallen Nancy, I quickly added, "Nancy, I'm sad to say, you are right."

After a poignant pause, gales of laughter erupted simultaneously from each of them. Now that I had exposed their agendas, with the reality that rather than who was right or wrong, we were here to figure out why, in the midst of their desperate need to love each other, they were so afraid to love, we were finally able to actually begin our therapeutic journey.

I've been talking a lot about heterosexual couples in the traditional marital situation. I hope you are willing to apply some of what I've advocated to other couples or twosomes who are not necessarily married, as well as to the family or group situation. Every couple who comes to me has had a communication breakdown of some sort, but each pair has its unique elements. The relationship falls apart for many reasons.

Ron and Jane were doing fine until she fell in love with his best friend. Grace and John were very much in love, but when their first child was born, for reasons they couldn't ascertain, everything changed. Victor got along well with Tom until Victor's drinking problem got out of hand. A grown mother and daughter haven't spoken for three years, and finally the daughter calls me requesting that I facilitate their reconciliation.

A father and son who work together in business have built up a case against each other: the son, who is virtually paralyzed with fear and therefore unable to perform his duties, gets a second job executing the same tasks he was negligent to do in his father's business. Dad is infuriated and senses his son is about to leave Father in a lurch. More important, to Mom at least, is that these two may end up never talking to each other again.

A lesbian couple wanted to adopt a baby and was having a controversy as to who will be the one primary parent since legally there can be only one "mother." A divorced couple wants to meet with me to see if they can reconcile differences because their child is torn over his allegiance to each of them. I request that Chrissy's husband come in to help me understand her better but also, to learn more about him so I can ascertain how much she is being "dumped on" and how much she is provoking such behavior in her husband.

A former priest wants to get "married" and needs help to see if this man is the right one for him. A happily married couple has their world blown apart when she finally confesses that what he had suspected all along actually did occur: she had an affair ten years ago but called it off after a few rendezvous but never told him until now. An adult family asks me to hold a meeting with their college student so they can confront her about her phoning them in the middle of the night every time she and her boyfriend have an argument. Parents of a grown homosexual man request a meeting with me and their son to help them understand their son's lifestyle.

I've just offered you a dozen scenarios other than traditional couples or family therapy where people might elect to get help for communication breakdowns.

I've mentioned my husband, Will, who is a psychiatrist. I bet, during this whole conversation about love, you've been dying to answer the question: well, if she's such an expert on love, what's with her and her husband? Okay, I'll tell you. We've been married for almost fifty years and still counting. After fifty years, he's starting to get on my nerves! (Just kidding. One would wonder, though, how anyone doesn't get on anyone's nerves after fifty years.)

But I know you have more questions such as: "What's it like for you, a psychologist, to be married to a psychiatrist? How do you keep each other straight?" Okay. Okay. Okay. Here's the answer you've been clamoring to hear as to how we keep each other straight:" I know who he is, and he knows who I am."

I apologize for being flip, because as I advised you, if a person asks a serious question, I must respect your right to ask, and I must either answer your question or tell you I don't want to answer it. Being clear on who we are means we won't make false assumptions about each other (we don't make up stories), and we will be sensitive to each other's needs.

Will and I have been through our storms and castles together without murmur or resistance. When things got rough, we knew we were in it for the long haul. This is essential to weave into the fabric of a relationship: we're here to stay and no matter the conflict, we always assume good intentions (there it is again) on the other one's part. I read in some research paper somewhere that people who describe themselves as being in happy marriages don't necessarily fight less; they plain don't like to quarrel and will both do anything to resolve the fight when they have it so their disagreements don't last very long. I believe Will and I fit into that category. Besides, our best indicator of a good relationship: we laugh a lot, a whole lot!

Another fact I'm sure you want to know about us is that we can put together a healthy and delicious dinner in twenty minutes! We can clean up said meal in less than ten minutes. We're like a well-oiled twosome machine. That's really saying something.

Phew! This love stuff sure is comprehensive, isn't it? I even got into my own love relationship just now. Who knew when we started talking about love we would go on this long? (You should see how much I cut out of this discussion!) You and I have to get some sleep at some point, don't we? I'm glad we did put in the time to investigate how love helps to lighten each other's hearts, nourish us to go on, and give us meaning in our lives. Issues around love are at the bottom of most psychological troubles. It certainly is at the core of those who suffer from eating disorders. Hey, funny thing, that's where we're going next, to visit with the people who abuse their bodies as a way to deal with their love. See you there.

LETTUCE, POPCORN, AND CEREAL

As an eating disorders specialist, I always have to be aware that I could easily get sucked into the mindset of the patient. Sufferers live their disease twenty-four hours a day, seven days a week, and all they think about is food, diets, exercise, and body weight. It's easy to fall in line with them and start to get so focused on what they put into their mouths. I could forget our mission and end up commenting on their food rather than their reasons for abusing it. For them, the kitchen is an eerie place. It has power beyond comprehension. How can a haunted kitchen simultaneously serve as such an overpowering magnet?

Food abusers definitely bring out the mother in me, and just as it is for the loved ones surrounding these cheerless human beings, it's gut-wrenching to watch eating disorder patients hurt themselves. They have every right to nourish themselves, yet they deprive themselves of one of the pleasurable necessities of life, or they use the food against themselves and over-nourish only to have to find ways to undo what they couldn't stop themselves from doing.

But this is why I am the therapist and their families are who they are. Their families and friends are counting on me to be objective and not do as they do—wring my hands in frustration and resort to lecturing or pleading with my patients to eat or spew forth angry outbursts or slip into my own depression. We all know these personal reactions won't help people who are beyond logic. They probably feel guilty for causing their loved ones pain, yet they believe they are totally out of control to do anything about it.

Why did I call this portion of our conversation "Lettuce, Popcorn, and Cereal?" You guessed it! These three foods are about the only substances some people will allow themselves to eat. I could add peanut butter, but sufferers usually end up including this substance only after they've started treatment and visit a dietitian who helps them get more protein and "good" fat into their bodies.

By definition, humans are human. Period. Humans are not perfect. *Perfect* to some people means to be superior to others. *You all have to eat to live, but* I *don't.*

But humans have to eat to survive. Therefore, to strive to be perfect is to deny your existence as a human being.

CAROL

Whenever a college student, named Carol, gets a B on her transcript, even though it's probably the only B out of an all A report card, she thinks to herself, *B is for bad.* In her mind, one B constitutes a failure.

I proposed to this student the following hypothetical dialogue:
"Who are you?"
"I am the best."
"But that doesn't give me an idea of who you are. What do you like to do?"
"I like to be the best."
"What are you good at?"
"I'm good at being the best!"
This young woman lives with an insurmountable burden to be perfect. She has no self other than that which is measured against other people. She can't say, "I like to draw; I'm good at writing; I

love to go to the movies; I want to be a scientist; I have a passion for gardening, etc." She is the embodiment of perfection.

Well, maybe not, because she thinks she's fat. And as long as there is someone whom she views as thinner than she, then she is *not* the best. And her obsession will cause her to be in a frenzy until she is the thinnest. She will go to any length, be it vomiting, restricting food, or compulsive exercising to reach an unattainable goal.

Some of you have this problem in varying degrees. Perfection becomes a form of control. As long as you are perfect, then you can make sure bad things won't happen to you. If you prepare a better dinner, then maybe he won't go out drinking tonight; if you never make or admit to having made a mistake, she won't seize upon your weakness and hurt you; only if you have a perfect movie star body will others love you.

We all live in this world. In real life, we want to know, "Am I acceptable?"

To eat or not to eat, that is the question. Do I deserve to eat? This is another question.

People who struggle with eating obsessions experience their symptoms twenty-four hours a day, seven days a week. Despite their appearing as if they engage in intentional, destructive practices, they are captives who have no volition remaining in their emaciated selves. By the time I see them, they are at a point of no return from their indomitable, involuntary actions. They and their families suffer unconquerable heartache.

To keep this discussion of symptomatology down to a minimum, I thought I'd show you a quiz I devised to help people determine if they have a problem or not. By showing this to you, I can avoid having to delineate an exhaustive list of boring symptoms. You'll get the general idea of the array of indicators when you see the quiz.

EATING AND BODY OBSESSIONS QUIZ
©1991 Phyliss Shanken

For each of the following questions, select the number that best reflects your answer. 4 = extremely or always; 3 = very much or often; 2 = moderately or sometimes; 1 = rarely or slightly; 0 = not at all or never. Then add up all the points.

1. Does your body size or shape disturb you?
2. Are you afraid of getting fat, regardless of your weight?
3. Do you think about food when not at meals?
4. Do you eat even when you are not hungry?
5. Do you ever avoid going out because you feel too fat?
6. Do you fear situations where food may be present?
7. Do you skip meals to lose weight?
8. Do you weigh yourself more than once a day?
9. How often do you go on diets?
10. If you go on a diet, do you choose extreme or fad diets, which are difficult to follow?
11. Is your eating out of control? For example: if you eat one item from the box, you feel compelled to eat all the items in the box. You wake up in the middle of the night to eat. You eat too much to the point of feeling sick.
12. Do you ever feel that your dieting is out of control? For example: you find it difficult to permit yourself not to be on a diet, and you don't allow yourself to eat anything that is not a diet food.
13. Is your exercising ever out of control? For example: if you don't exercise when you are "supposed to," then you put yourself down. You exercise to lose weight more than one

hour a day. You exercise as punishment for "being bad" with food.

14. After you eat, do you ever "put yourself down," or feel depressed or guilty?

15. Do your feelings about yourself depend on what you have or have not eaten? For example: if you eat "good foods," diet foods, you feel worthwhile. If you eat the "wrong foods," then you feel unworthy.

16. After you eat, do you have obsessive thoughts such as: "I shouldn't have eaten that!" or "How many calories did I just eat? I'll skip dinner."

17. Do you have obsessive thoughts about your body, such as: "If only I lost ten pounds, my life would be wonderful?" or, "I hate her for being thinner than I am!"

18. Do you ever eat massive amounts of food at one time (binge)?

19. Do you hide food or eat food in secret places so you won't be discovered?

20. Have you attempted to control your weight by harmful and drastic measures such as: vomiting, spitting out food, diet pills, use of laxatives, diuretics (water pills), enemas, vigorous exercise, fasting, or other means?

If you scored approximately 20 (twenty) points and above, it's possible that you may have an eating obsession, which could significantly affect your emotional well-being or potentially lead to a more severe eating disorder. You may wish to talk to a friend, family member, or other helping person about this problem.

Here's another way to look at symptoms. Imagine "I" is the body who has a voice. Here are just a few of the phrases an eating disorder patient's body might utter:

"I want to disappear so I will waste away to nothingness."

"I want to be stronger than other human beings—human beings need food, but I don't. I'll show you my bones to prove it."

"I won't eat my mother's food (ideas, love). If I do, it will mean I don't have my own mind. The thinner I get, the more independent I am."

"I feel so empty. I am like a cavern that can never be filled up. Therefore, I eat until I almost burst, but at least then I'll finally feel full."

"I need you so I take in your food, but then because you betray me by not feeding me what I want when I want it, the food you gave me makes me sick, and I throw it up so you will know how you hurt me."

EMILY

Some patients are afraid of treatment because they don't know what life will be like without their eating disorder. Emily, an anorexic girl whom I treated and prided myself on keeping her out of the hospital, told me many times, "All I am is an 'anorexic.' I don't even have a name anymore like, 'Hey, you over there, *Anorexic*, come here!"

My job was to help Emily find the original self that had gone astray. Yet her true self was masquerading in a body that was trying to convey something to me and to everyone else. We, the spectators, in the enigmatic matinee become baffled as to her message. All we see is skin and bones or excessive fat or a lost little girl trying to make believe she doesn't need us anymore.

Here's how I think about treating eating disorder patients: imagine you are holding a baby chick. You need to squeeze hard enough so the wiggly little chick won't run away, get lost, and left to its own devices, get hurt. But you shouldn't clutch on so hard the chick could be crushed and die. You need to know exactly how much pressure to exert. For her own survival, you firmly and lovingly embrace her, but you always use self-restraint.

JENNY

Eighteen-year-old Jenny was absolutely beautiful! Contrary to what most people believed about her having everything just because she was such a knockout, in fact, she was miserable.

Before I go on about Jenny, I want to talk to you about the plight of beautiful people. Despite the belief that beautiful, famous, and rich people have no reason to worry about anything, they have problems too. If you are a good-looking person or if you have a particularly attractive trait such as gorgeous eyes or figure, here is a view of what you might face:

As Jenny did, you may feel like a fraud as you question the attention you get for your other achievements. You worry and feel guilty that you are receiving special treatment only because you are good-looking. In that way, you feel like a cheater. Everyone else is clamoring to look wonderful, and you just happened to be born this way. Your looks have become your only source of reinforcement, so you fear that if you lose your looks, then you will be ignored, rejected, or forgotten.

As a little girl, Jenny could sense people's eyes on her when they gawked and made a fuss to Jenny's beaming mother. For some people this staring at one's physical attractiveness is flattering, but to beautiful people who deal with it all the time, it may be very uncomfortable. It can feel as if your beauty is actually a disability. In later years, Jenny felt guilty from this attention as if she had deliberately gone after it.

In high school, Jenny was accused of seducing other girls' boyfriends when she was merely being friendly. The more attractive she became, the more her peers treated her as a non-person. No one asked her if she set out to attract someone else. This assumption is made merely because of how she looked.

Of course, she was seen as a snob or as conceited. Jealousy toward her was plentiful. She overheard family as well as acquaintances saying what amounted to the following: if they could just have what Jenny had, they would live happily ever after. With strangers, she was dismissed as stupid (the "dumb" blonde), or discounted ("How can you be upset when you are so pretty? If I had your looks, I wouldn't complain about anything!").

When a very young Jenny confronted her father because he wasn't listening to her, he retorted, "Sorry, I couldn't concentrate on what you were saying, because I was distracted. I was thinking about your beautiful smile, how all the guys are going to be chasing after you."

These accolades were confusing to Jenny, because she was too young to be flattered by sexual references. She had been told so often as a youngster that she was breathtaking, and now she was being told her beauty would help her to "take over" men.

As a teenager, due to her father's discomfort with Jenny's burgeoning sexuality, he began to distance himself from her. She suffered the loss of her dad's love, and she began to crave other people's interest in her external visage. In her relationships, with her beauty as a backdrop, she felt empty when she didn't hear the words, "I adore you," or "You look magnificent." It's as if a drive state had been set in motion and she was a prisoner. By age sixteen, Jenny starved herself to a dangerously low weight and was hospitalized for three months. She gained enough weight to finally be discharged.

Jenny maintained enough weight on her body to get her elders off her back, and then, as many anorexics do, she staggered into bulimia. Her kind of bulimia took the form of bingeing on large quantities of food and regurgitating the food immediately after ingestion. A typical binge might include: a dozen doughnuts, a half gallon of ice cream, three chocolate bars, a liter of coke, and a bag of potato chips. She exercised at the gym or at home many hours a day. These extreme measures were designed to help her deal with her teetering self-esteem, her chronic need to be perfect and in "perfect" control and her confusion over who she actually was, her own self, or the object of her mother's mirrored perception of her.

Many of my patients come from mothers who were either fat themselves, who hated fat and were constantly dieting, or who feared fat and conveyed this to their average-weight daughters by constantly discussing their daughters' body weight. I've treated some of these mothers who hate themselves for hating their fat daughters, but they feel helpless to change their perception.

Jenny's mother was one of these mothers with whom I held a delicate restraint. Jenny's fear about her own body originated from mother's fear that Jenny would have to endure the teasing mother had suffered as an obese child. Mother commented about Jenny's body when Jenny was as young as two years old. Jenny grew up with a horrific fear of getting fat. This was further intensified by all the comments she heard about her being such a beauty. If beautiful was all she was, then if she gained weight, since she believed she had no other redeeming talents such as intelligence, athleticism, or creativity, where would she be?

Mother and daughter didn't know where one of them ended and the other began. If Jenny's mother withdrew from the family, Jenny thought Jenny had somehow hurt her mother. If Mother saw that Jenny appeared unhappy, Mother felt it was her responsibility to make it better for Jenny. Sometimes Jenny wasn't unhappy; she was merely exercising her right to privacy and alone time. When Jenny was angry with her mother, Jenny hurt herself by not eating or by cutting herself.

As is true in many eating disorder families, both Jennifer and her mother were like Voodoo dolls for each other: stick a pin in one, and the other writhes in pain. If Mother mopes around the house, daughter starts feeling depressed and doesn't know why. If Jennifer doesn't eat breakfast, Mother takes to her own bedroom. Between them is a thin partition, as if each one is picking weeds in a separate garden, but at any time, they remain confused as to which flower patch is which.

By the time Jennifer came to me, she had gone through three other therapists and several dietitians. She was not a very cooperative patient, or so she was depicted when her father first called me. I saw Jennifer in treatment twice a week for individual sessions and once a week in family therapy. As I have found with many chronic eating disorder patients, Jenny was not the recalcitrant teenager she was cracked up to be.

This kind of patient usually has a history of hiding hordes of food or vomitous secretions so no one will discover her shameful secret. She resorts to lying and manipulating others. So many therapists start out by taking a hard line and act as a disciplinarian just as the parents have been reduced to doing.

I, on the other hand, don't believe in this kind of approach. It just wouldn't be any fun to do therapy if I resorted to confronting patients before I even knew them. If engaging in therapy isn't enjoyable for me, then I might as well not do it. I also think I wouldn't be very good at it either. So I spend a great deal of time commiserating with my haggard patients as they complain about their former treatment. It's probably one reason I have a good record of holding onto this kind of patient. And sooner or later, I do confront patients. I'm not afraid to do it, and it's very healing if implemented at appropriate times. But the way I confront is never to tell a person I know she's lying, or as many other eating disorder specialists do, that I won't treat her any more unless she gains a certain amount of weight. I will never abandon someone.

Okay, so now I will show you by excerpting parts of sessions with Jenny how I use food- and body-related words in therapy.

In family therapy, Jenny rebuffed her father's compliment that she was looking healthier these days. She didn't say it at the time, but I knew she viewed "looking healthier" as meaning she was fatter, because when she was gaunt, no one said she looked healthy! Later on that week, in individual therapy, I referred to the interaction and said, "You were 'throwing up' what your father fed you. You starved yourself of his 'good food.'"

At the end of that session, Jenny smiled and complimented me, saying that over the past months since she began therapy, I had helped her so much.

Due to her having "fed me" her love, I quickly retorted, "Uh oh!"

She knew what I meant. I fully expected her to pull away from me, and it was confirmed the next week, when she cancelled our appointment. At the second session of the next week, I said, "Last week, you told me you were so happy to be here, and then this week, you cancel and 'throw me up,' the one person you said was here for you and who could nurture you. These days, you must be worried about loving me too much."

She refolded her bare, skinny legs that emerged bashfully from her mini skirt and with reluctant tears, she said, "I just couldn't get out of bed that day."

Months passed, and Jenny didn't run away any more every time she felt too close to me. She regularly kept her appointments and found a new way to distance herself from me, but this way was more healthy—she got angry at just about everything I did and said.

She experienced anger and physical emptiness as synonymous. Therefore, she was physically hungrier these days. Her increasing hunger made her even more furious. To have an appetite, especially for my love, was a shameful state of being. It meant she needed someone, and when you believe you can't exist without someone else's love, you lose who you are. In essence, you might as well waste away into a whisper.

One day, she told me, "Last week, I left here and binged on the way home."

Quick on the uptake and with unwavering eye contact, I bluntly said, "Last week, I didn't answer your question, and you were angry and felt I didn't feed you the way you requested. You felt empty. You had to fill up the empty space and also stuff down the anger, so you used food to try to accomplish both."

EMILY

Often, when I met with Jenny, she reminded me of Emily, the anorexic young girl who had told me all she was, was an anorexic and that she had no other identity. After beginning to show more progress in treatment, Emily became frightened that she had begun to eat some snack foods between meals as she had done before she became anorexic. In my mind, I translated her fear into the reality that she was beginning to relate to me and permit me to be important to her.

In her sessions, she suddenly changed from relating easily with me to stopping herself sometimes in mid sentence and becoming withdrawn and quiet. When the timing was right, I said, "Emily, I believe that you turned off when you realized how much you enjoyed the idea that you and I were hitting it off so well. It's like you have begun to 'snack' on me, and now you're afraid you'll get fat."

Jenny also reminded me of Emily, because Emily fought my nourishing her yet had gotten to the point where she knew she couldn't live without my support and love. Isn't this the same kind of dependency a newborn experiences who is totally at the mercy of another human being for survival? For both Jenny and Emily, their power was in their refusal of my "food," but I was there to help them out of their misery and bring them back to life, so they wanted and needed my nourishment. They resisted with all their might.

Emily used to say, "I feel fat."

Each time, as if we hadn't addressed this topic before, I asked her, "What does fat feel like?"

I truly wanted to know Emily's use of this dreaded word "fat" and it's meaning specifically to her. Emily wasn't the first nor the last woman to say this. To feel fat is to feel ugly, dirty, evil, ashamed, "too much," disgusting, unlovable, and so much more.

It's not a physical description of a body accoutrement. It's actually a *feeling*. Feeling fat is just about the worst sensation in the world.

JENNY

When Jenny said, "I feel fat," I asked her to elaborate. Emily had taught me what she meant, but I couldn't and wouldn't take if for granted that Jenny's "fat" feeling was the same as Emily's. At any rate, I knew it was important for Jenny to work on honing down the meaning of the phrase to its pinpoint truth. As a result, I learned more about Jenny's underlying, irrational beliefs.

Jenny's fantasy was that if she didn't eat, someone would force her to eat. In the hospital, for a period of time she had a naso-gastric tube inserted through her nose and into her esophagus so liquid nutrients could be poured through the tube. And for the longest time, even when she didn't have the tube, she was not permitted certain privileges unless she ate a specific amount of food. By refusing to eat, she was increasing the likelihood of her external environment's being the dictator of what she ate rather than her being the mistress of what goes into her body.

But Jenny's fear went beyond the reality she fostered by her restriction of food. She actually had daydreams of food or other objects being stuffed into her mouth with her nose pinched shut. Because she expressed this fear, I was always on the alert for anything that might lead us to a history of sexual abuse. If a person has no recall of such abuse, I don't go after it. I'm not into putting ideas in people's heads. I merely kept a watchful eye, because this concern on her part, which also emerged in dreams, may have indicated a past record of some kind of oral coercion. Very often, girls repress these events; these taboo incidents are so demoralizing, terrifying, and confusing that the little girl doesn't even have the words to tell a protective adult about it. Also, when there are no words, it's more likely a person will repress the horrific event.

So, with Jenny, I was always careful how I addressed her with my ideas and interpretations. On one particular difficult day, I looked into her eyes, and with a gentle smile on my face, I said to Jenny, "I'm not trying to stuff this idea down your throat. You are in charge here of what goes in your mouth and what goes in your brain."

On other occasions, I presented ideas so that Jenny wouldn't be afraid of my overtaking her. I thought aloud and permitted the ideas to float in the atmosphere. My thoughts were then readily available to her, but it was very obvious I wasn't force-feeding her. Here is how it went:

"Jenny, what you just said reminds me of the time your father cut your mother with glass. I wonder how that fits? Now, I'm associating to this week when you felt the urge to cut yourself... Oh, that connects with what you said when you first came in to the session today. You said you felt like 'cutting' the session with me, meaning that you wanted to avoid me and cut me out of your life."

Here I was thinking aloud and modeling a way of processing. I said it as I thought it. I opened up my problem-solving process to Jenny for her to voluntarily take it in. At some point, I asked, "What do you think? Am I on track?"

Sometimes I just remained silent and waited. Sometimes, I talked even if Jenny didn't. In her early sessions when she was more silently resistant, as she spent the bulk of the sessions running her bony fingers over the purple lines in my "stupid" sofa, I talked for entire sessions, sharing my associations in my own life that related to what Jenny had already said or based on what I knew of her from her parents and from our family sessions. I even guessed at what she might be feeling and associated to my own teen years and how I felt about similar events in my youth.

There are no forced feedings. Control is such a big issue, and I dare not try to take her over. I did a soliloquy. I even commented on my insights such as: "I feel good about the way I processed that topic! Hmm, this is a new thought for me. I'm glad I brought it up. I learned something new today."

Even in her more wordless days, Jenny smiled at my antics, even if she didn't verbally respond.

Jenny was talking about her previous hospitalization. She described the horror of being forced to eat when she didn't want to and how out of control she felt. I said, "That reminds me of when I was three years old and I was at day camp where all I ever ate was peanut butter and jelly sandwiches. One day they served mushroom soup. They told me my mother said I had to eat whatever they served, and I couldn't have my old standby P B and J sandwich. (Imagine serving mushroom soup to a three-year-old!) I was forced to eat it. I can still remember the horrendous taste."

EMILY

Emily was angry that I wouldn't answer her question. We know that so many anorexics need to be perfect and good, yet they have no other way to fight back except unconsciously through their bodies. They are angry because deep inside not always known to them they believe their identity has been stolen from them. While simultaneously "being good," they fear being taken over.

Impeccable Emily was concerned about knowing the rules of therapy and felt compelled "to do therapy right." Whenever I made an interpretation, she tended to beat herself with it, thereby sending me the message that she wanted me to feed her, but when I did, I was to feel that I had been aggressive toward her. I believe that this was designed to render me impotent so that she could be rid of me. Aloneness was the safest place for her, since this is how she had always survived, while at the same time, aloneness helped her to avoid the pain of relationships but at the same time, created pain in and of itself.

Referring to the "should I do this or that" kind of question I hadn't answered, she licked her parched lips as if she were in a desert with no water anywhere in sight and said, "I feel like I'm at a fork in the road and don't know which road to take."

I said, "Yes, I see you there at the fork, standing alone. That's the way it always is—you—alone … I see myself hiding behind a tree."

Her left eyebrow rose up sharply in concert with her voice. She said, "I guess I have to invite you to come out, or you won't come out from behind the tree."

Because this young woman was so hard on herself, trying exhaustively to do it the right way, I responded, "It wouldn't be fair to you if the only way I'll come out is if you have to ask me."

Covering her wounds under a begrudging smile, she tried again, "I guess you'll come out only when you want to."

I interpreted, "That's not fair to you either. It would be like your father who was available only when he was good and ready, not when you necessarily needed him… I see myself peeking out once in a while, reminding you that I'm here. If you seem ready, I will probably ask, 'Would you like me to join you? Would you like my help?'"

We went on with this story together for many sessions. It became our little inside tale, another way to intensify the connection while at the same time maintain some distance from the rawness of the resistance and the fear of her acknowledging my importance to her.

One day Emily talked about wanting to think on her own rather than having to go along with everything her mother said. She suddenly couldn't remember the word she was thinking of and asked, "Is it *emancipation* or *emaciation?*"

I explained the difference between the two words and noted her confusion. For her, the only way to be independent of (or *emancipated* from) her mother was to starve herself and end up *emaciated*.

Later, I said Emily would be *emancipated* when she gained enough to be normal weight. She misheard me and thought I said she would be *emaciated* when she became independent.

I was so impressed with this juxtaposition of the two words from a young lady who, if tested, would probably score in the genius range, that I asked her permission to tell my colleagues and others this poignant anecdote. Emily, too, got such a kick out of having this cognitive blind spot over a psychological issue that she readily agreed.

(Uh oh! Did I just blow my cover? Yes, this little anecdote did really occur with someone who was not Emily as depicted in this account. This is one of those little vignettes where I was given permission to print but not allowance to tell the whole story so I imbedded it into Emily's account here as if she, fictitious Emily, had really said it, which she does here but she actually (or I, the writer, actually) "borrowed" it from someone else who gave me permission! Wow, that was a mouthful! You get it though, don't you? And don't you find it clever of me to incorporate it here? Say yes. You know you're thinking it!)

We worked a great deal on Emily's need for perfection. In one session, Emily lamented that she was being selfish to leave her mother home to clean the house while the teen went to the mall. Since this was one of those "perfect" anorexics (to me, perfection and anorexia are synonymous terms) and very parentified (which means she was more the parent to her parent than she was the child), and in an attempt to normalize her attitude, I told her that adolescents, by definition, are generally inconsiderate.

She said she had never been inconsiderate, even though her mother had accused her of such. And I knew how much she felt responsible for her mother's well being. Emily so wanted to please her mother—or better yet, not cause her mother any discomfort.

Without castigation, I gently answered her, "Doing anything for yourself—feeding yourself—becomes aggressive to someone else. No wonder eating is bad! When you take care of yourself, what starts out as loving and wanting your mom turns into biting, gnarling, devouring, gobbling, and destroying her."

JENNY

Because it was necessary to see Jenny three times a week, and because the family's finances were in peril due to the cost of all her hospitalizations, I treated Jenny for a lower fee than my usual charge per session. She knew my real fee and that I was giving her a break to insure our being able to work together. This lower fee was, in essence, one of my gifts to her. We both felt that she was ready to stop binge/purging, but now she was solidly locked into a difficult habit to break.

I promised her that if she didn't binge/purge for three days, I would give her a free session, and we would do whatever she wanted during that session. I had given Jenny a choice between her love for me versus her love for her habit. Which would win out? She abstained for the three days, and as part of the free session, she elected to go for a walk with me. I had offered this plan to remind her that she had it within her to stop her binge/purge behavior. Now we knew she had the strength.

After a few more months of on-and-off binge\purge activity, I told Jenny that I was no longer going to continue to pay for her binges, that her habit was expensive. (A single binge could cost as much as twenty-five dollars!) If she could afford to pay for these "treats," then she could afford to pay me my full fee.

We designed a plan whereby Jenny was to pay me for every binge. We figured out a price based on the difference between my fee and what she was actually paying me divided by the average number of binges per week.

In one particular session, she was angry at having to pay me but afraid to directly express it. She tottered into my office, and with a sardonic smile threatening to break through at any moment, she dumped a huge pile of pennies on my couch and very pretentiously counted them out one by one. Don't you think that little stunt gave us plenty of grist for the mill?

About six months later, Jenny reported that other than when she had stopped for three days in order to get a free session with me, yesterday, for the first time in years, she abstained from bingeing and purging. I congratulated her and thanked her for allowing me to share her joy. "You carried me with you. You felt sated, and you didn't have to throw me up." The barrier she had placed between our two hearts had finally begun to melt.

BONNIE

The kitchen, which symbolizes safety and security, is often viewed as the hub of the household. The family gathers there; neighbors may drop in for a cup of coffee. Bouquets of warm fragrances emanate from the kitchen and cause your mouth to water.

But if you are a compulsive eater as forty-five-year-old Bonnie was, being in the kitchen can become a nightmare. Because it's where the food is housed, just the thought of the kitchen, as well as restaurants or dinner parties, may provoke feelings of helplessness, depression, and fear.

Bonnie resorted to dieting, losing, and regaining. On numerous starvation diets, juxtaposed between overweight binge eating episodes, her metabolism decreased, and her cravings for food increased.

With this kind of yearning, for Bonnie it became too hard to fight off the wrenching impulses, and each time she gave in, she felt guilt and self-loathing. She looked in the mirror. She called herself a fat, ugly pig. Because she associated "being bad" with eating, even if she were entitled to eat for sustenance, her disapproving voice remonstrated her time and again.

During every waking minute, Bonnie suffered the agony of having to fight off the forces within herself. She avoided any association with food, yet she was lured back to the torment: "Maybe this time, I can conquer my compulsion!"

But food served also as her friend. It eased the anguish of loneliness, rejection, and fear. Food was often used to "stuff down" her anger, grief, or disappointment. Popping that potato chip into her mouth helped her to temporarily numb or divert herself from pain.

Unconsciously, by eating compulsively, she was attempting to deny her dependency feelings: "I can feed myself. I don't need anyone else!" or, "I won't allow myself to take in your food (your love, your advice) because then you'll be able to control me."

Bonnie gorged herself as a way to symbolically prove to the world that she could do whatever she wanted whenever she wanted to do it. No one could tell her what she was allowed to put in her mouth. Her mother, who used to monitor her every crumb, could no longer hold the threat of withdrawing love as a way to try to dominate her.

I told Bonnie in the therapy, "You are trying to salt and pepper me to your taste. In so doing, you are denying that I am a separate person with my own way of preparing and offering food. You are trying to tell me that it must be your way or no way. Let's look in your life for clues as to how you lose out on getting sustenance because you try to control the other person." We found some clues in her relationship with her husband, Frank.

Bonnie married a man whom I suspected had an unconscious need for her to be unattractive so he would be secure that she wouldn't run off. He joined us in therapy a few times and didn't deny his fear of losing her.

Bonnie protected Frank as well as herself by remaining fat. Also, Bonnie's fantasy was that if he didn't want her, she could have any other man she wanted, but only if she lost weight. Having been promiscuous as a teenager, only when she married Frank did she stop her wild sexual encounters. Within weeks of her wedding, she gained ten pounds. She fantasized that if she stopped abusing food, she would become beautiful again and not be able to control her sexual impulses. In fact, she feared that without her "fat" brakes on, she could easily become the town prostitute.

Bonnie's fury over her husband's treating her as a sex object sometimes caused her to have temper tantrums, which left her breathless and empty. After his chauvinistic comments or insensitive sexual advances, she snuck into the kitchen for an, "I'll show him!" snack.

Bonnie's mother had pressured her to "clean her plate" while concurrently ridiculing her for being fat at a time in Bonnie's life when she wasn't actually obese. Not only could Bonnie retaliate against Frank, but even though her mother lived on the other side of the country, as Bonnie feasted, she sent unswerving messages to Mom. In so many words, she chanted, "Hey, Mommy dearest, I did what you wanted. Now you have to look at my ugly body." Then she stuffed another doughnut in her mouth.

All this hadn't become conscious until we were well into our therapy. I remember the day Bonnie first started to verbalize her rage. We discussed her aggressive feelings toward her husband and mother. She recalled the time her mother verbally attacked her because she had gained yet another pound. I reminded Bonnie she probably wanted to take that unit of weight and "pound" her mother with it.

Over many weepy sessions, she then was able to understand how she used eating and fat accumulation as a weapon. Also, even though "thin is in," Bonnie unconsciously needed her fat to "pad" herself from pain, to prove she was big and strong, and to camouflage her sense of emptiness and inferiority.

Large people who have become so because of a fear of dependency may be afraid of becoming too "small." Bonnie numbed herself to prove that she was big and strong and didn't need anyone. At midnight, in secrecy, she gorged herself on food to fortify herself and establish her independence. Nighttime was the worst. In fact, sometimes she awoke to find herself in front of the refrigerator but had no memory of leaving her bed.

BONNIE AND EMILY

Obese compulsive overeaters such as Bonnie are the flip side of the same coin of the anorexics such as Emily. Listen to them as they interact with each other in a group therapy session:

Bonnie lost forty pounds. "I freaked out, because I felt my hip bone for the first time in years." (Without her fat padding, her small, vulnerable self was now exposed.)

When Emily, who had started gaining weight very slowly, heard Bonnie's comment, she spluttered, "Oh no, I get upset when I *don't* feel my bones!"

For Emily, it was the clavicle bone, which she pinched each morning before deciding whether or not she would be permitted to eat anything more than a leaf of lettuce that day. For her, her bones proved that she was strong. Fat is soft; bones are hard, whereas for Bonnie, naked bones are evidence of weakness. Fat is strength.

After Emily and I worked together for a while, in the beginning or the end of a session, she sometimes reached out for a hug. One day, I said to her, "Emily, your body is telling me to go away. Your bones are sharp and piercing. They cut into me and hurt."

PENNY

For many patients, their bodies become important evidence used in a paradoxical love test. If you love me when I'm thin, then you don't love me because you must not have loved me when I was fat. Sooooo—"Screw you, I'll get fat again."

Penny, the youngest of five children, had always been chunky. Almost from birth, Penny's family had called her Rolly Polly Pudgy Penny. She hadn't been home for a long time, so Penny took the long trek back to California for Thanksgiving.

A few months before she left, she became clinically depressed, so much so, she couldn't eat. Traditionally, she used to overeat as a way to deal with anxiety and depression. This was the worst depression she had ever suffered, so in this case, she just couldn't eat. For the first time in her life, she lost weight without really trying, but her despondency was miserably distressing. For her, it was the least desirable way to get skinny! When she arrived at her parents' house where the rest of the family celebrated the holiday, her ears rung with boisterous greetings, "Penny, you look great!"

Penny was crushed. She told me later, "All the family cared about was how I looked. They didn't even see how depressed I was."

Needless to say, when Penny returned to her own home, she gained back all the weight she had lost plus some more for good measure.

ALLISON

Allison was one of those patients where I found myself resisting the urge to take her home to my house to live. Often when she took a drink out of the water bottle she was never seen without, this action seemed familiar to me, as if she already lived in my home and I was seeing her do what she did every day. I believe I had this sensation because she occupied my mind so much.

One day at home, Allison was upset because her mother seemed withdrawn, and to Allison, that meant her mother was unhappy about something. Being enmeshed with her mom, Allison always assumed that she was the source of her mother's discomfort. Allison was all set to skip dinner because she couldn't eat when she felt depressed. She went to bed early, but thirty seconds later, she got out of bed and went into her mother's room to ask her mom what the problem was. She then prepared and ate her dinner and remarked to me later, "I can't believe how easy it was to eat. I didn't even have to force myself."

In the following session, when Allison reported this event to me, I cheered her on, praising her not because she ate dinner, but because she took it upon herself to check reality and didn't rely on an *imagined* story about her mother which would implicate Allison as being the culprit and she pushed through her frustration and anger and didn't hurt herself as a way to deal with her mom.

191

In this case, she was able to reverse an old dysfunctional behavior because she had gotten the straight scoop from her mom and determined that her mom had a headache due to work stress, which had nothing to do with Allison.

POLLY

I always look for a *secret* when I treat people with eating disorders. Their covert activities are the patients' way of using their bodies to attempt mastery of an earlier conflict.

A bulimic patient, Polly, grew up in an alcoholic family. This was an upstanding family in the community. The children were forbidden to talk about their father's drinking problem. Polly never brought kids home from school, because she was filled with shame and embarrassment, and anyway, how was she ever going to explain to her friends her father's erratic behavior if she was forbidden to talk about it?

Now, the Polly I see before me in my office is replaying her early life trauma through her body by having everything look fine on the outside by being normal weight and president of student government at her university while secretly bingeing and purging in the privacy of her dorm room.

MEN

Since we're talking about secrets, by now I'm sure you're asking the question: what about men? Don't they have eating and body issues too? Last I heard, one in ten eating disorder patients are men and maybe a higher percentage than that, because many men do a great job of keeping the secret. Even obese men avoid suspicion because our culture accepts heavy men much more readily than we accept overweight women who are more likely to be accused of being greedy, lazy, and over-stuffed. People aren't as liable to assume that this man is padding himself nightly with enormous amounts of precious food in the same way as the alcoholic who imbibes his drug of choice for some of the same purposes. Either one can sleep it off, wake in the morning, and go to work. An overly skinny man, particularly one who exercises, is seen as a man who loves his exercise rather than one who is obsessed with his appearance and his fear of fat.

Another reason men are hush-hush about food-related problems is that anorexia and bulimia are often seen in the homosexual population where there is a greater emphasis on appearance and attractability. Heterosexual men usually don't want to risk being lumped into a homosexual identity.

Many men have issues regarding the symbolic use of their bodies to make a point, but the same symbols women use may have an opposite meaning. For example, whereas a woman makes herself big and strong to cover her weakness and dependence, a man may fatten himself up to cover his hard masculine self. Since fat is more of a feminine physical manifestation, a man might be shirking his perceived masculine duties by acquiring or wishing to attain fat. (Just about everywhere you look, *the wish is the same as the fear, and the fear is the same as the wish*. For men or women, fear of becoming fat is most likely equivalent to the wish or *need* to *be* fat!)

He may also eat as a way to dull or avoid pain or to remain a pudgy baby rather than a responsible man. In his treatment, as with any woman I treat, I would again be looking for what he is trying to express through the language of his body.

Fewer men seek help for eating problems. It's hard to know, therefore, how many of you are out there. I have seen a few men with anorexia, bulimia, or binge-eating disorder (which is the binging without the purging seen in other forms of bulimia), as well as general compulsive eaters who are obese.

Since the men I've treated for eating disorders present even further complexities, I hope you'll forgive me if I postpone discussion of men's experience with eating disorders for another time when I can go into it with full flavor.

Let's take a break from this lugubrious topic. I have just the lighthearted answer we both need. After you've had a rest, let's move on to an exploration of funny things that happen on the way to inner peace.

FUNNY THINGS CAN HAPPEN ON THE WAY TO INNER PEACE

Sometimes I admonish myself because I'm having too much fun in the office. This is okay, but I have to be on the lookout for naturally funny people who are accustomed to being the life of the party and who may use humor as a way to avoid uncomfortable topics. The unconscious game some comical patients play is called *Entertain Your Therapist so She Won't Probe into the Tough Stuff.*

I've had some real comedians frequent my office. These were mostly men who maybe hadn't ever allowed themselves to feel much of anything. They use their gift of humorous gab to distract themselves and others from real down-to-earth pain.

HARRY AND SALLY

Remember, in our discussion on love, I told you about Harry who made light of his wife's comment about getting along better with her mother, and he retorted, "That's because she [his wife's mother] is on vacation." In our joint session, Harry, Sally, and I got a lot of mileage out of this one interaction.

We learned that part of Harry's initial attraction toward Sally was Sally's actual laugh. Sally didn't just titter; she produced an explosive sound as if she were filled to the brim with perfumed, volcanic air that was stored and waiting to spew out. After she exhaled her wide-grinned torrent, she would bend over, inhale as if she were taking in her last breath, and convulse loudly all over again. Harry just loved when she expressed herself in this way. He felt as if he were the only man in the world, maybe even on top of that world, and an entire audience of cheering people were waving their arms and throwing him kisses. He felt a few inches taller by the end of his performance.

As Harry said, "There's no sensation any better than seeing and hearing Sally laugh!" after which his eyes unabashedly revealed their characteristic sardonic twinkle.

When Sally laughed at his one-liners, quips, and witticisms, she needed tissues to wipe her face, because tears oozed down her cheeks like an irreparable leaky faucet, heartening Harry to smirk like a mischievous little boy. Sally noted his enjoyment of her merriment, and this gratified her nurturing nature. It encouraged her to guffaw even more. Therefore, as will happen when you laugh, her playfulness and creativity were stimulated, and she fed him some "straight man" lines to further encourage him. Their repartee provided a regular Gracie and Allen act.

The only problem was that Harry's gift of putting across his gaiety had a limitation: he felt compelled to divert, dilute, and deter his disturbing feelings. His only coping mechanism appeared to be his humor, which was witty and endearing and which scored him points at work, social gatherings, and with his wife.

But often times his tactic turned against him. Particularly with his wife, he made light of her most serious and emotional interjections as if he didn't care how she felt. Or if he used cruel humor or ridicule and her feelings were hurt, he would retort, "Come on. I was just kidding!"

Don't you just love when people do that! You not only feel hurt by what they say; now you are stupid for having taken it seriously. Well, righteo, guys, if you say it, you pay it. Don't ask the other person to take the fall for your insensitive jibes, which are designed to help you escape reality. Stand up like a man and take your lumps. Move on rather than pawning the responsibility on to the other guy for taking it "wrong."

To those of you who have been victims of the be-all-and-end-all funny man, when the funny people declare, "Don't you have a sense of humor?" or they say, "Oh, I was only joking. Can't you take a joke?" after they've just poked fun at you, do not allow this to throw you off. Just quote Shakespeare who said, "A jest's prosperity is always in the ear of he who hears it, never in the tongue of him who says it." If someone tells you a joke and you don't think it's funny, then it's not funny.

Yes, I know most of the guys who engage in this joke-and-reverse practice do so because they are trying to help minimize their loved ones' suffering. If making a joke about one's own difficulties works as a detour for the joker to diminish the impact of what ails him, why wouldn't he try to help the significant people in his life to do the same? The problem is: the rest of us don't always think the same way as he does, and what works for him is not necessarily helpful to us.

Many couples and parents don't understand that we each tick to our own clock; we each have to paint our life's scenes in our own way. This concept is most difficult to acquire. Besides, as Will Rogers said, "Everything is funny as long as it's happening to somebody else!"

Understanding the hurtful aspects of humor was very hard for a facetious guy like Harry. When you've gotten through rough times using your humor as your pillow, your weapon, and your escape route, why would you want to give up this exceptional gift just so you can more exquisitely experience your own misery, let alone someone else's?

Many men prefer to make other people laugh rather than to laugh themselves, whereas we women are more often the actual laughers much more than we are laugh producers. Did you ever notice that most women laugh more than men do? At a party or family gathering, look around at who's providing the levity and who's truly tee-heeing. You'll probably find the women giggling and smiling way more than the men.

Then take a gander at the kind of humor the men are expressing, and you will probably note how aggressive it often is, taking the form of putting down a group or a person. If the women are joking around at all, and it's unlikely they will be if they are in a mixed crowd, they are probably pointing out their own stupidity or awkwardness in an attempt to make the others feel better about their own frailties.

I'm not criticizing men or women. I'm just asking you to look at ways you use humor in your life. The more you use humor to get closer to other human beings, the better chance you have for humor to help you enhance your relationships.

Harry served as a good example of a guy who attempted to use his comicality to control other people's reaction to him. He and I worked individually to learn more about how he developed his wit as a tool to deal with the world. The goal was not for Harry to give up his delightful and droll slant on things. I wanted to liberate him from being locked in by his talent, since he felt compelled to always be funny. If his friends didn't see him yukking it up with jokes, they asked him, "Hey, Harry, what's the matter? You seem down today."

That's the problem with the resources and limitations of funny people. What is a positive trait becomes limiting when it's used in a rigid way, when the person has no alternative but to be a certain way all the time. In Harry's case, I think he was pretty lonely and scared. What was he if not funny? In a way, isn't it similar to beautiful Jenny's plight? (Jenny is the young woman whom I talked about when we got into eating disorders, who had no identity other than to be pretty.)

I really felt for Harry. I had to be careful not to exhibit my sympathy, because if he allowed my truth to invade his semi-safe world, it would be as if I robbed him of his fur-lined clothing, and he might feel crushed upon the realization that without comedy, he had no other way to ward off impending doom.

I have seen people who can put on a positive front and appear as if nothing ever bothers them only to have them crash and become severely depressed as soon as real crisis hits. Their denial apparatus worked most of their lives, but this one event threw them, and they had no other defense mechanism to put in its place. I had to take it slowly with Harry.

Also, if Harry learned to differentiate between connecting humor and alienating humor, he would be able to retain his fun-loving nature while simultaneously maintain a feeling of being a whole person with more to him than a man dressed in a meager, imaginary clown costume.

I wouldn't confront him with, "Harry, give up your façade, your armor, and get real so you can connect with others and not be so lonely." Imagine how frightening it would be for him to cope with the nothingness he feared was inside.

If Harry were a performer, he could have been in the seat of many performing comedians.

As I've seen with many funny men, I wondered if maybe Harry was trying too hard to be lighthearted. I imagined him at a party. Did he come across as if he had to keep up the monologue forever? Like Sisyphus, who was doomed to push the rock up the hill only to have to push it up again, if Harry stopped talking, might he be right back where he started? When I meet people like this, despite my observance of his audience's laughing at attention, I invariably soak up what I sense as his depression as if it were puddles of water magnifying a dry sponge. I suspected this could be true of Harry as well. But Harry was not conscious of the depression that threatened to erode his false sense of well-being and which served as his cover.

Harry was the first son of a working-class family, which eventually increased in size by five more children. His mother was a busy lady who would stop her work and clap her hands then cover her mouth as she giggled over Harry's antics. His mom's reaction was one of Harry's few positive early memories.

Even though Harry's father was strict and rigid, Harry took his chances on misbehaving and frequently got into trouble. But at least his siblings laughed and secretly cheered him on. He seemed so brave to defy his highly intelligent but uneducated father.

In school, he felt stupid, having no extra coaching at home, and he wasn't motivated to study. He assumed he would end up working in a factory as his father did. His only source of self-esteem came from his ability to make his classmates laugh.

Only after months of our work together did Harry give up his practice of thinking up jokes before he went anywhere as he had done since adolescence. He rehearsed his drollery at home or in the car so he would not be left off guard in awkward social situations. As he put it, "I would never go out of the house 'naked!' As long as I have my jokes handy, I am properly dressed."

What he loved most was to make the girls giggle and chatter away in response to his funny faces and weird noises. Using his body as a musical instrument, he could produce unique sounds. His favorite ploy was to tap someone on the back and cause a hollow pop to echo forth. This gave him a chance to touch the girls without appearing "fresh." Harry was the class clown, emcee, and stand-up comic all rolled into one.

Gradually, I found myself laughing less at Harry's witty remarks and feeling more in sync with his sweet, vulnerable nature. As he stopped relying on his comic intelligence to control the reaction of others, he discovered other talents such as his ability to listen and really count as a support person to his children, something he had never felt competent to offer. In addition, he learned to differentiate between humor for fun and humor that can hurt someone else, in other words, humor at someone else's expense. You see, when he didn't need to be the comedian anymore, he didn't have to, out of desperation, jest over other people's foibles in order to achieve his goals of being accepted and noticed by others.

Sally sure did appreciate this new man who could now look her in the eyes and see further into her soul than ever before. And much to his dismay, she continued to find him hilarious, and she persisted in offering him her rollicking, fun-loving laughter.

I strive for opportunities to laugh with my patients. After all, aren't they here to deal with their tension, stress, and pain? Isn't it my job to help them discharge it as well as to help them determine the cause of their misery so they can work through their conflicts once and for all?

I use laughter therapy to help people lighten up over very difficult issues they face. I facilitate the process that Steve Allen described as, "Tragedy plus time equals comedy."

It's important for you to note, however, that I do not introduce laughter therapy unless my patients want to give it a try. I seriously get into their dilemma and empathize with all the painful emotions attached to it. If and when I think it's appropriate, I ask, "Do you wish to lighten up about this?"

Before I share with you some examples about how I have actually used laughter therapy, I need you to understand a few more things about what I mean when I say you play with your pain (a phrase I learned from Annette Goodhart, author of *Laughter Therapy: How to Laugh about Everything in Your Life that Isn't Really Funny*).

You don't deny the pain. You laugh *because* of the pain. You laugh even though it isn't funny.

Imagine a person who comes to me, and when I ask him why he is seeking my help, he says he is depressed. I immediately start laughing my head off.

Nope, this isn't what I had in mind. There is much forethought that goes into this smiling intervention. We've got lots of work to do before we employ laughter as a healing maneuver. We've got a whole bunch of crying to do. We need to understand what is going on in this person's life.

We are talking here about playing with your own pain. When you play with someone else's pain without their permission, that's ridicule. You want to play with your own pain in order to make yourself laugh. The physical act of laughter helps you release the heaviness inside that builds up like a volcano, which, if there is no release, can hurt you both physically and emotionally.

The rule here is that you need the other person's permission to poke fun at his or her pain. This means the person is usually a peer, someone whom you trust, who would feel comfortable saying to you, "That's going a little too far. Please stop."

Given all the disclaimers, I will now tell you how I helped Suzanne by using laughter therapy.

SUZANNE

Remember Suzanne? When we were talking about the helping process many hours ago, I told you about how we used humor to help her release her guilt and anxiety over having had an abortion. We turned on our imaginary television and made up a situation comedy sketch about a family of three girls, one of whom is a make-believe Suzanne who, on the same day, tell their parents they are pregnant.

On another occasion, we got into Steve Martin's Saturday Night Live routine where he goes through an energetic, enthusiastic plan and then says, "Naaaaaah!" Remember how she got into that when we talked about how she imagines doing great things and then retreats for fear of failing?

In addition to her other troubles, Suzanne was diabetic and didn't always take good care of herself. She was sometimes ashamed and embarrassed about her condition and, in other instances, she was in denial. She reluctantly admitted in a moment of supreme trust in me that she felt the diabetes was God's punishment for her previous transgressions. Part of my work with her was to help her accept the reality of her physical problems, which, contrary to her guilty feelings about her earlier abortion, were not her fault. For her to acknowledge the disease would be to accept blame for having caused it.

One day, I was trying to get Suzanne to face up to her situation. In my usual free associative style, I told her I was reminded of a TV show I used to watch but had never heard anyone else speak of it. It was a Kung Foo off-shoot of the old Keith Carradine character. The lead character was a cop. The Zen master, who was actually the cop's father, and the cop both thought the other one had died in a fire many years before. (This doesn't have much to do with the point I'm making, but as a secondary motivation, I was secretly hoping one of you would remember this show and join me in reminiscing about it.) In the beginning of each show when they introduced the characters, the main cop would say, "I'm a cop. It's who I am. It's what I do!" I just loved when he did this—I think it had to do with his confidence, determination, and unambivalent love of his work. I made sure never to miss the beginning.

I told Suzanne about the show and my favorite part and suggested that she say, "I'm a diabetic. It's who I am. It's what I do!"

She was reluctant, of course, but eventually followed through. I suggested that she get a T- shirt with those words on it. We had some fun with this and periodically, over the course of our time together, I spontaneously broke into song. I turned it into a cheer with all the hand movements to go with it.

We both laughed and produced a cacophony of the kind of sounds people make when they not only think the situation is funny, but they are getting a kick out of themselves as well.

Would Suzanne ever be able to think about her diabetes again without accompanying the thought with a little chuckle? In so doing, she was attaching the tension release of the laughter with the painful reality of the disease.

AGNES

In a similar fashion, I helped Agnes to accept the truth about her limp and the necessity of using a walker to get around. After she and I had traveled together to the land of loss where Agnes had been stuck for five years before coming to see me, I asked fifty-year-old Agnes if she would like to lighten up about the loss of function in her leg. I intuited that even though we would be lighthearted and silly, our engaging in something outrageous would help her to make a breakthrough.

I pointed to a quotation on my office wall that says, "When your heart cries for what it lost, your soul laughs for what it has." She hesitantly agreed to see what I had in mind.

At the next session, I brought in some crepe paper and small pompoms and asked her to decorate her walker while we continued to talk about her necessity to use it. After a while, I said, "Now that you have dressed it all up, you should probably give your walker a name!"

By this time, her playful nature had been stimulated, and as she stepped back to admire the colorful array of paper loops, which were each topped off by a blob of multi-colored pompoms, she said, "I dub you Miss Merry Lightning Rod."

As we talked about what behooved her to produce this name, she told me she had a silly fear that if she were walking in the rain and lightning struck and hit her metal walker, she would die. This tragedy could occur at any time.

"I know it's stupid, but when it rains, I just don't go out. In fact, a few weeks ago when I cancelled our appointment, it was because of the rain, not because I was sick. I was too embarrassed to tell you." With her right hand, Agnes tugged her lower eyelid, exposing the white portion of her eye as I had seen her do whenever she was anxious.

"I've never told anyone that little truth before. Do you wonder why?"

By imagining her walker as a protective lightning rod rather than as an instrument of her destruction, Agnes had turned the tables on her fear. Agnes and I laughed our way through this conversation as I pretended to be lightning and she raised her walker and zapped me back. By the end of the session we were like two giggly little girls. Her lightheartedness was evidenced by the way she strutted out of my office. Yet leaning as always and caressing her decked-out helpmate, her trusty, beloved walker, anyone might have thought she was Cinderella about to enter the coach to go to the ball.

Sometime in the middle of the next session, as she talked about how impossible it would be to get around without this equipment, she started to appreciate her instrument of mercy. Agnes blurted out, "I love my walker!"

Agnes quickly put her jeweled hand to her rage-red lipstick as she gasped in delight over her spontaneous declaration. It was a crowning moment for both of us. As she was leaving and as I stood by the door to escort her out, she turned around and reached out to me. We embraced in one gargantuan hug. What a great day that was.

SANDRA

I asked Sandra, who had rheumatoid arthritis, if she was willing to try using laughter as a way to deal with her chronic pain. She was desperate enough to try anything. We established that she would be grateful if we could just find a way to alleviate her suffering for short periods of time so she could at least climb steps at home or maybe even walk in the mall for a few hours.

There wasn't much to the strategy except for Sandra to learn how to make herself laugh out loud and for her to learn how to say, "Ouch!" The last part is simple. Believe it or not, the first part, getting yourself to laugh out loud, especially if there's seemingly nothing funny going on as well as to try to accomplish this when you are in pain, might be an enormous task.

I asked Sandra to find a spot on her body that was presently paining her. In Sandra's case, this wasn't hard to do. She was to put pressure on her elbow until it hurt but not to the point of agony, just enough to let her know the pain was there. When she did this, she was to shout, "Ouch!"

We had to practice this a number of times, because at first she was inhibited and worried people in my waiting room would hear her and wonder what in the world was going on. Also, she had always been a good little girl, trying to be perfect so as not to be a burden to her parents, both of whom worked all day and complained when they came home that they were too tired to take any nonsense from the kids.

Okay, we got the "ouching" down pat. Now, we had to work on the laughter. Sandra was feeling so self-conscious that it wasn't too difficult to get her started. She had a little snicker that she evoked whenever she was embarrassed, and we were able to take off from there. Eventually, with drama, she could shout, "Ouch!" And then as I instructed her to do, she recited the words, "Tee hee," and then she really poured on the laughter.

We repeated this ritual again and again, with her pressing on the sore elbow, "Ouch! Tee hee." It was so silly that her laugh became throatier, and she wheezed in hysterics. After a while, I asked her about the pain in her elbow. She was unable to make it hurt even when she pressed on it harder than the original time.

Sandra was astounded. She was giddy by then and giggled all the way out the door. She couldn't wait to tell her husband what had happened and was hoping they would try a short mall visit that Saturday.

Yep, it was hard work to make herself laugh, but Sandra wanted to have these respites, and she felt more in control to make them happen.

BONNIE

Bonnie, the large woman I talked about in our discussion of eating disorders, learned how to use laughter to work through her pain over her body size and shape. Before she lost her first forty pounds, throughout many sessions we worked on helping her to deal with the actuality that she was fat. Even saying the word "fat" was difficult for her. She, like so many other obese people, wanted to deny how she looked. It was as if she were a toddler playing peek-a-boo by putting her pudgy fingers over her eyes, kind of saying, "If I don't see you, you're not there." She never looked in a mirror. I guess we could say she didn't want to see her fat, and if she didn't see it or say it, it must not exist. So even getting her to call herself fat was a momentous feat.

I believe before you can lose weight, you must face reality. As frightened as you are of the scale, you must face the numbers they reveal. It's so scary to see the digits shining in your eyes, making you want to blind the reality but piercing through to your brain nevertheless.

Just as I did with Suzanne, I asked Bonnie to speak of her body parts in real terms. I questioned her: "So, Bonnie, when you look at your fat, what do you say to yourself about being fat?" Or "Bonnie, how do you think you would feel if you weren't fat?"

So when it came time for Bonnie's son's forthcoming wedding, we had made progress as she fretted over the fact that some of her family and friends who were to attend might think or say to each other, "She's still fat," or, "She sure did let herself go," or, "You mean she still hasn't lost weight?" or, "Bonnie has such a pretty face. If only she were thinner."

Bonnie's way of handling the agony of her lifelong challenge to look like everyone else was to blot out her thoughts about these potentially agonizing occasions. In the past, to protect herself from noticing how people stared at her or purposefully averted their eyes, she adopted an icy, austere facial expression, one of being impenetrable to the pain. She fantasized that she could actually prevent others from observing her distress over not looking ordinary and acceptable. However, this facial expression actually worked against her, because many people, after observing her belligerent face, believed that Bonnie preferred them to keep their distance from her. Therefore, because she didn't get the love, support, or recognition she so desperately craved, Bonnie felt empty and lonely most of the time, which of course, was impetus for her to stuff herself even more in an attempt to fill in the empty space she imagined inside of her body.

My goal was to help Bonnie accept the reality that others most assuredly noticed her unusually large body. Bonnie needed to acknowledge her pain over that fact rather than to employ her standard method of trying to obliterate her view of these torturous situations. I wanted to find a way for Bonnie to discharge the tension surrounding her fear over being isolated and ridiculed.

I was the bearer of the bad news. "Bonnie, your fears are well founded. Most people will notice your body. Many will ponder silently, but others may turn to their spouses or friends and utter those comments you so abhor."

I even role played with her, reciting the unsaid but imagined cruel words that might be in the minds of her guests. The more I made these statements, the less she was able to block out the reality. Even if she tried to wash these ideas away, we agreed that no matter how much Bonnie tried to control the reactions of others, people would think what they were going to think, regardless.

I said, "I have an idea! How about approaching each guest and magnanimously throwing up your arms, while announcing, 'My, I'm large!'"

Bonnie nervously laughed at this idea. "Are you serious?"

"Serious or not, can you imagine yourself saying that?"

We played with this for a while, my making the comments and Bonnie's repeating, "My, I'm large!" in as joyous a way as possible. Each time, we laughed harder and longer.

Knowing how laughter can help people bring out their creativity, I assigned Bonnie some homework. "Bonnie, for the next session make a list of all the things that you could say to each guest. Be as imaginative as possible. Stretch your laughing soul to conceive of statements of fact about your size rather than considering aggressive comebacks."

Seeming to have a new lightness to her, Bonnie returned to my office with a bounce in her step. She presented her list of scenarios. Here's what Bonnie imagined she might say to her guests:

"I'm *enormous…ly* glad to see you."

"I'm the mountainous mamma."

She envisioned a circle of fat people with their hands clasped as in a choral performance, following her around the wedding banquet room singing, "Hmmmmm."

"I'm *humongous…ly* happy that you are here."

"I'm so large I can hug you from both sides."

We both laughed as Bonnie shared these accounts. Gradually, she worked off the tension around her negative body image and the fears of what people thought of her. She said she wasn't worried about the wedding any more.

However, we agreed that at the wedding if Bonnie did become tense at any point, she could conjure up the pictures we had laughed about. Then she should laugh and greet each guest. I predicted that the guests, therefore, would tend not to distance themselves as they would have in response to her previous, almost hostile facial expression. Because of the laugh, she would naturally have a smile on her face. Her friends and family would be encouraged to reach out to her.

After the wedding, when I stepped into the waiting room to greet Bonnie, I saw a lighter woman. She almost raced me into the office and exuberantly reported the results of our preparatory work together.

"I had the best time of my life! I even stood in front of everyone to make a speech. I had always been afraid to dance even when I was thinner and younger. But I actually danced most of the night. My guests had such a great time. It was because I was playful and 'light!' All the laughing we did helped me to see that just because I try to blot out thoughts of what people see, I can't pretend any more that other people are blind to my fat. Now it's okay that they see it. I saw some of the pictures guests had taken with their cameras. I don't look that bad. I think I actually look okay! I'm beginning to accept who I am. The best part is that I'm not afraid any more. I can laugh about it now."

ABE AND ESTHER

Here's how I helped an elderly couple find their way back to each other:

I gave Abe and Esther an assignment, which was to be carried out the next time they argued. At the rate they were going, they wouldn't have to wait too long to carry out my orders.

I said, "The next time you are about to argue, I want you to think about what we reviewed today. Remember our talk about how you both get caught in a childish battle, which you have enormous trouble ending. You each make your point, and neither of you will budge. You realize that you will have to either say you are sorry, or let's stop fighting, or isn't this silly. But you worry that your spouse may not be ready to end, or you just don't want to give in. Here's what you do: excusing yourself for a minute, go to your underwear drawer and put your underpants on top of your head. Then return to the argument and say, 'Now where were we?' The tension is discharged, and you are now both unstuck. Neither one wins or loses, and maybe now you can really talk!"

I suggested also that if they are not at home, they could produce one of the clown noses I had given them to keep handy for just such an occasion.

This couple never did go through with the assignment. But here's what did happen: shortly after our session where I recommended the silly resolution, they were at each other's throats again. Before the fight even escalated as it usually would, because they remembered my suggestion, they both burst out laughing. They really had fun together that night.

The discussion of the plan in my office served the same purpose that tickling does for a young child. You never actually have to tickle the child. You merely act as if you are going to do so, and the child laughs as if you are actually touching him.

KEVIN

Do you ever hear yourself saying, "I shouldn't be laughing right now because I'm depressed." Could it be that you are holding onto your misery as if it is a monument of your very being? Here's how I worked with the very serious Kevin and how I taught him how to lighten up and emerge from his woe-is-me nature.

First, we'll need to review his history to get you up to snuff since it was a long time ago that I first introduced him. Kevin was the fifty-year-old man who came to see me at the behest of his lover, Diane, for whom he had babysat as a kid. He was married to Darlene, a woman he thought was self-sufficient, but almost within minutes of his marriage to her, she turned into a semi-invalid who could be demanding. He owned an auto parts store, which I visited once the way his father would have done if he hadn't died when Kevin was four. After Father's death, Mother became an alcoholic and for a time, the town whore. She was absent because she was in several treatment centers to "dry out." At these times, Kevin stayed with his aunt and uncle, but when his mother returned, so did Kevin's bellyaches. In high school, he was the star on the baseball team. He is the one I had compared to Randall Cunningham, because he had so much talent but didn't have good receivers to catch the ball. I wanted to take him home to my house to live.

Contrary to the usual contagion that laughter produces, Kevin's laugh was not infectious at all. When he laughed, it was more like scorn with a smile attached to it—although he would have denied this, I'm sure, because he wasn't conscious of his fury—putting me in the position of having to decide if I wanted to go along with his brand of mirth. Sometimes the sounds came out of the blue from his lungs like a squall or a sudden violent gust of wind often with rain or snow.

Kevin's lover, Diane, had remained in the picture during the whole time I had been treating Kevin. On one particular day, he described a fight they had had. Diane complained that he didn't allow her to make him happy. Whenever she massaged his back, he would just walk away with no acknowledgement of how she made him feel. In reality, he loved when she did this but was afraid to tell her so for fear she would stop. (Remember how his mother would giveth and then taketh away, especially when she got drunk?)

"What's her problem? Why do I have to bow down to her just because she deigns to touch me?"

"Kevin, when you get like this, furious and sarcastic, it usually means you are afraid of something underneath. What's going on?"

He rubbed his nose with his index finger, sliding it back and forth like a saber saw. In his usual avoidant style, he looked away as if examining the books on the shelves.

I waited. I had plenty of time.

"All right, all right. My mom used to do that when I was studying in high school. It was kind of freaky. But I really like it."

I asked, "Did you ever not like it?"

"Yeah, when she was drunk. That's when she would do weird things, and I never knew how to react."

We examined all the nooks and crannies of this one event and learned more about his relationship to his mom. We spent a few sessions exploring it. Then we got into how good he felt when Diane was kind to him, especially because Diane didn't withdraw her affection except when she was upset that he didn't validate her advances to him. When he and Diane got into this controversy, Kevin berated himself and called himself a miserable, depressed guy who had to be a real drag to anyone.

"What do you get out of this view of yourself, Kevin?"

He knew what I was driving at. We had been here before. I always look for the gratification when someone does things that make him unhappy but seems compelled to keep doing even though he is free to choose another path.

"Why do you ask me such tough questions? Why don't you answer it for a change?" His nostrils were dilated. He was glaring at me with moist eyes, and he was sawing his nose again!

Kevin went on, "All right, all right. I think she gives me more when I'm miserable. And you do too for that matter!"

Hmmm. Very interesting observation on his part. Was he picking up my maternal feelings for him and being gratified by this but scared at the same time that he would lose my attention once he felt better or not depressed? I looked into myself and determined that I felt just as loving toward him when he felt good about himself as when he was down and out. I based this on my emotions during those few occasions when he had allowed me to see his joy.

Having explored this in myself, I could now ask him what he meant by my giving him more when he is depressed versus when he is upbeat. His fantasy was that I, like his mother, would feel guilty about having treated him abusively. When she slept it off and came back to him in the morning, throughout his childhood, he had developed a certain pathetic expression that was the signal for his mother to make amends. He would droop his shoulders, tilt his head, let out a deep sigh, and look up toward the ceiling. Since his mom always came through with the "lovey" stuff in any case (or that's what I surmised, because I figured she was a loving woman who wanted to do right by Kevin but the alcohol got in the way), I hypothesized that Kevin developed the magical idea that it was his posture and stance that got him what he needed.

Over the next several weeks, as Kevin and I came to understand more about his holding onto his wretched self-image, we looked at what his despair cost him with his son, Dirk, with his wife, Darlene, with his employees, and now with Diane. We determined that he was ready to give up this dysfunctional behavior, which may have worked when he was little but was no longer necessary now; in fact, it was a form of self-abuse in a way. Here is where the laughter therapy came in.

First, I had to teach Kevin the concept of laughing for its own sake and not to feel compelled to attach laughter to a comical event. This meant that he had to be willing to try exercises where he would deliberately laugh for no reason. I asked him to stand in front of a mirror each morning, look into his own eyes, and say, "Tee hee." If he felt the urge to laugh out loud, he was to do so. If not, he was to try to force it, or as I said to him, "Fake it till you make it!"

He was to try this when he was in his car and any time when no one was around so he wouldn't feel too inhibited. He was to work himself up to be able to laugh for three minutes. I told Kevin, "Three minutes of laughing is supposedly the cardiovascular equivalent of ten minutes of rowing. Hey, Kevin, you don't need any water, and you don't even need a boat!"

When he smiled in response, I said, "No, don't just smile. Laugh out loud when you think something is funny!"

He did so, and as soon as he laughed, I did as well. I feel I have permission to crack up only when my patient is doing it. Otherwise, I might be using my patient as a foil for my own wish to laugh, not because I am truly trying to help my patient. I must always keep in mind our mission, especially when I'm doing laughter work. However, on this occasion, in order to help him loosen up by making a fool out of myself, I demonstrated for Kevin how I do it.

You know how contagious laughter is. In no time, Kevin was holding his stomach from the hearty exercise. Once Kevin bought into this whole concept, we were ready to proceed.

I asked Kevin to make his face as pitiable as possible and also to adjust his body to reflect his wretchedness. He was then to say, "Tee Hee," after which, he was to get himself back to normal again. Of course, we then repeated the process over and over from miserable Kevin to normal Kevin. We both laughed uncontrollably at times when he did this.

Then, I asked him to do it again, but whenever he was normal looking, to say with conviction, "I used to be a depressed person, but now I'm a hap-hap-happy person!" He was to force a laugh at this time.

Well, when he said these words, I'm sure you figured he didn't have to force a laugh; he could hardly get the words out without snickering and then downright hee-hawing.

We had a grand old time in these sessions. I can't imagine Kevin's ever being able to pout and drop those shoulders without remembering how we laughed about it. He was ready to give up this formerly unconscious way to manipulate others to give him what he had thought he didn't deserve in the first place—love, attention, and respect.

BETTY

I'm always intrigued by people who are ashamed of being stupid or poor. Often formerly poor people are especially mortified by poverty as if they, as children, had any control over how their parents did or didn't provide for them.

I'm thinking of Betty with whom I role-played a pretend interview for a job where she was to convince me that I shouldn't hire her because, as I instructed her to say with a straight face, "I'm a previously poor person." Later we added another *P* word, and she said, "I'm a pathetic, previously-poor person."

When she really got into it, spontaneously, she threw in her own *P* words. By this time, she couldn't get them all out without giggling hysterically, "I'm a pathetically, pretty, painstakingly, previously poor person in my poverty."

I added, "That's precious, Betty. You're pretty punchy too!"

As we parted at the portal of my office, the people patiently waiting were pretty well perked up and pondered the perfect pandemonium we had produced in my pad.

KATIE

Katie was the courteous, obedient, approval-seeking young adult who mourned the loss of her unborn child, and her aunt tried to console her by saying, "This is for the best." She had broken out of her shell by throwing my accent pillows across the room. As I remarked when I first introduced Katie to you, the tantrum marked the beginning of her healing. She was the one who cried on my shoulder and used the crying towel so when she sobbed her mascara wouldn't ruin my clothes. She took the towel with her when I went on vacation and at the end of therapy.

We also discussed Katie's lamentation, because she was bursting with emotion but surrounded by people who neutralized feelings and were very good at it, leaving her feeling isolated and lonely. I had helped her by modeling what it looks like to be excited on the outside and taking the risk to show it to others by saying, "Great! That's wonderful!" when she talked about stopping at the store on her way to her next appointment. She followed suit by pronouncing her love for me.

I also referred to Katie in our discussion of the impact of fathers on teenage daughters. I mentioned that Katie's dad said she resembled his sister, Aunt Rose. Aunt Rose was fat! Katie was devastated.

I once told Katie, who punctuated almost every sentence with an, "I'm so stupid," that what she needed was a stupid therapist to match. I remember how she had been looking down at her car keys, and she suddenly looked up at me and said, "Are you joking?"

I certainly didn't want to hurt her feelings or in any way appear to be poking fun at her. I said, "I'm not kidding. I think you would do well with a stupid therapist. You know, I'm pretty stupid. I think I'm it!"

I've often referred to myself as being a very slow processor. Because I digest so much before I propose hypothetical ideas about what people are saying and because sometimes I am seen looking up and to the right as if my eyeballs are going into my brain, and minutes will go by before I respond to people, I can appear very stupid. My patients have gotten used to me, and a veteran client usually lingers expectantly for any length of time, no longer uncomfortable with the silence as he or she had been in the past, waiting for what's going to come out of my mouth.

Katie said, "Phyliss, you're not stupid."

"I can be as stupid as anyone. And, you know what, I like being stupid sometimes. Why not? I have a certain way of processing thoughts, and it's unique to me. Anyway, what's so bad about being stupid? We all can't be born geniuses."

Because I had introduced the stupid therapist concept to Katie, a few months later when Katie was espousing some irrational and distorted perceptions, I was able to say, "Now, Katie, at this moment, you are bordering on stupid."

She got a big hee-haw out of that one, and with those few words, we were able to break through and look underneath ideas she had taken for granted.

SANDRA

Sandra, the woman with whom I worked to help her with her rheumatoid arthritis, often referred to herself as "stupid." An intelligent woman, she used the word "stupid" in a loose way, particularly when I made interpretations that she had difficulty understanding.

I knew that her lack of comprehension had to do with her emotions, not her native intelligence. Even though I reminded Sandra that it takes time to incorporate new ways of looking at oneself, she continued to put herself down. And the more she did this, the more uptight she got, and therefore, the less she understood. This self-imposed confusion was a sabotage technique. She fogged up her natural intelligence when the things she was smart enough to know were too painful for her to examine. She also used personal putdowns as a way not to look further into herself.

One day, Sandra came into the office and said, "I read an article on stress. There was a list of things that you do to create stress in your life. I checked off all twenty items. I'm so stupid. I cause my own problems."

Attempting to crack through Sandra's usual self-sabotage, I said, "Sandra, you are very smart. You got a hundred on that stress test!"

She laughed, and I joined in as soon as I knew that she was aware I wasn't making fun of her but merely helping her to see how she sabotages herself. Using laughter as a tension discharge, she felt freer to look more closely and less harshly at herself.

I hope our conversation on funny things in therapy helps you nourish that core within you. And if I have failed to accomplish this wish, then you and I can always guffaw over the fool I made of myself trying to make it happen!

Before we go on to talking about the best humor producers of all—children—I would like to yet again quote an anonymous wise person who said, "Imagination was given to man to compensate him for what he is not; and a sense of humor was provided to console him for what he is."

GIVING CHILDREN
A SENSE OF SELF

Sometimes parents are upset that their children are in therapy. They complain that psychologists don't really help; they just induce patients to blame their parents instead of helping people learn how to take responsibility for their own actions.

Well, guess what? For the most part, parents are not to blame any more than their parents' parents were at fault. Do you think I'm blaming parents when I tell you about people's past life events? When I tell you how my patients adjusted to their parents' frailties am I pointing my heartless finger at all the moms and dads of the world?

Most patients feel guilty talking about their parents. Parents of children and adolescents often sabotage therapy of their offspring, telling their children the therapy isn't working so they're not going to pay for it anymore. This withdrawal of resources from their children may occur even though the children want to continue treatment.

I'm a parent and a grandparent. Neither you nor I were born knowing. Even after I learned to be a psychologist, I wasn't prepared for the personal plethora of worries, impossible decisions, difficulty in dealing with the unexpected, and the questions, concerns, and developmental challenges of my children, not even counting the skinned knees, terrifying trips to the doctor, breaking up the sibling rivalry, conferences with their teachers, and then, when you finally get some sleep, they have grown into their own teenage selves and tell you you were all wrong the way you did it, and when they become parents, they will do it the right way. This is how it goes. Life rolls along, and these declarations of independence and assertions of how they know better sound familiar to you, because maybe you heard yourself saying similar words to your parents about twenty-something years ago.

One of the greatest challenges your parents had to face was giving you the power to be who you are as opposed to molding you into a mere replica of themselves.

Were you ever embarrassed by your parents when they said, "Oh, he's just being shy," but you thought you were being cautious? How about when they scolded you, "Don't be so negative," but you thought you were just asking an innocent question? They said, "Don't make trouble," but you believed you were really expressing a fear. Did you ever feel laughed at by your parents? They were probably chuckling because you were so cute. You misinterpreted their behavior, because at the time, you were trying to express a serious thought.

Remember when your parents used to speak to other people about you as if you weren't there? Did a relative or family friend ever question you, and your mother answered the question for you as if your mother actually had your brain, your mouth, and your voice? Did your parents ever ask you to show off so others would see what great caretakers they were?

Did your parents sometimes pressure you to be different from who you really are? Did your father ever tell you you'd make a good teacher, as if you never told him you wanted to be an artist? Did you ever feel that you were bad because you weren't doing things the way your mother did? Did you look at the frowns on your parents' faces and believe that by being your own self rather than being the self they imagined for you, you were *hurting* them?

Your vision of yourself was tied to how your parents viewed you.

We know now that your parents' gestures probably weren't intentionally designed to rob you of your "self." Nevertheless, you started out your life trying to please them. By being what you thought they wanted you to be, you subsequently forgot who you are!

I'm a proponent of providing an atmosphere conducive for your children to find themselves. Without this acceptance, they are in danger of becoming "invisible." Yet even as you follow this edict of forsaking your own possessive needs and/or your urge to hold onto your brood forever, you can really be in for it when they are old enough to tell you off! They are able to confront you because you helped them find and maintain their own voice. For any parent, even if you've done your job, you might question as I did: *Why didn't I raise them as guilty little dependent automatons? I could have saved myself a lot of heartache!*

Nevertheless, a sense of self is the perfect present you can give your children. You don't even have to go to the store to acquire it. The most precious offering you have to give is already available within you. It's an intangible. It's your special token that they can carry wherever they go. It's the gift of helping them find the "self" that is rightfully theirs.

AGNES

Remember Agnes? She's the woman who by laughing and being playful learned to love her walker, which she needed to get around because of loss of function in her leg. The question for Agnes and me was to figure out why she had such difficulty with her angry feelings. Remember, she had this secret fantasy that her metal walker would absorb lightning when it rained and ultimately electrocute her.

Agnes recalled as a child being told whenever she got hurt that she must have done something to cause it. On one occasion when little Agnes fell off her bike, she overheard her parents telling her aunt, "Oh, Agnes always falls off her bike. She likes to get sympathy." In other words, Agnes was the agent of her own pain. Agnes came to believe that she caused all of the misery in her life.

As an adult, when she started having problems with her leg, underneath, she assumed she was at it again, damaging herself just so people would feel sorry for her. Agnes was furious that her previously active life was thwarted by this medical condition, and she had nowhere to put the blame but on herself. Therefore, she needed to be punished for deliberately causing herself to lose her ability to walk. What better way than to be struck down by lightning!

Agnes might have unconsciously chosen any form of retaliation for having been a bad girl. We wanted to find out why she specifically selected lightning as the weapon. Here again, Agnes absorbed the messages she was sent.

During thunderstorms, when she cried in bed at night, her father angrily entered her bedroom and scolded, "Agnes, stop being so dramatic about it. You know better than that. You know thunder won't hurt you. You just don't want to go to sleep now. You're always trying new stalling tactics."

Of course, Agnes stopped crying (out loud, that is). She was so ashamed and didn't know where to put her fear. As we talked about this in our sessions, she kept telling me how silly she had been to fear being struck down by lightning.

As she made a trail with her fingers on the outside of her nose and then over to her cheeks and pulled on her lower lids to expose the red inside her eyelids, she resembled an extraterrestrial creature. She exclaimed, "I always make mountains out of mole hills."

Of course, I asked a typical shrink question, but this wasn't a rote inquiry. When people come up with these clichés, quite often they've been inculcated with these exact phrases at specific times, and frequently, they received these words of wisdom as a child. "Agnes, what makes you say you *make mountains out of mole hills*? Did someone specifically tell you that?"

"I don't know." She sheepishly snuck a peek in my direction the way she might have done as a child.

"Think about it, Agnes. Run the video tape in your mind."

"I remember my sisters actually singing the words to the tune of 'Ring Around the Rosy' and my mom giggling, especially when they got to the 'all fall down' part and they sang, 'molehill, molehill, we all fall down.'"

Here comes another shrink question, "How did you feel when they did that?"

"Well, I figured they were right. It was Christmas time, just before New Year's, and I made a New Year's resolution to myself that I wouldn't make any more scenes—ever!"

"Did you stick to your promise?"

"Oh, yes, I remember vividly withholding tears. I was a real crier, and they always made fun of me, even my parents, but before that day, I was never able to hold my tears in. I got very good at holding my tears back, but boy did my throat hurt from the lump. I didn't get too excited about anything either, at least not in front of them. Since I was the baby, they never took me seriously anyway."

I guess, at that moment, I became the dramatic one. Tears welled up in my eyes; I actually experienced her early throat contractions. I contained myself and tolerated the staggering stone forming in my throat.

"Agnes, I feel very sad right now. I feel as if you were robbed of your right to feel what you feel, and you learned to deny your entitlement to any intense feelings. You assumed what you felt wasn't even real."

Then I started getting angry for Agnes. "How dare your family take away your claim on your unique feelings!"

Okay, I know I just told you I don't blame parents. This declaration still holds true. It wasn't necessarily their fault in that they probably weren't setting out to inhibit Agnes for the purpose of hurting her. They had their reasons, or should we say, they had their hang ups, which they sent along to Agnes. Passing on our vulnerabilities is what we all do as parents, whether we mean to or not.

Also, I'm not trying to set her against her parents as we therapists are often accused of doing. But Agnes simply needed to get in touch with what she had mislaid in her life; she lost more than a healthy functioning foot. She had given up her birthright to be her own person and her entitlement to feel her feelings and still be a good person. So my getting angry and feeling sad about her deprivation was important. By expressing my gut feelings, I was giving her permission to be annoyed about what she has missed in her life because of these early communications from the people whom she loved and who loved her.

I also knew that even if temporarily she would blame her parents, as we worked more on her issues and continued in our therapeutic process, she would inevitably accept her parents for the good and loving people they were but be freed of the verbal chains they had imposed on her. She would take responsibility for her behaviors and defenses and become her own person, not a reaction toward or against her parents, but a unique personality, closer to what she might have originally been had her psyche not been tampered with.

As an aside, I need to tell you also that there are hazards to therapy. She, like Katie, whom I described as feeling very lonely when she finally broke free to express herself and then found the people around her putting her down for it, was in danger of becoming unleashed yet surrounded by friends she had sought when she was looking for others who would discourage rather than encourage her to express herself. It was as if these chosen, constricted people were selected to further imprison her, to help her keep down the storm that was brewing inside. (Note the use of the word "storm" to describe what was hidden deep within Agnes. I linked this stormy image with her fear of the lightning storms that would strike her down because she was bad. It was Agnes's own anger that was threatening her.)

But as Agnes melted off the heat-sealed guardians, the friends she had set in place to inhibit herself, she was in danger of becoming a lonely oddball. When you are different from others, isn't it true you become self-conscious over your singularity? And to be sure, those who are unlike you will most assuredly remind you of your dissimilarity, especially if they are shook up by your "oddball" nature. Isn't this what may have happened when little Agnes, as a child, was so "out there" with her emotions but living in a family who got scared off by intense feelings? So if Agnes were to feel her isolation because she was now a liberated "emoter," would it be any worse than the loneliness she had felt as a child in a family who sent her signals that she was wrong to be the person she was born to be?

Let's look at an opposite scenario. How about when you "show off" your child? This is probably the hardest for all of us. "Tommy, show everyone how you can sing 'Mary Had a Little Lamb!'" Even if Tommy enjoys the kudos he gets, if his parents are consistent in this approach over time, he gets the message that his parents have strong needs for him to take care of them by showing off what he can do rather than who he is. If he's embarrassed to perform and is pressured to do so, he might inhibit himself from showing his parents what he can do so they won't present him as a decoration to others. Maybe, if he's angry, he'll even fail at things so they won't have anything to display! You get the drift. One behavior on the parents' part can produce many offshoots of survival mechanisms on the part of the child.

Your child gets an A on the test. Of course, you are pleased. But this is not *your* grade; this is his. Find out first how your child feels about the grade before you do all the emoting for him.

JENNY

Jenny, the anorexic woman who believed that she was a beautiful trophy for her parents to show off, exemplifies how we can be proud of our children yet send them signals that hurt them. This is not our intention. Nevertheless, in these cases, my job as therapist is to help the person find the original self that had gone astray. As I said about Jenny, her true self was masquerading in a body that was trying to convey something to me and to everyone else. But all she was doing was reenacting what had been told to her all of her young life: "Look at Jenny. See her young body? Isn't she special because she has that body?"

Jenny pleads with us in the same reverberating cadence to hear her message as she tries to manipulate her natural-born skin, muscles, and bones: "Look at me. See the me inside the beautiful. Please see me. If I'm not here, then you can't see me. If I waste my body away, will there be anything inside for you to see?"

Another way we parents can contribute toward depriving our children of a sense of self is how we deal with their pain. When my children and I were at the playground, I used to have to deal with other parents, who didn't necessarily understand where I was coming from with this issue. If my daughter, for example, fell off the swing, I didn't immediately run over to "fix" her up. I would wait on the park bench as she looked over at me. Maybe she was even trying to decide whether to cry on not.

I would ask, "Are you hurt?"

As she ran over to me, she might answer, "I have a boo boo on my knee."

Even then I didn't rush into action. I might ask, "Do you need my help?"

I took nothing for granted. This little person has her own body, emotions, and thoughts. She, not I, decides if she is injured enough to require an adult's help and /or comfort. Maybe she can handle her crisis without my help. Wouldn't my believing that she is capable of managing her fear and pain facilitate the strengthening of her own self-concept?

On occasion, if my son, for example, fell and didn't come running over to me but just looked over at me about to cry, the other parent sitting next to me, observing what must have looked like total apathy and neglect on my part, might start to get up and gesture toward my son to help him.

Then I had to say, "No, please don't. He will let me know if he needs me."

Imagine how that looked to the other doting parents. Every once in a while, these playground days could be embarrassing ones, but I held firm in my commitment to preserve the "self" of my child and forgo my looking like a wonderful mom.

GEORGIANA AND JAMES

Remember Georgiana, James's wife, the woman who checked off "excessive dependency" and "compliance" on the "How I Protect Myself from Loving You" rating scale? Just to review, I'll tell you that James checked off "becoming aggressive," and whenever he was aggressive, Georgiana became more dependent and compliant in an attempt to get him to love her and to stop putting her down, but the greater she clung to him and showed him how much she needed him, the more he felt duty-bound to push her away.

In her early life, Georgiana was not allowed to feel pain. If she did, her mom, Grace, would whimper and beg Georgiana's father, George, to make his daughter stop crying. At night, through the common wall of hers and her parents' bedrooms, Georgiana overheard Grace, a small-framed, shaky woman, complaining to George that their daughter had a weak constitution just like Grace had. Mom was sympathetic to blonde haired, blue-eyed Georgiana, who wore prescription glasses by age four. She told Georgiana's dad, "Poor Georgiana, she'll probably never be able to take care of herself too well. The kids at school call her a scaredy cat. When she gets a bad mark, she cries, and then the kids make fun of her. She's such a sickly child just like I was."

Her father, George, didn't always agree, but sometimes, after hearing Grace's litany of Georgiana's frailties almost verbatim from the night before, he would sigh and say, "I guess you're right." Then he would roll over and go to sleep.

It wasn't as if Georgiana's parents would resolve anything about how to handle their perceived pathetic child's affliction. It seemed enough for Grace to procure George's validation of her viewpoint, because only when he finally assented did she terminate the list of defects.

The more Georgiana's fears about every day functioning were reinforced, the more timid she became. Whenever she was physically or emotionally upset, she was "fixed" up immediately by her dad, whom she came to adore. If she showed the least little concern about anything, he told her not to worry; he would never allow anything bad to happen to her. If Georgiana didn't have time to finish her homework and, as usual, Grace had gone to bed with a headache, he finished Georgiana's assignment for her.

She really believed she was a weakling. Obviously, her dad did too, or he might have asked Georgiana to struggle through a challenge. Because of this conviction and also from what she observed between her parents, as an adult, she was doomed to end up with a man who was required to be very strong, strong enough to take care of little old her.

She mistook aggression and bullying for fortitude. James tried to appear as "the man," but underneath, due to his fantasy that his biological parents had "dumped him" into the arms of an inadequate couple who served as his pseudo parents, he felt unlovable; he wouldn't allow his need for love to show through at any cost. He took up bodybuilding and covered up his sensitivity with muscle. He married a dependent woman whom he could take care of and whose fragility made him feel even more physically powerful.

He needed her to need *him*, so instead of admiring her contribution to their dyad, he did what he could to knock her down, further insuring her permanency in the relationship. However, the way she clung to him and tried to please him turned him off, because it reminded him of the secret about himself that lurked inside. He hated the dependent part of himself that was just like Georgiana, but of course, he wouldn't allow anyone to ever find out who he really was—until he got into therapy. (No wonder he was so afraid of me!)

So, here we had obsequious Georgiana, who saw herself the way her mother painted her and the way her father molded her by making everything better for her so she wouldn't have to suffer. I recommended that I see Georgiana in individual therapy alongside of the couple therapy so we could work on helping her find the resilient self that had been there all along but which had been chiseled away from her by her well-meaning parents who couldn't see her as separate from themselves.

KEVIN

Kevin once said languidly of his son, Dirk, "Allowing someone to go off and do their own thing is like putting them on a boat, and they go away and never come back."

I had responded, "Yes, and you are left with your inadequate self, the same self that lived in your mother's house. You got a reprieve because you had a child of your own and you were going to be the best dad, and that would make up for your own inadequacy, but now that you've put him on a boat, there's only you again. You need to figure out who you are and accept that person. It's the only way you can actually separate from another human being. So when Dirk rants about how much he hates you because you are this way or that, you can say, 'You're right, I am that way, and I can see how that angers you. It is who I am.'

"Because you know and accept who you are, you can take in what your child tells you, and by having this new information from an 'expert' in your house, you can work on making change."

So far, I've been telling you about the good stuff when therapy has worked out well for the participants, and my interventions seem to be paying off. Here's one where I really screwed up. It didn't work out well for the family I was treating, but at least I learned something. I have since made a rule for myself: be careful about giving people what they demand in therapy, especially if it goes against my typical way of doing things.

POLLY

I briefly mentioned Polly in our discussion of eating disorder patients. Polly was the bulimic patient who grew up in a respected and well-known family in the community. Secrecy reigned above all else. Polly's obsessional thoughts about her attractiveness were part of the conspiracy to have things look good to others. Her popularity and having been elected as president of her university was taken for granted as a necessity. This ability to cover the bad stuff with good-looking traits mirrored her upbringing where she and her siblings were tacitly forbidden from talking about their father's drinking problem. In actuality, no one in the family had ever specifically said Dad was an alcoholic. Polly just knew alcoholism was something one doesn't verbalize out loud.

Once when she was seven, she had asked her daddy what he was drinking, and out of nowhere, he slapped her on the face. Polly was to remember the incident for the rest of her life and to be careful about allowing her curiosity to get the better of her.

One other time, after studying alcoholism in high school, she asked her mother if the reason her father got in bad moods was because he drank too much. Her silent mother removed herself to her room. Of course, Polly didn't get an answer and certainly never asked it again. She never brought kids home from school, because she was filled with shame and embarrassment and knew she couldn't find an acceptable way to explain to her friends why her father acted so "weird."

Polly replayed her early life trauma through her body by having everything look fine on the outside by being normal weight, an honor roll student, and president of student government at her university, while secretly bingeing and purging in the privacy of her dorm room. Eventually, she was bingeing and purging four and five times a day, didn't leave her room except to buy food, and began wasting away. Her parents pulled her out of school, and they desperately beseeched me to help their daughter.

After we met for a few times, I asked Mom and Dad to come in for family sessions. I had planned to invite Polly's younger brother and sisters to join us later. Our goal was to help them figure out how they could get Polly to take more responsibility for her eating disorder, and they wanted to know specifically what they should or shouldn't do to help. At this time, I knew about Dad's drinking problem, but Polly hadn't told them we were discussing it, and she forbade me to bring it up.

My pledging to seal my lips on this subject didn't really present much of a problem, because we had plenty of other things to talk about. For one, I had heard Polly say that when she went out on the weekends, her parents wanted her to check in with them so they could monitor her comings and goings, and she resented this.

In the meantime, Mom and Dad were annoyed with me and how the family therapy was going. Despite Polly's raving about how I was different from the other therapists she had seen and how much better she felt she could relate to me, her parents were demanding faster results. They wanted to visibly see the progress. They refused to accept Polly's take on it. Remember! It all boils down to how things appear.

Within this negative environment and given the restrictions on me, we were still able to learn some more about how the family functioned, and this was very helpful to Polly. For example, when her parents complained about Polly's mother finding candy wrappers hidden under the mattress and Polly readily confessed to having done it, through our discussion, Mom told us how when she was a teenager, she had done the same thing. This was so sweet and supportive for Mom to share. Polly and Mom narrowed the rift that had developed between them ever since Polly had left for college.

During one session, Polly was complaining about having to check in when she returned from weekend activities. While she was away at school, she came and went as she pleased and answered to no one. I was trying to mediate because, of course, I could see both sides: Polly's need for freedom and her parents concern for her welfare. At one point, in an attempt to help Polly as well as her parents to recognize the separateness of each, I said to Mom and Dad, "Polly's job is to grow up and leave you in a healthy way, and your job is to worry about her. All parents worry. It's built into our job description. But worry or not, we still need to let go."

Polly's parents really didn't go for the form of exploration we had been employing in our sessions thus far, nor did they seem enamored with my words of wisdom. Each time we met, Father would say to me, "Look, we keep coming here, and you ask questions, and we answer, and where is it getting us? You should be telling us what to do."

This man could be kind of scary, and I admit I wasn't in my best and most innovative frame of mind. Covertly, I think I was expecting his temper outburst at any time. Also, through my sensitivity with Polly and knowing how frightened she was of his volatile nature, which could reveal itself even in the midst of a tender moment between them, at times, I identified with Polly and felt as if I were the one who was his daughter. So perhaps my own anxiety clouded my thoughts.

We had established that when Polly came home on weekends, her parents were already asleep. The rule was she was to come into the bedroom and wake her Mom to tell her she was home. However, Polly wasn't only resentful of having to report in— she followed the rule regardless—but what did bother her was that her father slept in the nude, and she was embarrassed to see him like that. She even ventured to say that she thought it was inappropriate for a twenty-one-year-old daughter to see her father like this.

I remember vividly when she brought this up to her father. He raised his voice to an almost alarming level. Polly's mouth appeared to be glued shut, yet she was fighting to speak even though her tongue was so parched she could hardly sputter words of agreement or protest.

All Polly's father heard was that she was objecting to the rule about reporting in when she had returned home. He didn't hear about the other discomfort.

We went on to other subjects. Once again, Dad and Mom both registered their frustration with this therapy process. Mom said, "When are you going to tell us what you think? When will you tell us what is going on in Polly's treatment and whether she's getting anywhere? We're paying a lot of money. When are you going to tell us what to *do*? Why don't you ever give us advice?"

I had felt such pressure to give them what they wanted, and I thought if I gave a little advice, that should appease them for a while and maybe settle them down so we could make better use of our time. I thought, also, if I gave them something, they wouldn't sabotage the therapy by pulling Polly out of treatment, which although they never stated it, in my mind was always the threat.

"Okay," I said, "I'll tell you what I'm thinking. I know you are looking for more guidance from me. I think Polly is too old to be going into your bedroom in the middle of the night. This is your bedroom. It's not really appropriate for an adult child to go into your room at night. Your bedroom should be a private place."

There was a ringing in the air from the silence that followed. Polly's father stood up and said, "I am leaving now. This is over. I've had it!" whereupon he walked out!

The three of us remaining, as if in a freeze frame, looked awkwardly at each other. Polly was already in tears. Her mother stood up, her eyes darting around the room. In staccato fashion, she moved toward Polly and grabbed her hand, which Polly promptly pulled away. A small gurgle came from the direction of Polly's mother. As if this bizarre sound could travel by megaphone into Polly's ears, Polly jerked her head and slapped her hands to the sides of her face, almost putting her hands in her ears as a young child might do.

Her mother's flushed and sweaty face was quivering as she said, "I have to leave. Polly, let's go."

Polly looked pleadingly at me. My heart was pounding, and all I wanted to do was throw my arms around her and say, "You can stay, Polly. You can stay."

By then, however, I knew it was all over. I felt so sad for Polly, who had in our few months of therapy developed a connection with me, one that is so necessary for progress in treatment, particularly with eating disorder patients. Given her history of having had therapists with whom she felt she couldn't relate, what was she to do now? All these thoughts flew across an invisible screen in the brief snapshot of stillness following her mother's command.

Polly sauntered out the door like a little girl following her mommy who is convincing her this will be a wonderful first day of school. Just as I thought all was lost, Polly returned to my office, out of breath. She grabbed onto my shoulders and nearly crushed me in a squeeze. I was so taken by surprise that our heads actually bumped up against each other.

When she blurted out, "I'm sorry. I'm so sorry," at first I was confused as to whether she was apologizing for having hurt my head or for the way her parents had acted or because we weren't going to see each other again. She leaped back into the hallway, racing to catch up to her mother.

I never saw Polly again. I did call her parents and tried to help them deal with their anger and the crush they must have felt when they thought I was criticizing them, but of course, this was just a gesture on my part. I knew it was over.

I decided I would never allow myself to succumb to the pressure of my patients to give them what they want just for the sake of holding them in therapy. I have to keep a steady stance, doing what I know is the right thing to do, and not run scared of losing patients, particularly families. This family was complaining a lot but hadn't fled therapy. It was only when I gave them what they wanted that they ran amuck.

The reason I shared this account with you was to talk about parents of grown children and some of the problems they face. The issue about giving patients what they want in therapy is just something that went alongside of this discussion. Please forgive me. I guess I just needed to vent. The loss of Polly lingers in a very soft place in my heart. For Polly and me it was as if each of us was flailing our arms in search of each other so we could finish our job together. Hopefully, the family found another psychologist. Nevertheless, Polly's and my unique bond would never be duplicated nor explored. Essentially, our linkage was dead.

Why do I miss Polly maybe even more so than other patients of mine? Because those whom I send off into the world because the time is right, because the person doesn't need me anymore and is glad of it, despite the grieving part, carry me with them and them with me. We're bonded as in no other human relationship. I feel deprived of the joy I felt, for example, at Dick's funeral where

I cried for the loss of him, but I had the memory of his unique spirit to serve as a salve to my sorrow.

I hope Polly has gotten good treatment and maybe is even out there in the adult world functioning healthily. She was a cool kid, and she deserves to have a good life.

There's another set of people who come to me for help. These are often parents of grown children who are dealing with the crush of what most people call the empty nest syndrome, which is an awareness of the loss of your usual role, because your children are gone from the house. Sometimes, the person or people are aware of the problem, and when they visit me, they state it as such. There are other people who embark on therapy for one apparent reason only for us to find out their symptoms are masking an empty nest adjustment reaction.

MARGARET

Margaret was one such woman who came to me for generalized anxiety, but after we got started, we unleashed a bunch of other problems. You may recall that Margaret was the person who checked off "counter dependency" on the "How I Protect Myself from Loving You" scale. After she found out how distressed Don was over which woman he wanted, Margaret or the woman with whom he was having an affair, she resisted showing Don how much she wanted to be the chosen love mate.

Self-sufficient Margaret never showed anyone how much she wanted to be loved, so when her daughter took off for California after college and obviously was doing her own thing, Margaret's empty nest reaction hit her like a ton of bricks. Here was her daughter being independent just the way Margaret prided herself on being, but particularly because Don was still deliberating about his choice of lover, Margaret felt abandoned and alone.

When I asked her about her reaction to Krista's departure, petulantly, she said, "I didn't come here to talk about Krista. She doesn't need me anymore. I came here because I was nervous all the time and for no reason. And who wouldn't be? Don is giving me the runaround."

I retorted, "Yes, that's true, Margaret. Your reaction to Don's problems are causing you a lot of anxiety, but we need to talk about Krista's leaving. Granted, Don's behavior is devastating to you, but it softens the blow of Krista's leaving to deflect our discussion onto your situation with Don."

I went inside that place I go awaiting visions, fantasies, and associations particularly to her pain. I recalled the way swarthy Don with his forget-me-not eyes had faced Margaret in my office as his lips curled in contempt; yet, I had seen his face soften when we engaged in a reminiscence of how he had felt when he first met her. My next association was to a statue that was being stoned by the town's people, and of course, the statue couldn't feel the pain of the rocks hitting against its borders. Cracks were forming in various parts of its body.

Margaret passed the time while she was anticipating my next words by looking down at her car keys and jiggling them softly. She was accustomed to my silent deliberations.

"Perhaps it's a blow to your ego to think you would be upset to say good-bye to Krista just like you wouldn't give Don the satisfaction of showing him how distraught you are that he might not want you."

Margaret pursed her lips and took the deepest sigh I think I'd ever heard. I got distracted trying to see how long it would take before she took another breath.

"Don has nothing to do with Krista. Krista doesn't even like Don. In fact, that's probably why she's moving so far away, to get as far away from him as possible!"

"Then you must be pretty angry at both of them. He's leaving you in his own way, and she's forsaking you just to be rid of him."

I noted a moistening of Margaret's eyes and her quivering lips as she tried to hold back every emotion, which had been hibernating in the chambers of her broken heart. Coincidentally, the crystal that was hanging by my window emitted rainbow rays as the sun shone through it, causing a green light to rest on Margaret's face, which resembled a muzzle. She suffered anxiety because, unconsciously, she was afraid the emotional volcano would erupt and inside, rather than an explosion, to Margaret it would feel more like an implosion.

People who compensate through a rigid self-sufficiency or counter dependency may look strong and independent on the outside, because they are protected by a shell that hardens over time. Frequently when under stress, their brittle covering cracks open, and a torrent of emotion gushes out like a squall—or at least, that's the fear. Their anxiety is their fear of basically "losing it." It feels as if they might go crazy; they most likely won't. It's just that their defenses are shaky as they pretend to themselves they've got everything under control. In contrast, all those stormy emotions seem unmanageable like a spoiled, hyperactive child who refuses to go to his room when you command him to go: "Feelings, go away! I said go away! Why aren't you listening to me?"

"Feelings, you are going to kill me, and I must stop you."

That's why we, my patient and I, need to carve out a little opening so we can get a glimpse into the tempestuous cavities where the terrifying emotions reside. We take an eyedropper full of frightening feelings and allow them to ooze out one drop at a time.

When it comes to mothers' having to deal with empty nest feelings, it's not a simple exploration. It can feel, as we eventually ascertained it felt for Margaret, that your whole world is going up in smoke. It's a death of a very sundry kind.

And what do you do with your anger at your child for betraying you by going away? Margaret's anger threatened like a venomous snake to destroy everyone she loved and desperately needed. However, she wouldn't allow herself to prostrate herself before Krista or Don. Even though helping Krista to become independent was to be the plan all along, unconsciously for Margaret, the trouble was when Krista was born Margaret made a hidden bargain with Krista that Krista would never leave her mother even if Margaret had to stifle Krista. But since Margaret was a counter-dependent type, she betrayed herself by modeling behaviors that taught Krista never to rely on anyone for anything. The best-laid unconscious plans had gone awry.

Margaret did eventually get in touch with all of this, but it was surely a painful journey for her. Of course, the way to go was to not only explore her ambivalent feelings toward her husband and child, but to find her own "self," who had the capacity to be her own woman. After many sobs, and when this final development came to pass, Margaret's pervasive anxiety lifted.

As we move up the parental development ladder from birthing newborns to empty-nest syndrome, we arrive at the in-law stage, a time when parents must learn how to incorporate their sons-in-law and daughters-in-law into the family album. This can be an enriching stage of life as it has been for me. What happens when this in-law relationship isn't so great, and then your adult child has a baby of his or her own?

ABE AND ESTHER

Into the picture enter the dysfunctional married couple, Abe and Esther. (They were the couple to whom I suggested they put their underpants over their heads when they fought.) In addition to this troubled marital relationship, they now had to face (drum roll please)—the wicked daughter-in-law!

Even before they became parents, Abe and Esther had already anticipated being grandparents someday. This wish for immortality through their offspring was one of the wishes they had in common, and it bonded them.

In our sessions, when we talked about Heidi, the "bad" wife of their do-no-wrong son, it was one of the few times these two saw eye-to-eye on things. Esther would lick her lips as if she had been in the desert with Moses for forty days and nights, and then she would launch in.

"I told my son, 'You'd better set her straight. You're gonna have this baby next month, and don't you want your child to have a grandmother?' And he said—"

Abe quickly interrupted, "That girl has a hold on him. He can't see it. She saw from the beginning what a catch he was, and she sunk her claws into him. He didn't even see it coming. I tried to warn him about her."

"That was wrong," cited Esther. "You shouldn't have gotten involved. You should have waited for him to see for himself. The more you complained, the more he insisted on seeing her just to spite *you*."

Abe's nostrils dilated and quivered at the same time. I knew him well enough to know how pissed off he was. "Look, Es, if you would have backed me up, maybe he wouldn't have gone through with it. You undermined me with this just as you always did when he was a kid until he ended up having no respect for my opinion."

I asked Abe to elaborate on this accusation.

"I used to discipline Stevie, and she would secretly tell him not to worry. When I was out of town and I had grounded him, she let him go out with his friends. Do you believe a mother would do that? Don't you think that's wrong for a parent to do?"

Abe often asked me how I professionally viewed something. Due to this couples' volatility, I elected to answer many of his questions that required an educated answer rather than a, "Why do you ask?" which wouldn't have helped him. I think my not answering his questions would have turned him away from treatment with no guarantee he would ever cooperate in couple therapy again. I wasn't going against my rule of not giving my patient what he asked for out of fear of losing him in treatment. I based my decision on his very needy nature: Abe required "feedings" of information, and at this point in the therapy, I was the likely one to abate his hunger since Esther gave him virtually no support. Also, I was modeling for Esther how little it actually took to appease him. Far better it was to feed him some answers even if at the risk of his taking my words as absolute and perfect proclamations of how it should be done.

I said, "It makes it difficult for a child when parents openly go against the wishes of the other parent. Children get anxious when they think they can drive a wedge in the marriage. It's important to present a united approach to children. The best way is to have a conference with your spouse and fight it out behind the scenes, and when you figure out what is comfortable for both parents, then you inform the child."

Esther's shoulders drooped, and she bent her head almost to her knees. A shrill yelp—was it a cry or a shout? I couldn't tell—erupted from somewhere in the middle of her body. "Who the hell do you think you are, Abe, blaming me? You were so unreasonable when you punished him. I had to intervene, or the kid never would have gotten out of the house! Kids should be able to let off steam with their friends, and if they're always being banished to their room, how will they ever grow up?"

Esther sometimes had some very wise things to say. Abe, in the meantime, for some reason remained silent as if to say, "You got me on that one!" Did he feel duly indicted, and by his lack of articulation was he admitting guilt over his stringency with Stevie? He looked at Esther in a curious way, half acidly and half affectionately.

I didn't check out my hunch. I reserved my wish to quiz him on it for another time. I didn't want to intercede on this "moment" between him and Esther.

241

Esther, perhaps realizing how she had twisted the dagger too deep into his heart, refrained from going further in her remonstration of him. Her secession of the cross examination of him was intriguing to me, and this softening endeared me to her. I had seen Abe behave similarly toward her. It was as if they both knew just how far to go with each other, and in the interest of fair play, they backed off just before the other person was crushed beyond repair. Their relationship at these heartrending moments was rock solid.

At various times during our work together, I reminded Abe and Esther of their mutual sense of justice and how this interplay was a plus in their stormy relationship. It helped them when I remarked on it. We pulled apart their weaknesses, but all couples need to be able to rely on their strengths in order to get through the therapeutic process and end up in one piece—hopefully one united piece!

They didn't fully realize it yet, but I believed it was their concern over their son and his marriage to the "wicked witch" and their fear of potential loss of access to their mutual grandchild that had brought this zany but engaging couple to me.

When we talk about parents, either being one or being the product of one, invariably we are talking about how to cope with loss. We don't have to lose children through death to be in touch with our grief. Every time we look at a newborn baby and then check back on that baby within a few weeks, we see time passing right in front of our eyes. It's a scary thing: your children have never and will never belong to you. They are gone before they arrive.

There are many kinds of losses in your life, and how you deal with what you no longer have, what you thought you would always possess but realize will never be, and what you do because you fear you will lose what you have all fits into a larger discussion, which we will begin immediately.

PASSING AWAY

I believe our concept of death and dying underlies almost everything with which we struggle in our lifetime. Even when you're happy, you may not be able to sustain your happiness for fear you will lose your treasure, or you worry that your contentment will "die" and "be" no more. When we talked about love, weren't we dealing with the same issue—reticence to love another person because you will lose him or her? When you suffer the loss of someone or have to give up anything you once possessed, such as your ability to walk or see or hear, you grieve in a similar way you react when a loved one dies. When you lose hope and must abandon your dream of becoming rich or famous or married or having a child, in your woebegone state of mind, you might question if life is worth living any more.

Many of the most precious things in life last but a season or two, and then you and I find ourselves looking backward and craving what we once had. When your children grow up, you feel joy for having done a good job of getting them to this point, but your efforts result in bringing you to an alone place.

Throughout your life, the more you learn how to cope with loss, the better shot you have at living the abounding life possible for you. Otherwise, you spend your years dodging imaginary bullets and getting *ready* to live your life rather than *actually* living it. The question is: are you prepared to take the risk of breathing and thriving even though death (or loss or disappointment or failure or devastating illness) will inevitably come your way?

CHRISSY

Chris is the woman who we talked about way back in the beginning of our conversation whose first memory was of red blood oozing down her mother's arms. There was always a question as to whether Chris's father, who was privately very affectionate with her, had in fact molested her. At least he was guilty of having spied on her when she undressed, because she had seen him watching her as he hid in the closet. Her parents fought a lot over his coming home late and over her mother's bogus suicide attempts. Chrissy saw herself as the bad little girl who was somehow the cause of her mother's self-induced violent actions. However, she knew she had saved her mommy's life, and she was to be responsible for her mother ever more. She vowed never to let down on the job. Any time her mother expressed displeasure, Chrissy immediately changed her behavior and used Mommy's reaction as her gauge to determine whether or not the action was okay. Chris became a nurse and set out to rescue others even when these actions often caused pain to herself.

Frightened of her father, Chrissy blamed mother for staying with him. Father's odd behavior had increased, and one night, he produced a gun and pointed it at Mommy, "So you want to die! I'll put you out of your misery!"

Mom didn't die that day, but Chrissy warned herself, *You never know…*

Predictably, Chris ended up in very abusive and dysfunctional relationships with men who "needed her." She eventually married one of them, had three children, and then divorced "the loser." When she came to see me, she had been remarried for about five years to a somewhat better choice but not much improved from her earlier predilections. Her mother had died years ago, and her father, whom Mother had finally divorced about five years after Chris left home, now lived with her and her truck driver husband, Jack. Daddy, as she continued to call him, held an unduly firm grip on her emotions, which were similar to the tight physical clutches he used to have on her as a child in those late night encounters. She was constantly under the scrutiny of Jack for including Daddy in everything they did and thereby not meeting Jack's needs to have her as his own.

Chris had developed what the doctors called Chronic Fatigue Syndrome. In addition, she experienced anxiety attacks where for hours at a time she felt as if she couldn't catch her breath.

Chris was also the person who, even though I really liked her and didn't consciously feel angry with her, I imagined the joy I would feel if I could punch her in the mouth! I visualized myself demanding, "Wipe that smile off your face, young lady!" I talked earlier about how I analyzed why I didn't fantasize hitting her in the stomach. I used this daydream of mine (which I did not share with her) to help her see how she covered negative feelings with feigned happiness. However, ultimately, she was unable to keep up her charade, because somehow her invisible aggression seemed to vibrate in the air and unconsciously send a message to those around her. In turn, she became the recipient of their sadistic reciprocity.

We already talked about how Chrissy made up stories about her husband, Jack, who if he showed any emotion whatsoever, she immediately assumed he was trying to manipulate her to do something for him, all because she confused him with her mother, who exhibited distress as a way to manipulate her, and she didn't check out what he meant when communicating his displeasure.

As you know, in previous sessions I had interpreted that she was behaving toward me the way her mother had behaved toward her with the see-how-you-hurt-me stance. When I described this to you before, I had said, "You couldn't give up her misery just yet." As a child, she had lived with her mother's pathetic locution, and by now, suffering for its own sake had a life of its own. Chris would feel naked without her gloomy despair.

It's funny that I had used the word "naked" to describe her feeling. As history served, her mother walked around the house naked, and if strangers or if any of her siblings' friends came to the house (Chrissy herself never invited anyone into the house), Chrissy would shoo her mother away into the bedroom, which was her mother's favorite resting place. Chrissy remembered the daily vision of her mother's bare feet straddled apart at the end of the bed. Her mom's legs were about all she could view from the hallway. She wondered, *Is mommy resting, or is she dead?*

Throughout her life, Chris always stayed busy, because she felt shame in being or expressing helplessness, and if Chris took to her bed ill or fatigued, it reminded her of her often bedridden mother. Passivity was a no-no. Yet, how can you rest if you are exhausted from serving everyone around you? And she was always tired, which was why her doctors diagnosed her with Chronic Fatigue Syndrome and prudently referred her for psychological treatment, because they suspected the etiology of her problems might be psychosomatic.

When Chris was twenty-five, her mother died. Of course, Chris was the one to discover Mom. Chris had used her old key to enter the house. By this time, Mom and Dad had been divorced for about five years, and except for her younger brother, Norman, her siblings had scooted away from the dysfunctional household at the first available opportunity.

Chris called out, "Mom, are you there?"

Hearing no answer, she investigated. When she arrived in the hallway and observed the same vision from her youth of her mother's bare legs at the end of the bed, she sighed in relief. Chris was never sure what she would find, and the familiarity of this scene was a comfort to her. Later, she recalled, "Why would I feel relieved to see her in that pose? Had I forgotten how as a kid I worried when I saw her like that?"

But this time Mom was dead, and her demise hadn't been from a self-inflicted fulfillment of her wish to be dead. Mom died of a heart attack!

Now I will open the door, and you may look in on a session with Chris. She's at it again, turning feedback I had just given her onto herself and hurting herself with it. Chris and I were taking another look at the way her mother manipulated her through fear of holy retribution. Mom used to say that just about everything was a mortal sin, especially if at the time she didn't like what you were doing or not doing. Chris's mother virtually molded Chris like a clay doll to become the end-all and be-all for anyone who could make use of her talents, and Mom accomplished this shaping through Mom's imaginary special arrangement with God. Consequently, Chris, the martyr, thrived on both hers and her mother's misery.

In this session, I had just said, "Chris, you may not actually like to be in pain, but you are gratified by your pain in the same way your mother needed *her* pain."

I saw Chris's flushed face change from what appeared to be angry, to teary sadness, to smiling numbness. It was an amazing transformation and put me in mind of Jekyll and Hyde but in reverse. Her mom had trained her well!

I added, "Chris, it seems that for you to be happy and out of misery is to be unfaithful to God."

"What a goof I am to want pain. Mom always told me that Jesus suffered and I should suffer too. I figured I wasn't suffering enough so that's why God keeps on hurting me, making me get chronic fatigue syndrome. I can't believe it. I can't really see it, but Phyliss, if you say it's true that I crave pain, maybe it is. And that makes me really dumb. What idiot actually wants pain? Are you saying I'm a masochist?"

When I think of Chrissy, at least in terms of our present discussion, I necessarily get into the issue of religion and spirituality. I've treated many patients who were devoutly religious, and some of these people have questioned whether or not they should be consulting me in therapy. After all, isn't it sacrilegious for a Christian to visit a Jewish psychologist, who first of all, wouldn't understand, and secondly, might sway you to become sinful or selfish as in, "Me, me, me?" In a number of cases, my patient and I had to explore his or her internal conflict over my Jewish identity before we could proceed. More frequently, the topic didn't even come up until the person was feeling emotionally a lot better and more confident to broach it. He or she procrastinated for fear of hurting my feelings or appearing prejudiced. Or maybe my patient doubted if it was okay to feel good, given that I was not a Christian counselor yet had a significant role in his or her newfound contentment. Would God approve?

Although I'm not a member of the clergy, in my psychological career, nevertheless, I have served as priest, nun, minister, and spiritual counselor. Here's an example of how I conveyed spiritual guidance with Chris.

In the same session where we were talking about Chris's need for pain, we once again revisited her distress over her mother's death, which had occurred more than twenty years ago. But, of course, when a person doesn't work through conflicted feelings about a parent, she cannot untie the self-imposed rope surrounding intense emotions of guilt, anger, and fear of retribution.

Chris said, "It's my fault Mom died." She didn't wait for me to query her. She was beginning to get the hang of the therapeutic process, so she elaborated without provocation. "Just that morning Mom had called me to say she wasn't feeling well. I was nasty. I said, 'Oh yeah, really!' like I was doubting her and making like she was faking it and trying to use it to get me over there. I told her, 'No! I'm not leaving work early. Ask Norman to come straight home after school for a change.'"

I wasn't going to try to talk her out of her guilt. Her guilt was here for a reason. No fair for me to strip it away. Anyway, if I had told her she was wrong to believe she was the culprit in her mother's death, she would have temporarily allowed my words, the words of a surrogate god (in her mind) to take her off the hook. Her reprieve would have lasted maybe ten minutes, and as soon as she left my office, she would be back where she started, staring at the gooey, black, guilty tar, which could have oozed down the face she examined in the mirror.

Melancholy Chris lamented, "I know I've been paying for what I did to my mom. Leaving home so young when Mom had all the other kids to take care of—I just found out my brother is really mad at me for leaving him with my mother. God has been paying me back for my cruelty to all of them. Look at my life." She gazed pleadingly at me.

Softly and with a deliberate slow rhythm in my voice, I responded to her earnest entreaty, "Chris, do you believe you deserve to be miserable and have bad things happen to you because you didn't save your mother's life that one last time? Do you believe God has selected you out from all the other human beings on this earth as a person to be punished?"

"Well..." She hesitated. Chris wanted always to get the right answer. "Yes. I know what you're going to say. My priest even once told me at Belinda's christening that one person can't be responsible for the results of another person's actions." Belinda was Chris's mother's name, and Chris had named her first daughter after her mother. After another pause, Chris continued, "But I can't help it. My mom really got through to me."

Here is another instance where I could have cried out loud for Chris, but for her sake, I constrained my throat muscles. Imagine a mother being so powerful as to literally rob her daughter of the right to be happy! If I were working with her mother in therapy, I'd probably be saying to myself, "Poor woman, she is so starved for love that she is unable to give it to her daughter, and how she is suffering because she wants to nurture her daughter but doesn't know how." However, today I was with Chris, not Chris's mother, and I could have screamed in protest, but I didn't want

Chris, by my reaction, to feel as if she were the one who had done something wrong by making me feel bad.

As if a metronome were controlling the syllables, I uttered, "Are you able at times to heed your priest's words?"

"I try, but I keep picturing my mother lying there on the bed looking so peaceful. She even had a sort of smile on her face. Phyliss, I've never told anyone this, but I actually imagined her saying, 'I got you!'"

Continuing in my modulated, melodious voice and without rushing, I said, "It looks as if she did get you. At least you allowed her message to influence your take on things. She took away any chance for you to ever feel good about yourself, your life, your family, your friends—" My voice broke on the last word, so I stopped my listing.

We both were quiet for at least three minutes, which in therapy-land can feel like a long time to someone like Chris. Then I said, "Chris, based on what I've learned from my clergy friends and colleagues, I know that God doesn't choose one person to go after for retribution. God is here for another purpose. He is here to help us have the courage to deal with all the things that go wrong over which we have no control. In the same way, prayer is not for the purpose of getting God to take care of you. You pray for Him to give you strength to cope."

Chris looked at me and cocked her head to the left, almost touching her left shoulder with her ear. I wondered if this was a pose she had struck in her early life. Not having a shoulder to cry on, perhaps she was using her own shoulder to rest her weary head. I imagined little Chrissy in her bed at night after she had done something to displease her mommy, or merely imagining she had done so, lying there bringing up her shoulder to her cheek the way she would have wanted her mother to do for her little girl. But Chrissy had to take care of Mommy. There was no way for Chrissy to be taken care of herself.

I leaned forward as I traditionally do when our time is up. Slowly, I rose up from my chair. Chris was trying to hold back her briny tears, and the corners of her mouth were turned down; the curvy line they formed made her look like a puppet, the kind whose mouths are hinged at the bottom of their faces under their chin. I reached out slowly in an inviting way rather than in a clutching manner. I was there for the taking. It was up to Chris to make the next move.

She lunged forward and grabbed onto me with all her might. I squeezed back in concert with her sobs, thinking, *Oh Chris, poor Chris, I wish I could take you home to my house to live.*

She sauntered out the door and turned and looked back at me in a sideways fashion as if to sneak a peek and maintain that I was all right. Chris was always taking care of me...

About six months later, Chris's father died, and we revisited this spiritual stuff again as we had numerous times since the session I just described. She couldn't admit to me that she was relieved of the burden of caring for him and of dealing with her deprived husband who had continually reminded her what a sacrifice he made for her by allowing her father to live with them.

For many sessions, we spoke about her dad and reviewed her ambivalent relationship with him. During this same period of time, Chris was in a quandary as to what to do about her job. Now that Dad was gone, she could look for something more satisfying and more remunerative. Until this time, she was sort of stuck in a dead-end minimum-wage endeavor. She worked for a very nice boss, which was a refreshing state of affairs for Chris, since she usually managed to find people around her to abuse her rather than to be kind to her. She had been unable to pursue her nursing career because of the demands at home. Now that she was free, she wasn't chasing her dreams, and I wanted to know why. She claimed that she just couldn't get up the energy to write a resume and search the want ads. (Remember, she suffered from Chronic Fatigue Syndrome.)

251

On a hunch, I reverberated, "I hope you're not now thinking you shouldn't advance yourself because you will be hurting your boss by leaving."

"I don't want to leave him in a lurch!"

"Anything you do in life has an effect on other people. If you get a new job and you beat out someone else to get it, those competitors may be hurt, but by taking the new job, you also benefit the people for whom you're working and the clients you will service. If someone else gets hurt because of an action in which you engage, it doesn't mean you are a bad person to have done what you did unless it was intentional or insensitive. When your mother intimated that she would kill herself, it was her decision about what she wanted to do with her life. Believe it or not, her behavior had nothing to do with you. It was the way she chose to cope with issues in her life. She may have implied that because you weren't turning out the way she thought you should that she would have to do herself in. But the action of killing herself belonged solely to her."

I was on a roll when Chris interrupted me and emphatically retorted, "I don't understand what you're trying to say, Phyliss. What's my mother have to do with my boss?"

"If you leave your job and your boss is upset, it's his problem. Your leaving isn't an intentional means to hurt him. You're just doing what you need to do to further yourself. It is the same as it was when you were growing up. You were just being you, a little girl who was trying to find out who you were and how you would live in the world when you grew up. You were a human being who makes mistakes in order to learn. What you did or didn't do had nothing to do with anyone else's welfare."

"But I'm supposed to be good, aren't I? Are you trying to get me to be selfish and be like 'who cares about anyone else'? Is this what you're trying to say? I go to church every week, and I say my prayers every night. I don't like to be selfish. I care about other people."

"Listen, Chris, you are a very sweet person, and you try hard to be good. But God wants you to develop yourself to be the best you can be. When you pray, along with asking God to help you, why don't you pray also for the strength to face your fears and take risks and be able to do what you have to do and develop your skills as a nurse to make a better life for you and your family? You're not supposed to use your faith as a way to sit back and wait around for this higher being to make your life easy. If you want to win the lottery, you have to buy a ticket. Life isn't easy, and God is not the one to make it easy for you. He's here to help you find your way, and then you are the one who must take the plunge into the unknown abyss and hope He will be alongside of you in the process."

"Okay, okay. I see your point." As soon as the sarcastic tone in her words slipped out, Chris's face flushed, and she put her hand to her mouth as if to smother the smoldering fury heretofore buried deep within her insides. She seemed terrified that more bad stuff was about to come flying out of her. No wonder Chris had so much trouble catching her breath!

"Oops. I did get on a soapbox there, didn't I? I get the feeling you didn't like it!" I was smiling affectionately. I rather enjoyed her talking back to me like a petulant child. Keep it up, Chris!

At any rate, I have shared all this about Chris to show you how sometimes I wear other hats in my role as therapist.

ESTHER

When Esther walked into the office after having been away for about five years, she presented herself with a detachment I hadn't seen before, as if part of her soul were lost somewhere else. She was arrayed in a soft and flowing chiffon dress because she was seeing me as a stop along the way to a wedding, which she was reluctantly going to attend. She also wore the burden of worry on her furrowed brow.

Although when we last met at our good-bye session five years ago, we had embraced and held each other tightly, on this occasion, even though my posture was open and ready, I was not offered a hug. I should have suspected there would be this distance today, because when Esther had called me the day before, I blurted out, "Esther, I'm so happy to hear from you!" When she acted the way one does in an awkward moment, as if she were straightening her clothes to fill in time and space, I withdrew a few drops of my enthusiasm.

I forget myself at times. I fail to remember that except for when people call me to tell me good news such as bulletins about babies being born or having graduated from school, after having terminated their treatment, they are most likely in distress when they call. Therefore, when I hear their long-gone voices, which used to be such a significant part of my office life, I need to pinch myself not to become too zealous about their return.

It didn't take long to find out what brought Esther back. Abe and Esther's son, Stevie, had been accused at work of propositioning his secretary and threatening to fire her if she didn't comply. Later the secretary recanted, but it was too late. Stevie had already committed suicide. When he hung himself on Saturday, Stevie hadn't known about the secretary's apology letter, which had already been in his boss's hands on Friday. His boss had planned to show it to Stevie when he came to work on Monday.

Dry-eyed Esther told her story. I allowed tears to flow down my cheeks. Death of a loved one is like having a sunbeam in your hand and then losing your grasp and not being able to get it back to hold. After you no longer can see or feel the sunbeam, you realize that no matter how hard you stomp around, scream out shrill cries, and after you beat on yourself, you will never ever see your loved one again. I think grief is about sadness, but it's even more about temper tantrums and rage. Its anger at everyone and everything including God and at every cell in your own body, because sometimes the only release from the agony is to literally hit your own head against a wall. What good will it do? Nada. But the container is flooded, and you must open the valve or burst. Yet you are quiet on the outside. You look withered and numb. But, deep inside, there just aren't enough walls on which to beat.

When someone you love takes his own life, there's even more with which to contend. In most cases, you want to punch the "living" guts out of the person. You want to take his face and bash it against the wall; you want to knock sense into his deceptive head for having committed an act that he knew would destroy you, and yet without regard for your soul, he did it anyway.

Stevie's death had occurred six months before I saw Esther for the comeback visit. It was because of the repercussions from Stevie's monstrous act that Esther was here. She had lost her son, but Esther was now obsessed with the possibility that due to Heidi's, her daughter-in-law's, animosity toward Esther and Abe, Esther might now lose her granddaughter as well.

For six months, Esther had been living with the reality of Stevie's passing, but I only just learned of it, and it was hard to close my mouth from having been openly horrified by the story. Esther had more important things to consider than my compassion. She told me the story and immediately moved on.

"Heidi is really getting us back for all the strife we've had all along. She knows she's in the power position now. When Stevie was alive, he brought Melissa to us every Saturday without fail. It was their father-daughter outing. Sometimes they all came over, even Heidi, for Thanksgiving and some other holidays. We even invited her parents, but it was tense. I'm beside myself, and Abe is just acting like a tyrant about it. He says to forget about it, but for God's sakes, we're her grandparents!"

Esther continued her tirade as perspiration exuded from her upper lip. Her forehead was now beginning to sweat. "I'll give you an idea of how mean spirited this girl is. When Heidi took Melissa on an airplane to visit Heidi's brother in college, she complained because the guards wanted her to put the infant seat through the conveyor, and the baby was sleeping, and she didn't want the baby to wake up, so get this, she tries to put the car seat on the conveyor belt with the baby in it! She gets so mad she actually sacrifices her daughter! She's so dumb. She brags about it at Thanksgiving dinner. You should have seen everyone's face. Stevie was really furious. You could see it all over him. Abe couldn't stop talking about it that night after they all left. I actually put my fingers in my ears to blot him out!"

As time went on, Esther and I tried to find a way for her to relate to Heidi, and the tension between them eased up a bit, at least enough for her to enjoy Melissa. Abe refused to let go of his vendetta and hardly saw Melissa. He absolutely rejected Esther's pleas to return to conjoint therapy. Based on what I heard from Esther, I postulated he was afraid if he came back he would somehow be forced to give up his stand.

Through Esther and other patients I've treated who lost someone to suicide, I learned about the heartache of unrelenting, unanswered mysteries as to why a person would give up his life and give birth to all the *what ifs* and *if onlys* that plague the survivors.

KATIE

There are other deaths that are not universally seen as *real* deaths. Katie suffered from the reaction of non-believers toward her grief over a miscarriage. Katie is the woman who was self-conscious about having her mascara stain my clothes, so I produced a terry cloth hand towel to cover my clothing. We later referred to it as the "crying towel." When I went away on vacation and she began grieving my absence, we decided she should keep the towel at home so she could have something of mine in her possession to help her through our separation.

Katie had lost her mom at age twelve and had to grow up so fast; she never had time to mourn. When she had a miscarriage, it brought back so much of what she missed with her mom. I temporarily took over the role for her. I felt as if her mom wanted me to do so. Katie is the one who punctuated almost every sentence with an *I'm so stupid*. I had told her that what she needed was a *stupid therapist* to match.

For the first few weeks, Katie's husband, extended family, and friends joined with her in her bereavement over the tragedy. Afterward, she was on her own—that is, until she entered my office. Thereafter, the haven Katie and I created helped her through the pain of dealing with the loss of an imaginary loved one whom she and her husband had created.

We've been talking about losing people who die. There are other wounds that cause people's coping strategies to be mobilized, such as losing physical function or loss of a job, loss of status, loss of money, loss of memory—the list is endless. Grief also plays a large part in the change process as people mourn their old, unwanted selves.

ALLISON

Allison is the young woman whom I talked about in our eating disorder conversation. She helped us in our demonstration of how eating disorder patients tend to have difficulties with separating themselves particularly from their mothers and deciding who's who. She was the one who was upset because her mother seemed withdrawn, and to Allison that meant her mother was unhappy about something, and because she was enmeshed with her mom, Allison always assumed that she was the source of her mother's discomfort. We knew we were making progress when she resisted the urge to restrict her eating but instead went into her mother's room to ask her mom what the problem was and then ate her dinner even though her mother remained withdrawn and miserable. Allison, in being able to separate her issues from those of her mother's, was able to nourish herself independently of her mother's mood.

After I praised Allison about this encounter with her mom, she said, "I have trouble when people say nice things about me. If I weren't anorexic, you wouldn't be praising me for what I did."

We moved into a discussion of her need to control what people give her, and this includes food, compliments, and advice. I had confronted her, asking, "Where is there room for me in this relationship?"

Eventually, Allison was able to work through her conflict of the *in*—taking someone in, loving that person, receiving their food—but because the nourishment is so satisfying, she would want more and be hungry for their love and take her chances that she would get enough, and if she couldn't have it all, she could handle her feelings about the deprivation, versus the *out*—keeping the person out, distancing herself away from the person, starving herself of the loved one, thereby being safe and protected from the longing for the person, but alone.

So the question became, what do we do now? Grow up? Stay sick? Be an eating disorder patient for the rest of her life?

As we've seen with many other patients I've presented here, Allison's identity was being threatened. During the last few months of Allison's therapy, she realized that in spite of herself, she was changing. One day, she said, "For five minutes yesterday, I didn't think about food, calories, diets, or weight. I can't believe I forgot to think about it. Is this what normal is?"

I bring Allison into our present discussion because of the many times I've heard that lament, "Who am if not an eating disorder patient?" Allison was joining the crowd. In her eager apprehension about leaving treatment, she had to face the reality that she was no longer "sick."

But Allison couldn't leave just yet. She had to work on her reluctance to move into a new identity and deal with her fears of loss of an old friend—her anorexia.

AGNES

Agnes dealt with the loss of body function because of her problem with her leg. Just like Allison's fear of not being an eating disorder patient any longer, Agnes had to face death of another kind.

Agnes's medical condition was the result of reflex sympathetic dystrophy, otherwise known as RSD. About twenty years ago, I suffered from this same disease. Because of this, I had more than my usual compassion to offer Agnes. I had been there! Fortunately, after about a year and a half of suffering, I went into remission and haven't had symptoms since then.

Agnes's condition hadn't improved, and now she was in danger of the RSD spreading to her other leg. She knew she had to relax about all this, because the stress could exacerbate her symptoms. As far as I was concerned, she wasn't too far off on this appraisal. I had no real proof, but one conclusion I had reached after hearing from all the people who responded to my published article on the condition was that those who called and said they had beaten this disease as I had were the kind of people who were sort of sturdy in their emotional make-up. They said they wouldn't allow the disease to best them. They exercised as they had before the onset; they set about to find creative ways to deal with the disease. So, one of the ways I wanted to help Agnes was to psychologically toughen her up.

Her anger over her loss was so strong; it turned on her and was threatening to destroy her just as her fantasy demonstrated: the idea of being struck by lightning. Her reaction was similar to one that a child faces who is afraid of monsters being in the closet; those ogres are actually symbols of the child's anger, which he or she is afraid will come back to haunt the bad little boy or girl who feels such terrible things.

One area I tried to help strengthen Agnes was to help her with her chronic worrying, which affected her relationship with her live-in, on-and-off boyfriend as well as her parents, who resided out of town but who came to see her frequently, particularly since she had been stricken with RSD. She knew she was a worrywart and that she just couldn't relax around them; she couldn't stop herself from ruminating over everything they did or didn't do.

The more we talked we ascertained that Agnes was upset about losing the people in her life who could help her. She worried that she would become totally debilitated and have no one on whom she could rely. She knew her worry wouldn't help her, but she fussed over her loved ones anyway.

We had already discussed the reality that Agnes had absolutely no control over her boyfriend and parents, but even so, to insure their always being there for her, she wanted to be in charge of their every move. Eventually we figured out that all her worrying was an attempt to act as if she really did have control.

I said to Agnes, "If you just worry enough and never let up, nothing could possibly happen. It's only if you stop worrying that disaster will hit."

Agnes wholeheartedly agreed. Her eyes widened, and she had a knowing smile on her face.

I continued, "So, what you developed as a way of controlling (or worrying about) an uncontrollable situation, has now taken you over, and you can't stop fretting lest you cause the bad thing to happen."

"I wish I could stop being so obnoxious to Charles. He hates when I badger him."

I was in sync with her. "It's like now you know your worrying is out of control. You had been attempting to worry enough so you could stop the anticipated grief over possibly losing your parents and Charles, but what you actually did to stop your discontent is to cause yourself and them more misery."

"So what do I do about it, Phyliss?"

Ah, there's the question we always ask when we learn something about ourselves we want to alter but have no clue as to how to change it. One thing for sure: you can't tell a worrier not to worry. She will end up worrying about worrying too much. To give up worrying is like a death, and that is why I have brought Agnes to your attention. Her issues belong in the death section of our conversation. She not only lost function in her leg; she was about to give up worry as a coping mechanism. Bring in the clergy. Hooray! We're about to have a funeral!

Well, not so fast, my friends. Agnes and I had much work to do. I said, "First, let's try to see what would happen if you gave up the worrying. Maybe we can find some clues." Once again, I was looking for the gratification in the use of her fretting and ruminating and wanting to explore what her life would be like without her trusty anxiety...

SALLY

At any time in one's life, a person notices changes, and if not conscious of her reaction, she may suffer a grief reaction in the form of depression or anxiety. Sally wasn't directly dealing with aging issues herself, although eventually, as all of us do, she would be facing her own growing old. Sally was the one who had been working on her relationship with her mother and said to Harry, "Aren't I getting along better with my mother?" and he joked that her newfound wonderful relationship was due to her mother's being out of town.

At the time, Sally was really beginning to enjoy being with her mom, and almost as a cruel joke, her mother started showing signs of Alzheimer's disease. Sally was beside herself with grief and anger. "Just when we start to get along, just when my mom is turning into such a sweet lady, now I have to watch her leave me in bits and pieces. I hate this!"

For a change, Harry knew to remain quiet and allow Sally to mourn the loss of something she hardly ever had.

I had a dream a long time ago probably around the time I was working with Agnes:

> I dreamt that I was an old lady. I was using a walker. Younger people were walking ahead of me, and I couldn't keep up. I kept imploring, "Wait up!"
>
> Suddenly, I put my hands tightly on the handles of the walker and flipped my legs directly into a handstand! I felt so good—the exhilaration I experienced as a child on the monkey bars when I hung upside down.

You learn so much as you age. When you get older, you get so smart; you change your perspective on many things. Every few years, I look back and say what a jerk I was a few years ago. Now I say, "Why wait a few years? Now I realize I'm a jerk now."

I'm just kidding. I'm not the kind of person who regrets my actions or berates myself today for what I did yesterday. I use yesterday's goof-ups as a learning experience. I just liked that little joke.

A friend of mine once said, "I want to have the last say in who I'm supposed to be!" Hopefully, by old age we can all say this.

WHOSE LIFE IS IT ANYWAY?

How do I, a psychologist, deal with my own needs when I'm being paid to be here totally for my patient? Suppose I'm struggling with crises in my life? How does this impact my patient?

I'm always astounded when my patients bring up issues with which I am presently dealing. When this happens, I ask myself, "Were they listening to my brain, which was trying to work through my feelings about my aging parents? Did they super naturally insinuate themselves into last night's dream about loss of a loved one? How do they know I'm struggling with choices in my life? From where did their statements about dealing with other people's false perceptions of them arise?"

I once heard myself say to a patient who was struggling with her son's not turning out the way she wanted, "You're job is to grieve the loss of your son."

Suddenly, clanging sounds were going off in my head. *Boing!* Duh. No wonder I had been depressed these last few weeks. Only now did I realize I had been somber because my son and I were not close in the way we used to be. He had just gotten married, and as thrilled as I was, particularly with our daughter-in-law, I had not properly mourned the loss of my son's and my old familiar, never-to-be-the-same relationship.

Earlier in our conversation, I said that if you don't grieve when you lose the person or thing and if you don't allow your sadness to flow at the appropriate time, your melancholy will burrow itself deep inside you and marinate into a depression. I had been sighing a lot lately and not sleeping very well, and having said what I did to my patient, I now saw why I had recently been so lethargic. Dealing with my patient's dilemma forced me to look into myself. I had been so in touch with what she was sharing about her son; it rocketed me back into my own life. Although my patient didn't know it, I was grateful to her for "sticking it to me." This is an example of how my life and my psyche intertwine with my patients' lives and vice versa.

You ask when else and with whom have I been in similar dilemmas?

I remember years ago when I wasn't as experienced as I am now; I had eye surgery for glaucoma and was having an allergic reaction to my eye drops. I was trying very hard not to share this with my patients, but I needed to wear sunglasses because of the glare. Consequently, my infirmity stood right out in the open.

As it turned out, because of my secretiveness, I caused more problems than would have occurred had I been forthright in the first place. You see how therapy imitates real life? In life, the more you lie or indirectly twist what you see, the more of a mess you create. It's the same with therapy. If you're not straight out there in therapy, you just prolong the reaching of your goals anyway, because you set up roadblocks that slow you down in your journey toward the distressing truth.

All I needed to do was to say, "I'm wearing these dark glasses because I had some eye surgery and the glare bothers my eyes."

Being a young and less experienced psychologist and trying to follow the rule about therapist anonymity, I caused alarm in my patients and, of course, their phantasms ran amuck. Later, in group therapy as we all discussed the impact of my wearing the glasses, we learned that some people thought I was trying an experiment with them, playing with their minds. (Oh, how I hated that one, because trickery and manipulation are the last things I would ever institute with my patients or my friends, family, and co-workers, for that matter.)

As the group felt safer and freer to discuss their fantasies—because when I realized what was going on, I came to my senses and asked them how they were feeling about my glasses—we learned more. A few patients thought I was targeting them because they, being the approval-seeking types, tended to look at me rather than to the rest of the group whenever they spoke. Some thought I was trying to hide emotions, maybe teary eyes, because of some horrendous problem I was having. These anxious people were very distracted and concerned about me. Some were angry. Why would I make them so uncomfortable on purpose?

Okay, I screwed up. But you know what? Nothing you ever do in therapy is wasted. Everything in the session becomes grist for the mill, and even if you as a therapist didn't intentionally try to bring on a certain reaction, now you have stuff to work on, because the situation most assuredly mimics other occasions in your patients' lives that might not have surfaced had I not, one day, sauntered into the group room trying to be casual as if nothing had changed.

September eleventh and my personal near miss of losing my son who had just walked through the World Trade Center five minutes before the first blast is another example of how my personal life can intermingle with that of my patients. I was worried sick about Greg. Alongside of my own angst, my patients were distraught over the crisis in the country, and I was attempting to help them. Like a good therapist, I asked them to apply what was happening today to events in their present and past life. In the meantime, I was chomping at the bit to get back on the phone to check up on the whereabouts of Greg. In most cases, I told my patients what was going on. I felt it was only fair.

How much of myself should I reveal to my patients? Oh, boy, here's a question about which we psychologists hold conferences. What are the ethics of self-disclosure?

What do I do when it's obvious I'm personally upset about something and my patient asks about it? For example, what happens if I open the door, enter the waiting room, and despite my best efforts to de-puff my bloodshot and teary eyes, I am unsuccessful in hiding the evidence that I have a life separate from my patients and which may contain heartache and stress? I recall times when clients asked, "Are you all right?" and I said, "Yes. I look this way because I just heard something sad."

This was true. I might have been crying because I just said good-bye to a long-standing patient the hour before or perhaps I had just heard some joyful news. But as I learned from the sunglass incident, it is better to be open and direct, keeping it uncomplicated—just the facts—than trying to hide emotions. I encourage my patients to freely express their feelings. Wouldn't it be hypocritical for me to do otherwise?

HARRY

A funny thing happened one day when I was working with Harry, the guy who was married to Sally and who joked with her when she said she was getting along better with her mother. You and I talked about how he misused humor to shut her down. I had compared him to many famous comedians. Harry and I worked on helping him to use his humor in a connecting way rather than in a distancing way.

Anyway, just before I was to see him, I got a call from a local diner saying I had won the grandfather clock that was being given away as part of their twenty-fifth anniversary celebration. I was beside myself with glee. Three minutes after receiving the call, I was sitting across from Harry and supposedly concentrating on *him*! I literally could not stop my mouth from grinning. It was the weirdest experience. I don't know if anything like that has happened before or since then. I tried to will my lips to go straight, but the corners turned up and betrayed me. I was biting my lip and trying to contain myself when I realized Harry had been joking around about something, so my smile appeared appropriate. But I hadn't been paying attention to him. I felt as if I were cheating him. I had to tell him what was going on.

Harry was quick on the uptake. He quipped, "And here I thought I was entertaining you by making you laugh! Well, you never know, do ya?"

Leave it to Harry. He could always be so simultaneously cute and clever.

For the time being, I had to go along with this digression from the task at hand. At the end of the session, I tacked on an extra ten minutes, which I often do if I feel I've spent some of our time on my needs. I've given the additional time when, for instance, my patient and I get into a discussion of restaurants, or they give me recommendations of places to go, or they ask me about myself, and I find it appropriate to share my reaction over something occurring in my life. Because there's a question as to whether or not what we're doing is pure socializing and not my being with them as therapist, I go overtime just in case. Otherwise, I would feel as if I stole minutes from them.

There's an obvious thin line between therapy and entertainment. Also, many times I truly enjoy myself with my patients. I have to assess whether my exhilarated feeling is because I'm enjoying what they are discussing or maybe I'm learning new things. Even though I believe I'm totally there with the person, nevertheless, I question: "Am I supposed to be having so much fun? After all, I'm expected to be working and sweating bullets for my money." As it turns out, the reality is I actually like the people with whom I work. This notion goes along with my belief that the more you know what makes a person tick inside, the more you are bound to like him or her.

DICK

I'll describe an incident with Dick, which will help us with the matter of the psychologist's self-disclosure. Dick was the man who had chronic heart disease and was always in danger of sudden death. Dick worried about his wife's being left alone with no one to take care of her. I told him I would watch out for her. I saw Alice individually in treatment as well as Dick, so if he had to die, he needn't worry about Alice.

Dick's was the funeral I attended and described earlier. The way I portrayed him in our conversation about how my patients and I are partners in pain was as follows: "In the meantime, a slow and progressive invalidism threatened his existence and frightened him terribly. It was as if he and I were companions, sitting on a bench, waiting for a dark cloud to creep in on him and knock him over. We kept each other company in the process."

Dick was the man who befriended my dog, Roxie, and Roxie greeted him by jumping on his lap as soon as he sat down. I bring Roxie back into our conversation because when I learned that Roxie had an irreversible condition, which meant that we had no choice but to bring her to the vet and have her put to sleep, Dick was the first person to whom I would have liked to turn for consolation.

As it was, so often I welled up in sessions with Dick. I described to you earlier how in his case, when I felt like crying, it was a tip off that he was isolating his feelings. I would say, "Dick, how is it that you are smiling and I feel like sobbing? I suspect I'm doing all the feeling for you!"

Now that I had this news about Roxie to convey to him, I was even more likely to cry for Roxie and for myself right in the session. Also, I would be crying for Dick, who was losing Roxie, but also because Dick was also dying, my sorrow made a deeper groove in my heart. I knew it would be healing for both of us to share our grief, but I questioned the ethics of expressing such raw emotions with him.

As it turned out, Dick and I sobbed together, and at one point we hugged and basically cried on each other's shoulders. What a precious moment for both of us. I believe this experience of sharing a piece of tragedy together helped him face his own dying process with healthy acquiescence.

When my twenty-six-year-old cousin, T'ai, unexpectedly died in a drowning accident while doing laps in a swimming pool, it was around the same time another close family member was diagnosed with cancer, another family member almost died of toxic shock, and my very good friend delivered a stillborn baby. In addition, I was scheduled to have foot surgery within a few weeks. I was in one of those places where it seemed as if everywhere I turned, tragedy struck. I must say it was maybe the only time in my career when in therapy sessions I have ever had fleeting thoughts such as, *You think* you *have it so bad? Wait till I tell you what happened to* me! Thank goodness I had the restraint necessary to spare my needy patient such details of my life!

Phew, those were hard times!

Despite the reality that my patients are not my friends or family, invariably, I start feeling close to them, and I have to remind myself of my role. Because of the restraint I must exert, I join the ranks of other psychologists who must deal with the loneliness of being a therapist.

I'm especially aware of this when, for instance, in a moment of intense affection for the patient when I greet or say good-bye to him or her, I blurt out a word such as "honey." Picture this: "See you at our next meeting on Wednesday, honey."

Oh, boy, this is embarrassing. I'm even blushing now as I confess it to you. Sometimes what accidentally slips out is a, "Looking forward to seeing you," or when I haven't seen the person for a while, "I missed you."

Also, when I feel close to them, I tend to nickname people. I forget I'm their psychologist and not their buddy. Through the years, I've gotten more polished. When I first meet the person, especially if he or she has a name like Judith or Robert, the kind of names that most people shorten, I'll ask, "How would you like me to address you?" Sometimes, I even tell them that I tend to nickname people and I want to be sure I call them what is most comfortable for them.

JIM AND PATTY FIELDING

What happens when I "bump into" one of my patients in all kinds of everyday places, such as supermarkets and department stores? I once unexpectedly met up with Jim and Patty Fielding in a home improvement store. I'm sure you remember them; they were the couple whose first session started out with the usual flurry as they and I got into a state of readiness to identify their reason for seeking my help. After a short pause, Patty glared at Jim and shrieked, "F— you!"

One Sunday, my husband and I were trying to figure out what wallpaper we should choose for our bedroom. Will had just finished making a very funny quip about our never leaving the store. I was doubled over, and tears were streaming down my cheeks from fits of laughter—a kind of typical scene in our household. We were really having fun together.

In contrast, we heard some loud yells from the aisle next to ours. The sounds came upon us so suddenly; we were shaken into sobriety. I had the impression that what we heard was a mother scolding her child. This is always disconcerting. I'm sure most people who observe an occurrence such as this feel embarrassed and frightened for the child. Nowadays, we might even imagine this child as being physically and verbally abused at home, and we concomitantly feel helpless to intervene. Will and I tried to tune out the background noise and go on with our job of looking through wallpaper books.

But the human barks were echoing more loudly. We were distracted from our chore and staring at each other in dismay. As the steamy shouts got closer to our reluctant ears, around the end of the aisle suddenly appeared Mr. and Mrs. Fielding!

I recognized her a few seconds before she peered over his bent head and observed me looking like a mute, open-mouthed statue. In the middle of her condescension to him, saying, "Jim, you idiot, I told you to get the one-inch *nails*, not the one-inch screws! Why don't you—" she stopped abruptly. "Hello, Phyliss," she said unabashedly.

Jim raised his head from his almost prayerful posture and smiled meekly. His flushed face said a lot, and later in our session the following week, he confirmed my hunch by acknowledging that he was, indeed, embarrassed and humiliated.

Then Patty did an interesting thing. She smiled. An even more intriguing change overtook her. She made a joke! "Well, Phyliss, I guess you got an earful on that one, huh?" Then she laughed!

Astounded, I recuperated from my original tongue-tied condition and said succinctly, "Yes."

"Jim and I are putting shelves in our kitchen."

Unimaginatively, I replied, "Oh?"

"You see, he was to get the nails, but instead he got *screws*!"

When she emphasized the word, "screw," I thought the choice of terminology was fitting since at that moment it was hard for me to imagine that this couple ever *screwed*!

I said, "Well, Patty, I guess people make mistakes sometimes!"

She chuckled. "That's true. Jim makes plenty of those. But, you know him, Phyliss." Magnanimously, and like a mother who knows better, she recanted, "Jim's okay. He's a good guy. He just gets mixed up sometimes."

Her upturned lips while she simultaneously clenched her jaw reminded me of what I call the grit-teeth smile. You never know where you stand with a person like this. Did you do a good thing or a bad thing? Is your smile just a cover for your disgust of me? The grit-teeth smiler maintains a lot of power over the afflicted recipient who remains forever in a quandary. I never like to make assumptions or pre-judge people without checking it out, but Patty's behavior was otherwise convincing.

Jim took her "compliment" about his being a good guy but getting "mixed up sometimes" as an invitation or maybe a cue that he was supposed to speak. "Patty, I thought you said *screws*!"

I could see we were all going to stand around in the wallpaper aisle for hours, that is, unless I took the lead. I introduced Will to them and then assertively declared that we were going to resume our perusal of the wallpaper books.

I'll never forget how they looked as they ambled away. She could have been a little girl leading her younger brother through a huge playground because her mother said she had to. Needless to say, there was much to talk about the next time we met in session.

Once when I was teaching a communications skills class for couples, I found myself in an embarrassing situation. Even though my class was not actual therapy, some of the participants eventually called me for psychological assistance and asked for an appointment. So, even if at the time of the class these people were not my actual patients, they could potentially become my patients. I was cognizant of my role with them.

One evening, I was driving my car into the very dark and crowded parking lot of the adult education center. I was afraid I'd be late to class. The person in front of me was hardly moving, and the person behind me started impatiently leaning on his horn as if I were capable at the time of doing something about the tie up. I basically ignored this aggression, as usual. (I'm very aware of death by road rage!) I parked and proceeded into the building.

The first thing I heard as I entered the classroom was Thomas's angry voice, "You sure get angry when people don't move their cars fast enough, don't you!"

At first, I thought he was talking to his wife; I had witnessed his fiery temper when addressing her. However, his red face was basically in mine—in my face, that is.

"Huh, what?" I was miffed.

Slowly, it dawned on me what he was getting at. "Are you referring to the guy who kept honking his horn?"

"Yes, I am. And guess who the guy was, *Phyliss*," he said tauntingly. "You're supposed to be teaching us how to get along better with each other and look at you!"

Uh oh. Here I was in one of my dreaded predicaments: to be falsely accused! I really hate when that happens!

The worst part about being falsely accused is that many times it doesn't matter what you say. No one will believe you anyway. This is why I never went into politics. The more you protest, the more damaging it appears.

Very aware of how guilty I appeared, mainly because I was tongue-tied like a little kid trying to wheedle her way out of having to finish all her dinner so she can get dessert, I protested, "No, I wasn't the one honking. It was the guy behind me. I must have been the car behind you, in the middle between you and the horn guy."

To the rest of the class, I proceeded to explain what had happened. Later when I recalled this incident, I imagined all twenty sets of eyes on me with twenty pairs of sucked-in cheeks saying, "Yeah, we know," and then the release of air you hear at the end when vibrating lips spew, "Tsk, tsk."

KEVIN

Once, while in a ten-items-or-less checkout line in the food market, just as the checker began itemizing my groceries, I recounted my packages and realized I might have originally miscounted. If you count two quarts of milk as two separate items, then I had eleven items, not ten.

"I never quite figured this out," I sheepishly asked the checker. "If you have duplicates of one item, do you count them all as one item, or should I count each separate item as one even if I have duplicates?"

The checker stared blankly at me. As I was waiting for the cashier to answer and as she tallied my groceries, suddenly Kevin appeared behind me! I was still wondering if my count was off when I saw him.

In our last session that very morning, just a few hours ago, I had been confronting him about the way he twisted reality to make things less anxiety inducing for himself. Lo and behold, now he had caught me red handed, or should I say milk-carton-handed, in the act of trying to get away with stuff. I had been impressing on him the idea that when he lied to himself or rationalized his actions to make them not really what they were, he was behaving as his mother had on the days after she dried up from her abusive, drunken state and acted as if nothing had happened. How about the way she "snuck around," bringing men into the house and stealthily pushing them out the door as if Kevin had no idea what was going on?

If he questioned her, "When I woke up, I thought I heard a man's voice," she would deny her clandestine activities. We had also talked about the way he used to lie and hide things from his mom to avoid repercussions and how he continued in the same vein with his present wife, Darlene.

In therapy, I was well aware Kevin needed extra reassurance from me about what he saw as real. It wasn't for me to take away his reality as his mom used to do by being abusive one minute and then all sweet and loving the next. She made him believe his feeling of rejection had been a figment of his imagination. Kevin needed to be able to trust me. Just recently I had compared him to a football quarterback who had no receivers to catch the ball, which left him emotionally "famished," empty and angry. He turned the anger on himself. I had urged him to take better care of himself and open up to capable receivers, people who can give to him. I told him I was his logical choice, because I was a reliable, responsible person in his life.

In junior high school, when Kevin's mom went out at night and sometimes didn't return until morning, he heard whispers from the other kids about his mother, but he found a way to close his ears to these "lies." He developed an ability to deny reality. At that time, Kevin couldn't face the actuality that his mother had become "the town whore." He used the "I didn't hear or see it" tactic and extended this to his relationships with women. If I didn't address his and my chance meeting and my breaking the rules, I would be in collusion with his mother and himself and reinforcing his use of a very dysfunctional coping mechanism.

Throughout his life, Kevin was often caught up in lying to himself. With women, he twisted the truth in order to save himself from their demands. His passivity eventually drove women crazy, one by one, and then he was out looking to get attached yet again. Finally, he married Darlene, who turned out to be a sickly woman who needed him to take care of her. Despite his earlier efforts to find a self-sufficient woman who would minister to him for a change, instead, he ended up with—yep, his mother!

Betrayals and reversals were at the core of Kevin's life, and the last thing he needed was a lying, conniving therapist. Okay,

I know it's a bit of an overreaction to jump to this depiction of myself based on X-plus-one food item in a checkout line. But, just as I believe you have to be the straightest you can be with your children, not budging one millimeter from the whole truth and nothing but the truth, you must be able to call it like it is. To say to someone, "I'm not late. I just arrived five minutes after I told you I would," is trying to paint your own reality. The fact is if you're late by one second, you are late. When it comes to telling it like it is, there are no in-betweens. Sure, when someone is a few minutes late, you can be reasonable in response to him. Nevertheless, the person is undeniably late, and for him to sketch it as anything other than what it is is fudging it, and it's untruthful, period. So, there was no way I could try to justify my actions to him other than to fess up and refer to it in the next session.

When I just talked about Kevin, I was sharing my experience about how my patient perceives my actions, which are independent of his therapy. Now, I'd like to talk about my personal life issues and how I grapple with these in the session and how my own stuff could complicate the therapeutic relationship if I don't watch out.

I'm referring here to my own hang-ups, private beliefs, and idiosyncrasies. I have to be careful about some of my pet peeves, of which I have few, but the ones I have are strongly felt.

In our discussion of children and the importance of preserving their sense of self, I talked to you about my dismay when parents speak for their children as if I wanted to hear from the parents and not from their children! I have a real problem with adults labeling children. Recently, a new mom said to me about her baby, "She's so fussy."

I thought to myself, 'She's not fussy. She's a baby, for gosh sake.'

I wince when I hear, "He's so stubborn." Come on. He's not stubborn; he's asserting himself!

One of the worst is when parents say their children are shy. I just don't get it. Why would you label your child's behavior and tell people your child is too afraid to speak to them when maybe it's just plain not true? It's adaptive for human beings to wait and see before committing themselves. Give them and me a break once in a while, why don't you?

You see how heated I get about this?

CHERYL

I saw a former patient, Cheryl, in a bakery. (I only briefly talked about Cheryl way back in the "Partners in Pain" chapter and how Cheryl's being "crushed" by misperceptions of criticism caused me to internally slap my hand and say to myself, "Shut up, Phyliss!" whenever I wanted to say to Cheryl, "Don't you get it? You're okay. You're abusive mother doesn't live here anymore!" I wanted Cheryl to see how she was treating her husband as if he were her mother. When in reality, he was just trying to please her.

Cheryl had done very well in treatment and had gone on her merry way years and years ago. She left therapy in a grateful state of mind. I treated her before she had children, and it was quite a while since we had seen each other. We exchanged positive greetings, and then she introduced me to her ten-year-old daughter.

Immediately after she told me her daughter's name, Cheryl pointed to her shopping cart and exclaimed, "Courtney made such a stink about not enough junk food in the house, so look what she made me buy!"

Even before Courtney interjected a protest, I was already wincing for Courtney. Her mother was publicly deriding Courtney for "complaining." Always conscious of potential problems preteens and teens have with eating and body obsessions, I was doubling my usual knee jerk wish to set this mother straight.

In the meantime, little Courtney blushed and said, "*I* didn't complain!"

Could it be that Cheryl wanted an excuse to buy this food, felt embarrassed, and pawned off the responsibility for buying it on her daughter? Perhaps Courtney had complained, but what's that to me? Why should I be made privy to her daughter's words or wishes? Was Cheryl worried about what I might think of what she buys in the market? I remembered how sensitive she used to be to the possibility that I might be judging her.

Of course, I wasn't in the office and not into my professional psychologist role. I would have asked her what was behind her actions. I would not have made any assumptions on my own. I guess you could say I was caught off guard. I said, "I'm glad to meet you, Courtney. I want you to know that I believe you!"

Did I damage Cheryl by saying this at a time when we wouldn't have another session to work through the issues my actions stimulated in her? Would it make any difference to Courtney that I defended her and basically said, "I see you for who you are, not for how your mother is trying to depict you."

To this day, I haven't heard from Cheryl, so I'll never know. I choose to believe, however, that my intercession might have helped Courtney a little bit and maybe even sent a message to Cheryl to put her fear of criticism (for being a bad mother who buys unhealthy junk food for her child) aside and for the sake of her child not use her child as a shield from scrutiny.

I know these are passionate words and opine much of my own agenda. Here I go defending myself when I say that regarding certain mistreatment of small and large people in this world, I have my own needs. I guess sometimes I want to cure the world, to provide safeguards against certain people's art of exploitation. I have to keep a watchful guard on my audacity when I'm doing therapy, but when I'm living in the "real" world, I try to forgive myself as I cope with what I see and hear.

Don't rest easy just yet. I have one more thing to throw into this discussion of my pet peeves. Let's include my beef about people who laugh at, ridicule, or put down groups of people by hiding behind what they deem as "humor" or taking the "can't you take a joke" stance. (Sorry, as long as I was on my personal soapbox, I just had to throw this whole subject in again.)

Well, all right, since you asked, I'll embellish on this topic. We should look at the power of our instinctive need to conform and how this requisite to be part of the crowd may sway us from following our own hearts.

The worst thing that could happen would be to be rejected and therefore left alone. At any one moment, we are either in the "in" crowd or we are on the outs. Which do we choose? Many people are afraid to stand up and say, "Stop! I won't laugh just because everyone else is laughing. I won't allow another human being to be hurt by ridicule and putdowns."

I have to keep guard over my rage reaction when I hear about ridicule of others or I see it in my groups. I try to educate people as to the repercussions of burying one's head in the sand and acting as if they are children and don't know any better.

That's all I have to say about that! Never mind. Let's move on.

MIKE AND NANCY

Now that I've reintroduced another of my hang-ups regarding the abuse of humor, I should talk about how when employed in a healthy way, being funny in relationships can be the greatest! I believe this fits into our present discussion, because we're talking about my personal issues and how they impact my work.

Mike and Nancy were the guys who never looked at each other, only at me, because in a competitive way, they each sought my approval. One day, very dramatically, I said, "Okay, after hearing both sides of the story, I now have the answer."

I then told each one that person was right. When I said, "Nancy, I'm sad to say you are right," after a poignant pause, they each broke out in gales of laughter.

I had assessed early in their treatment that these were the kind of people with whom I could joke. Mike was a very funny guy, and Nancy was fun-loving, and although she wasn't likely to initiate the jesting, as soon as he tried to lighten up her and me both, she readily became his partner.

When we join them in their session, Mike is teasing Nancy. "Hey, Phyliss, did Nancy ever tell you what she calls me when no one else is around?"

Nancy's face reddened. "Mike, if you tell, then I'm going to tell what you do first thing when you wake up in the morning!"

Before she had a chance to exhale from having said all that, Mike continued as if she hadn't spoken at all. "Oh, yeah, Nancy has some very interesting names for me, don't you, Nancy?"

Giggling, Nancy started to respond, but he interrupted. "Nancy is a Cutsey Wutsey."

"Yep, I have many nicknames for you, Mikey. I'm sure you don't want me telling Phyliss the one your mother used to call you."

But Mike once again missed the fun of responding to Nancy. Instead he continued with his own agenda until I intervened. "Mike, are you aware of what Nancy has been saying?"

"Huh? What?"

"You see, Mike," I pointed out, "you so much want to make her laugh, you haven't taken a breath to give Nancy a chance to join with you so you both can be in it together. When you say funny things, she laughs. Then she adds something to help *you* laugh, and you don't even hear her."

"What? What's the matter with my having some fun with her?"

"Hey, Mike, there's nothing wrong with it. It's great. Helping the two of you to laugh can't hurt anyone as long as it's not at any one's expense."

"So, then, what's the problem here?"

Nancy picked up the ball. "Mike, when you get on a roll, there's no way for me to get in. It's like you're a one-man comedy team, and I don't even have to be there." Nancy looked at me. "This is the way it always happens. He has to be the funny guy. There's no room for me."

Having studied humor in one form or another since I was a kid, I was right in there with Nancy. Also, gender differences came to light with this couple. Mike was so focused on producing laughs in Nancy, for the moment he forgot she existed.

Where my personal issue comes in here is from my own experience. Join me in mixed company, particularly when one person is identified by everyone as the funny man. If this funny man is more intent on being funny than on being with me, I will probably go underground—meaning I will desist from "bouncing off" of him when he makes humorous remarks. I'll probably maintain minimal contact with him as well as seek out other people's company instead, even if the "substitutes" are the serious type.

On the other hand, if the guy in the crowd opens his ears to my add-ons and looks me in the eyes and obviously is appreciative and/or amused by my offerings even if it's not the exact way he wanted to control the fun, then we're in business.

I really get a kick out of humor intercourse. I deliberately used the word, "intercourse." To me, interactive humor where one person says something and the other person, be it man or woman, takes in my joke, holds it inside of him then adds another element to it and then sends it back to me for me to take in, is like good sex. It's similar to the way we played as kids when we made up stories by one person writing or speaking a sentence and the next person adding another sentence. As you go around the circle, each contributor moves the story in his or her own direction, pulling it away from the former storytellers into a new place. But that's okay, because you're all in it together. It's the established goal to end up with a tale everyone has embellished.

Now you have a group invention. You've each given up a piece of your own self for the good of the group, but you feel energized because it belongs to everyone. You could have had your very own story, but then you would have had to forego the "joining" piece of the experience.

If you convey your humor by bullying your way into the laughing hearts of your audience and not including them in your gesture, as far as I'm concerned, you might as well be masturbating in public. I'm serious. (Just in case you were wondering.) Okay, it's fun to entertain yourself. Fine. However, if when you are making your jokes, you believe you are "with" other people, just be honest with yourself. If you truly want them to enhance your experience, then allow them in. If not, go ahead and masturbate. (Ooh, ooh, ooh. Them's mighty strong words, are they not? Look, I never said "self-pleasurizing" is a bad thing. If you do it, just call it what it is.)

All right, here's a concluding remark about this therapist's espousing her mission in humor heaven. Nancy had a real ally in more ways than she knew. And how lucky for Mike that I have this idiosyncratic passion about humor. Normally, humor is humor. Why dissect it and ruin it for all? Since these guys had me for a therapist, they were afforded the opportunity to heighten their love relationship and bring it up from the bedroom into their verbal intercourse and vice versa; they were providing more opportunities to intimately love each other.

Therein lies the art form of psychotherapy. This account highlights the reality that you take chances when you choose to give yourself over to another human being, a therapist, who is to serve as your assistant in personal growth. Even in other medical professions, there are standard ways of doing things, but there are variations based on the "flavor" of doctor you choose. This is why we have so many brands of clothing and food and so many ice cream flavors. To each his own. I think there's the same kind of variegation among therapists. Each of us puts emphasis on what strikes us as important among the infinite issues upon which we could highlight, and much of the choice is based on the psychologist's personal experience and personality.

Because of my lifelong study and interest in humor and due to my personal experience, it came to pass that Mikey and Cutsey Wutsey were destined to have some real hot times in the old town. Sometimes, I wished I could be there with them out in the real world to see them make "humor love" together.

Okay, where were we? Oh yes, we were still on my personal quirks and how these intermingle, interfere, or enhance my patients' treatment.

MARGARET AND DON

Politics and religion are similar in that people can get quite passionate about either or both. Therefore, this is a fitting time for you and me to talk about my being Jewish and how I work with those who have prejudice or fear about Jewish people.

Margaret and Don were the ones who came to me because after years of showing marginal interest in Margaret, Don totally withdrew. Self-sufficient Margaret found out that Don had been having an extra marital affair, and severely distressed Don couldn't decide which woman he wanted while Margaret awaited the outcome of Don's dire decision. They were one of the couples I described who filled out the How I Protect Myself from Loving You questionnaire. She used counter-dependency, and he used withdrawal.

One day, while Margaret was doing most of the talking, which was the usual scenario, in his chair across the room as far from both of us as he could possibly be, Don appeared extra restless. His crossed leg was popping up and down, and he was sighing loudly through what sounded like a foghorn. It always seemed as if Don's nasal passages were congested. I never quite knew why, but I wondered if there were tears lurking inside of him with no outlet and they had just settled in his nose. Margaret was repetitively denying her anxiety about her daughter Krista's going off to college. Margaret was talking a mile a minute and gulping back tears, so I held off for the moment from checking in with Don. However, his agitation didn't go unnoticed.

Finally, after Margaret's soliloquy of self-pity, I turned to Don and said, "You seem particularly restless today, Don. What's up?"

Looking as if I had just performed electroshock therapy on him, he jerkily tilted back his head and said, "Oh, it's nothing. Just something going on at work."

"Tell me about it," I requested.

"Oh no, it's nothing, just this Jewish guy who gets on my nerves is really bugging me."

"How does he bug you?" I asked as I moved into an internal compartment where I sometimes go when I need to keep perspective. I didn't imagine too many red flags just yet. Don might have just used the Jewish label many people will do when as a way to identify someone, they say, "Oh, Bonnie, yep, she's the fat woman who works in accounting," or, "Will is the bald guy," or, "Harry is that funny guy who told jokes at Sam's party."

I was pretty sure Don didn't know I was Jewish. He probably hadn't even thought about it. If a patient knows my Jewish identity and if he is a prejudiced person, he is most likely to refrain from elaborating on this awareness. I won't likely explore his feelings about my identity unless I glean something from his demeanor. Then, I'll ask about it. Most of the time, his discriminatory biases won't even come up, because the person steers clear of anything close to Judaism lest his tongue, having a mind of its own, divulge the truth in his heart.

Seething Don, who might have had smoke emerging from his ears, answered my question regarding what bugged him about the Jewish guy. "You know, um, Marvin is, eh, what can I say… so Jewish."

I asked him what he meant by that, and he said, "Normally, I'm not a prejudiced person, but when someone treats me the way he does, all bets are off. He's always plugging for my job and making me look bad with my boss."

Remaining in the screened-off area to which I referred earlier, I wondered, *Is prejudice a convenience? If the time is right, then you show open-mindedness and tolerance, but if someone crosses you, you turn into a bigot. I don't get it. You either do or you don't discriminate against someone. It has nothing to do with whether or not things go your way with the person.*

I asked, "How does Marvin's plugging for your job make him too Jewish?"

"No matter," hurried Don, "Let's just say he's a go-getter."

At this point, if I had perseverated on the Jewish business, I would have been going beyond my role. That would have been totally inappropriate and not constructive. My insistence on continuing the "Jewish" exploration would have been for my own needs to "cure the world" of prejudice, particularly of anti-Semitism. I could see the issue was not his Jewish bias but his concern over the competitiveness for his job and the dog-eat-dog atmosphere in which he worked.

Also, I was able to take a step back. I'm always interested in what makes people hate others in a particular group and why people tell stereotypic jokes that put down a race, religion, or disability, but this day was not the day to get into it. Later, I would think about Don and how he might be typical of others who conveniently use myths about certain groups of people with common heritage as rationale for their feelings.

The most difficult type of patient for me is dealing with anxious, passive patients. Basically, you can lead a person to understanding, but you can't make him take the plunge.

I once pep-talked a woman who had been terrified of driving to go in her car with me. She was an excellent driver but was afraid to do it. I asked her to have her husband bring her as usual.

He was to wait in the waiting room while she and I went for a drive.

MARGARET

I've worked with phobic patients who were afraid to make a phone call for a job, a call that essentially could change their life. To the formerly self-sufficient Margaret who gave up more and more of her activities after Krista left for college, I interpreted, "You said you love me, and if you succeed in your mission, everyone will think I'm the greatest therapist. Yet, you won't give me the satisfaction of making a little phone call."

I urged her to make the call right in my office. When she was too frightened to do even that much, I made the call for her and handed her the phone.

Even though this kind of directive therapy is not my favorite thing to do as a therapist, it can still be fun. I think one of my aversions to pushing people to do what they don't want to do even though it can produce great results is that this approach makes me feel like an I-know-better-than-thou kind of person. I much prefer to help provide the atmosphere for people to make change and then sit back and watch it take place.

But we psychologists don't always have the choice of those we treat and how we must do it. It's interesting, though, isn't it, that just as we saw with Mike and Nancy and their advantage of having me as a humor consultant, our patients have the advantage of different kinds of therapy with varying degrees of emphasis. The only problem is, of course, if the match up doesn't work out. How is the patient to know enough ahead of time to make the choice of which therapist to see? Sorry, I don't have the answer to that one. Beats me.

NATALIE

When patients give over their symptoms, it is one of the most loving gifts there are. I receive these with love for them and for their sacrifice. In addition, my being receptive in a gracious way is a healthy model to show how effective intimacy looks. At these times, it's hard to tell what is *I* as therapist versus *I* as human being.

At the end of a grief-filled session, Natalie, the young woman whose therapy consisted primarily of our looking at photographs of her deceased mother who died when Natalie was four, gave me a gift when she verbally "slipped" and accidentally called me, "Mom." Throughout our meeting, Natalie had delicately allowed herself to tiptoe on the buried sorrow deep within her heart-worn soul. With only a glimpse of a memory of having sat on her mother's lap and a hazy internal photo of a look her mother had given her when little Natalie was dancing in the kitchen, Natalie contorted her face in agony and cried, "Why did she leave me?"

Later, with her hands clenched in balls that seemed to bounce off her thighs as she hit them, she bellowed, "Why couldn't I have been like the other kids?"

Then she talked about her wretched kindergarten experience when the other kids pointed fingers, and like little judges sitting on a high bench, they chided her, "You don't have a mommy!"

(I'll bet if some of those kids knew as adults the indelible scar they had left on Natalie, the torment she faced every day of her life, the permanently imprinted badge of shame she wore, which was identifiable even in her dreams, they would have taken it all back.)

On the day of her emotional upheaval in my office, as she slowly lifted herself off of my sofa and sauntered to the door, Natalie looked at me as if I were her emotional overlord. With a Marilyn Monroe kind of rasp in her lumpy throat, she whispered almost to herself, "Bye, Mom."

I'd call that utterance a prized and precious present, wouldn't you?

HARRY

The day Harry cried in my arms is another gift I remember. In that session, he recalled his father's beating him for not cutting the grass behind the back yard fence. Good old Harry—or should I say good little Harry—was at it again, trying to get out of a chore (or a feeling!), and because he believed what you don't see won't hurt you, he thought he could get away with leaving a little grass for next time!

Harry chuckled when he made this statement. Levity, Harry, yes, sometimes it does help. When Harry quipped about this painful event in his past, there was a hint of mockery, but for the moment, his smile was so engaging, it temporarily took away the sting I had been experiencing as he told the story. I could easily imagine how he "got away" with being aggressive to people without their faulting him. But even more, I felt as if for the moment I had sneaked inside of Harry and felt the relief he must have experienced whenever he sculpted painful and personal knowledge into funny and creative humor.

Since this was one of two times his father had beaten him, and since it served as one of the instances he used throughout his life to brandish defiance of his father, it was a significant memory. As hard as Harry tried to wheedle out of getting in touch with his true feelings about the event, I wouldn't allow him off the hook. We were going to talk about this, by gosh, if I had anything to say about it—and yes, I had a lot to say about it. Harry trusted me enough then to go along for the ride.

He would answer my question and then immediately turn it into funny stuff. I would say, "No, Harry, don't laugh. Don't make jokes. Stay with the emotion. It's time for us to go into the reality of your pain. Harry, you can handle these feelings. Just let yourself go with it."

Boy, did he ever allow himself to take off. Here was the gift to me. Of course, I felt encouraged Harry would give me his trust and take the journey with me. I knew that he knew that I knew what it meant for him to sand down the edges of his crusty covering and permit entrance for himself and me into his private hurt.

As he started to let loose, I immediately got up from my chair and stood beside him. I put my shaking hand on his sobbing shoulder and quietly said, "It's okay, Harry. Let it go, Harry."

Thank you, Harry. I'll never forget the scene nor will I put aside the vision of the two of us at my office door, with Harry crying in my arms like a wounded baby. He gave me so much that day, and I am forever grateful to him for it.

KEVIN

Gifts aren't always nicety nice. One time, when Kevin had a broken ankle and he was resting his casted foot on a wooden chair he had brought in from the waiting room to elevate his leg, we had an "incident."

He got so angry that with his good foot he kicked the chair out from under his damaged one and screamed, "Phyliss, sometimes I just wish you would shut the hell up!"

Whew! Due to my being startled, I did flinch. I felt two ways about my reaction. On the one hand, I was glad he expressed his anger, and I thanked him for it. On the other, I wanted my office to remain a safe place for both of us; I had to remind him that I don't allow physical violence in my office.

Good for you, Kevin, for telling me off! Sometimes, I really can be obnoxious and pushy!

TIM

Okay, I'll balance that turbulent story with the one about Tim, the man who kept talking even though his wife was passed out on my multi-colored area tapestry rug. I saw him individually only a few times after he and Linda had already terminated treatment. He called me because he was having a problem at work and wanted my advice on how to handle his recalcitrant boss. By the third session, he said he didn't need to see me anymore, but since it was around Valentine's Day, and while at the store picking out flowers for Linda, he decided to buy a bouquet for me as well.

Since I was feeling a little down that day anyway, I was vulnerable to being more needy than I should have been. His gift was such as sweet gesture; I may have even blushed. Oops, not too cool, Phyl. Get a grip.

VICTOR

I received many "gifts" from Victor. These were intangibles of his opening himself up to explore the depths of his feelings by joining me where I "live" in the catacombs of the unconscious mind.

One day, he told me that he and Aimee had gone to a family Christmas Eve party. His father and mother arrived a little later than Aimee and he. He was in the kitchen. Sensing something from behind him, he could feel hands on his shoulders.

"Even before I turned around to see if it was my father, I had all these feelings. I knew it was him. He was touching me the way he touches other people in friendship, kind of putting his hands on my shoulders and then massaging. I could feel his willingness to touch me as well as a hesitation, like he wanted to make contact with me and pull back at the same time. I was very shook. He had never touched me before."

Victor relived the experience in my office. He smiled as he spoke of the incident, but also he was flushed and distressed, almost the way he had appeared when he first told me of his lovemaking with Aimee.

I said, "The shock of his touching you prevented you from experiencing the joy of getting what you have always wanted."

Victor agreed. He said his positive feeling had been overtaken by his shock.

"Victor, you must be sending out different signals. You are so different from how you used to be, and somehow your father must have thought that now it was safe." (It was at this time that I was reminded once again of my recent urge to hug Victor. I had been holding back. It seemed that I had always held back with Victor. Somehow I identified with his father, and when he described his father's having hugged him in his father's unique way of massaging shoulders "from behind," it was as if I had hugged him, too.)

In response to my saying that he had sent out other signals, Victor said, "Maybe I'll gradually get closer and be able to touch *him*."

"Why don't you talk to your father about it?"

Victor was very flustered. "Oh no, he wouldn't understand. I couldn't find the right words."

I insistently said, "Except for those first few years of therapy when you were in a dreamlike state, you've never had a problem finding the right words. You have a wonderful way of expressing yourself. You say things in such an uncomplicated way. No, Victor, it's not that you don't have the right words. It's that despite all your lamenting that he didn't want to touch you, you are afraid for yourself, afraid to get close to your father."

Victor then told me about how at work he touches men, but it takes him a long time before he feels free enough. "I'm afraid they will think that I'm coming on to them. My supervisor at work touches me all the time. He picks me up in jest, you know what I mean, the way regular guys do." Finally, Victor said, "Well, maybe I'll get to talk to my father about our becoming closer."

I could see the significance of this experience for Victor. I was very moved by it myself. My eyes watered. I simply had to underline what his interaction with his father had meant to him, "Victor, how wonderful for you. Your father finally touched you!" Victor was speechless.

Aside from the gift of allowing himself to share his feelings with me about his father, and due to his father's loving gestures of intimacy with his son (which I believe occurred because Victor was sending new signals to his dad), just after this discussion, Victor gave me the greatest gift of all—his manly courage.

Here's how it unfolded: in the next session after the one I just depicted, I asked Victor to imagine what it would be like if something happened to Aimee, if Aimee left him. He reassured me that he would continue to go to straight bars, that he would be terribly upset if she left, but that he knew he would seek other women for company and love. He reviewed for me a description of some of the women who in the past had shown an interest in him but in whom he had denied romantic or sexual interest. Now he realized how much he had denied.

During this discussion, a very large spider appeared and was crawling across the middle of my office carpet. Victor spotted it first and pointed it out to me. I said, half in jest and at the same time trying to get a message across, "Victor, protect me!"

Victor then proceeded to kill the spider and dispose of it. I thanked him and allowed myself to get into the feeling of having this man take care of me. Victor got the message from me that he had performed a manly deed, something a father teaches his son to do, but for now, he was to receive reinforcement from me instead. My reaction served to further enhance his budding self-image. I wonder how he would have responded to the spider if it had been about six years prior to this time. Even if he had felt okay about killing spiders, how would he have handled the feelings of being in the role of my protector? We were both smiling. I was thinking, *What a joy it is for me to be a part of this man's transformation.*

CHRISSY

At the end of her treatment, Chrissy brought me a small crystal sphere. She said, "I thought of you when I saw this, because you have taught me to see the rainbow colors of the world."

I graciously accepted her token of appreciation as well as its being a marker of her spontaneity. She had to feel comfortable enough with me and with herself to bring this to me. With obvious emotion, I welled up and thanked her.

The crystal is still in my office along with handmade Christmas ornaments, photographs, stuffed animals, mirrors, artificial flower decorations, and other tokens of remembrance from patients.

Here's my summation of our "Whose Life Is It Anyway?" talk: I am like a sponge, imbibing all the sorrow, anger, and pain of my patients. They leave my office, and I must find a place to carefully and tenderly store their emotional spirits. I dare not discard the products of our work together. Their intense, painful emotions and their heartbreaking memories must not be stored in a static container within me lest I transform into a depressed, pitiable singular spirit. I preserve all their secrets and hurts in a special vault reserved for very special things. Taking care of myself then becomes as important as nurturing the human beings who frequent my office. Because they need me to help them, I am dependent on their offerings as well as dependent on how I adjust to their "gifts." I must straighten out my wrinkled psyche and ready myself for the next life story that walks into my world.

CHANGE: IN SPITE OF OURSELVES

Suppose you know something to be true. It is what it is. Then suddenly one day an event takes place that is beyond your control or someone comes along and says, "Guess what? Sorry to tell you, but what you've been doing all this time to fix problems like these doesn't work anymore."

Automatically, you get shook up. Or maybe in order to survive this traumatic apprehension, you must shake yourself up enough to force yourself to change in a positive direction. Or maybe you land in therapy.

You turn up in my office. Your ways of coping with this problem aren't working anymore. If you're not already shaken up, I'm certainly going to vigorously jostle you around. Sorry, it's my job. When you arrive at my door with a dilemma, and if you are trying to use the old familiar ways to deal with it, I'm going to take a stab at your life's encrustation, crack you open, stir up all the fires inside of you, and do a rock-n-roll number on the vessel into which you store all your old methods of defense. Because our mutual job takes time, all the elements that have been floating around this shaker will settle to the bottom. Since you can't just sit around without any protection, you'll need to find a new way to deal with your problem. You'll have to swim to the bottom, sift through the sediment—against the current, of course—which contains the specks that were stirred up, and you'll have to find a new combination of coping skills.

Not only that. Once you find this new conglomeration of daily defenses, you'll have to stretch yourself tall enough to match up your skills to the challenge at hand. This is why you came to me in the first place. Your old methods were too shallow to reach the height of the stress. You needed to be stretched! (Not shrunk, as some people might say in reference to my work, but elasticized.)

"Change?" you ask. "Who needs it? Who wants it? Why bother?"

You go for it, nevertheless, because even though you are scared of what's ahead of you, internal forces compel you to move forward. You can't help it.

One day you decide, "I'm not going to take this anymore!" and you awaken out of your lethargy. You resolve to confront someone who has been "bugging" you; after months of fretting over being in a dead-end job, finally you push yourself to complete your resume. You overcome your fear of commitment and ask her to marry you after all.

In addition to internal pressure to change, sometimes positive or negative change is imposed on you from the outside, often without your asking for it. You are following your routines, living your life, and from "out of the nowhere" comes the phone call, the car screech, the letter, the "May I speak to you for a minute?" Your life takes a turn, and henceforth, it will never be the same. Now you unwillingly struggle with the emotional consequences of a newly diagnosed illness, a promotion, a car accident, an unexpected inheritance, a lay off, or loss of a loved one. Even planned change, such as giving birth to a baby or moving to a new and better home, can capsize your formerly "well-adjusted" life.

At other times, you need to accommodate to someone *else's* change. For example, your child, who metamorphosed over night into an adolescent, presently says he hates you! You must adjust.

Perhaps you are a CEO who knows that in order to "grow" the company, you have to disturb things and reorganize. Look out! Your employees are about to threaten mutiny, because they like things just the way they are, thank you.

To change is to *give up pre-tested methods* that may not be the most efficient but are certainly cozy and comfy. Heroically, you savor what you know, caressing the keyboard commands of your mental computer. "Alt-File. Save," is your mantra. If you lose your tried and true data, it would be like standing naked outside in the snow. No way! Alt-File. Save. Make a dozen copies of your proven methodology and attitudes.

A new challenge arises: you won't allow yourself to be caught without your old protection even if what you have stored is a mediocre solution to an obsolete dilemma. You say you want to grow, but at the same time, you want to covet yourself as you already are, so—neeeeever mind!

Entering into the change process voluntarily or having it imposed on you is like agreeing to kill yourself. You courageously and knowingly go into this devastating place every time you set out to live your life (as opposed to staying in bed all day!). In order to discover the "new," you need to mix up, redesign, or ultimately kill off the "old."

The initial heart thumping to an unsympathetic and offbeat tune where your internal self hears earsplitting clanging noises, you try futilely to silence your fears by acting as if this bad news couldn't really be foisted onto someone like you!

You calm yourself for about three minutes and then fall into a *depression*, which causes you to sigh almost every other minute. Hopefully, you have some really good crying bouts. (I say hopefully, because despite the fact that people say it doesn't make it better, nevertheless, crying can be so healing.)

You know you have to pull yourself together and get moving. It finally hits you that it's up to you to take charge, and waiting around for Mommy and Daddy just isn't going to cut it.

Over time, hopefully, as you deal with the anxiety of knowing what you have to relinquish in order to get to a better place, you begin to *accept reality*. Whether you like it or not, you must give up the fight to hold onto the old trapeze in order to be able to grasp the one swinging toward you. You have loosened the grip of your childhood fantasy that if things don't go according to plan, it's a catastrophe.

Some of your rigid attitudes begin to slacken. *If something bad happens to me, maybe I can handle it.* Or, *Is it possible I may have been wrong about my boss?* Or, *Maybe, I've been too hard on my kids. They have a point of view.* Or, *How come before my car accident, I never paid attention to people in wheelchairs?*

You begin to test the waters as you start getting used to the *new you* that is gradually emerging. You "pinch" yourself. *Could this be me? I am now a married man. How does a married man actually feel and act?* Or, *We may be downsizing, and even though I resent it, I will have to be part of the reorganization team. What ideas can I contribute?*

You incorporate the change into your attitudes and behavior. You have "worked through" the conflict. You no longer need to concentrate, test, question, or be bowled over by the alteration in your life. Instead of marveling over being able to birth a baby, you can now say, "I am a mother." This internalized change is now a natural part of your functioning. You have internalized a new identity.

If you try to fight the complete process by rushing toward short-term, quick-fix solutions that in the long run almost always fail, then you might experience unexplained anxiety and depression. Instead, if you flow with it, like a fever, which heats your body to kill off germs, the change process takes you over and performs its natural healing, creative work.

Becoming a champion of change is a tall order. All this is easy to say but so, so difficult to do. This is where *I* come in. I am your denial-busting monster. I'm the shaker-upper, remember? I ask you to embrace your internal hysteria and trust that you will make good use of the healthy troublemaker inside of you.

Whether as a psychologist, consultant, employer, friend, parent, or wife, my message is: I'd like to make it easier for you in one way, but in another way, I wouldn't. It's *your* mind, *your* history, *your* personality. How presumptuous of me to barge in as if I know what you should do! Momentarily, you are confused. Through personal research, when the cobwebs clear, you will know how to handle your predicament. Even if I had the power to take away your discomfort by directing your thoughts and actions, I'd be robbing you of an opportunity to learn and to repeatedly discover that you can handle uncertainty. The light bulb will unexpectedly switch on: *Ah ha!* Although painstaking at times, that kind of learning lasts forever.

In any one phase of change, people can get stuck for as little as a couple of minutes to many years. Let's bring Chrissy back into the picture to show how confrontation plays a significant role in the therapeutic process, particularly with someone in denial about traumatic events from long ago.

CHRISSY

Remember Chrissy's plastered smile? Do you recall way back in our discussion when I told you about how once in a while I had an overwhelming urge to punch her in the mouth whenever she flashed her synthetic, paper-doll grin? This puppet-like protective shield originated years ago and had frozen predictably on her face at very strategic moments.

My personal reaction told me Chrissy's smile was covering a deep fury within her, so deep she couldn't see it or believe it. The smile was a symptom of her early survival techniques, which had become quite dysfunctional by the time I saw her. Over the course of treatment, I was simply compelled to confront her.

"Chris, you're telling me how scared you were when your father was hiding in your closet at night, but you are smiling. I don't get it."

In one session, Chris was infuriated with her father, who was presently living with her and her husband, Jack. I confronted her. "Chris, you're angry. Wipe the smile off your face!"

Chris's smile in the midst of severe pain reminded me of the early researchers in behavioral psychology who were able to actually produce in the laboratory what they called experimental neuroses. They conditioned a dog to anticipate food every time a bell rang. Then they changed the rules so when the bell rang and the dog approached the spot where the food was to appear, instead of the expected food, the dog was given a mild shock. The dogs went nuts! They started acting the way we do when we don't know which end is up.

How does this apply to Chrissy? If crying is what you do when you are sad, then when bad things happen, how is it you are supposed to smile instead—unless, of course, your smile or cover-up will keep your mother alive, and alternatively, your misery will kill her? But she's the mom, the one supposed to protect you when you are sad. Instead you protect her with your smile. It's enough to drive anyone crazy!

Of course, because I felt as if I had a site map of the cobweb surrounding Chris, I simply had to confront her. What service did I actually perform for her? Why did I knife my way through her denial of feelings about the magnitude of her father's early actions and more especially about how she smiled in the face of sadness and misery? My brutal war of words was more beneficial than if I had gone along with her self-charade.

Ultimately, she was compelled to go deeper into her depression. This downer was merely temporary as she moved into frustration and anger over having developed this façade out of a survival need and now wishing it could have been different. She accepted the reality of her early deprivation, her longing to have had different parents, other life events, and an alternate outcome. She started testing new ways of coping, such as saying what was on her mind at the time she felt it as well as standing up to her husband and her father.

When we arrived at the "what meaning did all this experience have in my life" phase, I threw in my two cents. "Chris, if you hadn't gone through all you did as a youngster, you probably wouldn't have become a nurse. You wouldn't be the amazing mother you are today. It was a rough beginning, but your having to deal with it strengthened you."

Of course, in Chris's masochistic way, she poo-pooed my validation. But, you know what? I think what I said sunk in.

In due course, Chris moved on to internalizing a new change. By the end, the actor's smile was indeed wiped off her face, but not without some real painstaking work to push herself through the narrow opening to enlightenment—the hard way.

So when I disrupted Chrissy's unconscious "I don't want to change anything but I want to feel better" hell-raising and propelled her into the self-observatory, she necessarily moved forward in therapy.

Embedded in my in-your-face therapeutic interventions is the whole issue of separation. It's too hard to liberate yourself from bonds that were at one time your source of survival but have now become an entrapment without someone like me coming along and luring you to a place of exploration. Or maybe you experience some life event, which pushes you to question your old coping skills.

As long as Chrissy is fresh in your mind, I'll demonstrate what I'm saying about separation issues using examples from her life. Every time Chris vacuumed her carpet, she imagined her mother in shrunken form, standing on her shoulder just by her ear. Her mother whispered orders just the way she used to when Chrissy was a girl. "You have to do a perfect job. You never know when people will come into your house unexpectedly. What will they think?"

I'm wondering if you can relate to Chris's challenge. Are you one of those people who are separated from Mom by continents, yet you experience concern over how she perceives you? Or maybe Mom passed away years ago. Your old hang-ups with her may continue to plague you as you hear her voice directing your every move.

Why does she continue to affect you so much? Let's look back.

Did your mother acknowledge you whenever you mastered new things? If not, did she find fault with some part of your accomplishment? I'm sure you suffered for it. For example, while Chrissy's mother was hospitalized for minor surgery, to please her mother, Chrissy cleaned the house and made it spotless. When her mother returned, as Chrissy beamed nervously and expectantly with her eyes darting to and from the kitchen sink to her mother's eyes, her mother snapped her fingers and demanded an answer, "Where's the hand mixer?"

Chris was proud of herself as she responded, "I put it on the top shelf over there so we could have more space!"

Out of nowhere, Chrissy's mother burst into tears.

What's going on? wondered Chrissy. Like a good little girl, and in the same way a reader patiently waits to get to the last page of a mystery novel, Chrissy hovered around her mother. But Chrissy never found out "who done it." Her mother limped on her crutches back to the bedroom and slammed the door, leaving her desperate little daughter speechless and once again assuming blame for a victimless crime.

As an adult, Chris showed evidence of the impact of these kinds of experiences. She internalized a negative image. She felt compelled to seek approval from Mom and others for everything she did. Chrissy used to say, "But my mother always told me that no matter what, I should do good deeds for others!"

MARGARET

Did your mom overprotect you the way Margaret "protected" and clutched onto Krista? Then you didn't have an opportunity to take risks or make decisions and believe you were independent and strong. Even as an adult, you kept looking to others for the answers, always scared to make a mistake.

I don't know whether or not Krista suffered this fate, because while Margaret was in treatment with me, Krista did go off to college on her own. However, sometimes the effects of overprotection don't cripple a person until later on, say, after college or when a person gets married or gets into a significant relationship and gives decision-making power over to her mate or some other "worthy" person.

GEORGIANA

Georgiana's mother acknowledged her and even gave her space, but Georgiana never failed to pick up on how anxious Mom became when things didn't go the way Mom planned. So even though Mom gave Georgiana the leeway to be independent, maybe even forsook Georgiana because Mom took to her bed so often and Georgiana had no choice but to fend for herself, Georgiana absorbed the "perfection message" regardless. Georgiana developed a compulsion to be perfect as a way to protect herself from feeling out of control and to hold onto people around her whom she feared would go away if Georgiana didn't take the best care of them.

JENNY

When you have different attitudes or thoughts from Mom, do you become frightened, alone, and disconnected from her? If you give up your right to have independent thoughts in order to remain attached to Mother, then maybe you fear emotional separation from her. You can't change yourself until you work through this fear that by being yourself, you lose Mom. Sometimes the only thing that will bring you to inner peace is to cease from taking care of everyone else, including Mother, in preference to yourself.

In order to fully separate from Mom, first, you need to embrace her and appreciate how interwoven you both are. Then endeavor to differentiate yourself. In an attempt to become your own person, you may find yourself angry at her, but this is one stage of separation, and eventually you'll move on to accept her as having tried to be a "good" mom. It is you who will have to figure out how to live your own life and what to think and feel without her.

If your mother is still available, to make it easier on both of you, you may need to help your mom adjust by saying something similar to what Jenny, our bulimic young lady, eventually said to her mother: "Mom, I know you worry about me and you want to protect me, but it's your job to handle those feelings, and it's my job to figure out who I am."

It took a few years for Jenny to arrive at this emotionally independent place, but it was essential to her eventual relinquishing of her yes-no, in-out food behaviors. Give up Mom as your be-all-end-all, and become the person you were meant to be. Remember: having your own mind is not an aggressive act toward Mom. Knowing who you are and what you want is a right of passage for all human beings.

CHERYL

Cheryl used to protest, "I can't help it. I fought my mother all my life. Why would I start accepting her now?" In her case, she was using her early life experience as a rationale for blaming anyone who crossed her as if every person were her mother who was out to prove Cheryl wrong.

Very often, I reframed the misappropriation for her. "Your mother used to have power over you. You once felt small and vulnerable. You needed Mom. For her to be angry and possibly leave you was a devastating thought. But this is not the present day reality. Now she has no power over you. She is merely a person with whom you once lived." This statement fits under the rubric of my often-stated message, "Your mother doesn't live here anymore."

DICK

We're still talking about those early sequences of change and how you must either shake yourself up or have the upheaval foisted on you by someone else. If you happen to get "stuck" in the *denial phase*, let's say, unless I or someone else stirs things up, you could really cause harm to yourself. Take Dick, for example, the man who had chronic heart disease, the one whose funeral I attended. He was so frightened of death that he obviously couldn't stay overwhelmed as in the first stage. He had to pretend he wasn't sick at all! Sometimes, he ran up and down the steps in his house to the point of exhaustion. He did this under the guise of having chores to do or things he wanted to accomplish, but he and I both knew what was going on, at least, we knew this after he and I had met for a number of sessions and after Dick's wife complained unremittingly to him and to me.

I remember his steadfast gaze as he awaited my reaction to Alice's accusations. Almost as if to prove Alice right, whenever I went to the waiting room to invite him in, Dick was there striding to and fro as if in a race to cover the whole territory. He appeared to be tempting fate, or perhaps he was pretending he might not at any moment drop dead. I could see why Alice was so panicky about his every move. Dick had a sparkle to him. I think in general Alice's anxiety over the loss of him put a crimp in his spirit. At least in my office, he could play the "bad boy" and rebelliously deny the loss of that spirit.

Toward the end of our stint together, however, right around the time I told him about having to put my dog, Roxie, to sleep, he moved toward accepting reality. Then we were able to talk about how he wanted things to be after he died and who would take care of Alice. The hard part was over. His quality of life improved immensely once he allowed himself to flow with what was in store for him.

MARGARET

Margaret was definitely stuck in the *depression stage* for a long time. Even though she had consulted me along with her husband, Don (the guy who was having the affair), for couples therapy, the real work we did centered around her difficulty in moving out of a landscape of sighs and sleeplessness. She wasn't actually in denial. She knew her life wasn't turning out the way she had planned. She just was too pooped to do much about it. She knew she couldn't control Krista from leaving home. She didn't even have the energy to try to stop Krista.

The way I jostled Margaret out of depression was to help her get in touch with her anger about Krista's leaving her all alone to cope with Don's affair. Of course, since she felt so weak both physically and emotionally, she was a hard sell for me. In their own way, all my patients put up a good fight. I was persistent and so was Margaret. She never missed an appointment and took my prodding as an act of love. Much to her astonishment, she and I eventually arrived at the end of our therapeutic trail.

KEVIN

You could definitely say that Kevin's kicking the chair on which he was resting his broken foot was evidence of his *frustration*. When he yelled, "Phyliss, sometimes I just wish you would shut the hell up!" he simply wanted to escape what he dreaded—the reality that he was a man and a father and needed to take responsibility for his behavior. He also needed to grieve the loss of his son, Dirk, who had essentially rejected Kevin by not calling or visiting.

I had just been referring to an anecdote Kevin had shared with me months ago about how he had gotten pissed off at nine-year-old Dirk who had pestered Kevin to play ball. After Dirk's incessant pleas, Kevin lost his temper, and similar to the way he had presently kicked the chair out from under himself to emphasize his anger at me, he had picked up the dining table and turned it upside down, causing large holes to form in the ceiling.

Kevin wanted to relinquish Dirk's discipline to his wife, Darlene, but was forced to take on the role himself. He was wishy-washy and appeared apathetic about Dirk's development. From the day he poked giant holes in the dining room ceiling until the moment Dirk left home, whenever Kevin got angry at Dirk, in an attempt to control himself, he would glance at the ceiling to remind himself not to go haywire. However, Kevin learned later in one of Dirk's fits of rage that Dirk mistook this mannerism to be a message Kevin was sending to his son to stay clear lest you suffer the same fate as on that regretful occasion, which came to be known in the house as "the baseball incident."

So here I was, reminding Kevin of his shame and regret over this encounter with his son whom he adored. Kevin just didn't want to look at it. He didn't want to reach the painful place of accepting the reality of the impact he had had on his precious son. Aside from the four glorious years alongside his own father whose gigantic hands, dirty fingernails, slicked-down hair, and the ability to fix anything became like trophies to Kevin. Kevin had missed out from both ends—no father, no son. The closest he came was when someone would stop him in the street and say, "Aren't you Steve Herbert's boy?"

This was his greatest moment, to be associated with his daddy. Steve Herbert was a popular guy among men—a man's man. Kevin knew he could never match the impact his father had on people. "I'm like a little mouse sometimes," Kevin once told me in his clearer, more reality oriented sessions.

As seen with all patients who come for treatment, Kevin had his tricks of the therapy trade. At times, due to his need for bravado, he took great pains to disguise his sweet character, and if he saw the need, he could avert his emotions with alacrity. Kevin lived a private life within his own blustery nature, and he resided within this world while exhibiting a facial expression as if he were part of the conversation, but in reality, he was off somewhere in space.

For Kevin, unless he pushed through this frustration and his clash with the painful truth of his disappointing life, he was destined to bury himself in the mire of grief and regret. No wonder he flew off the handle at work! True, his outbursts had diminished immensely since his starting treatment. Instead of his displaying these symptoms to the outside world, he was showing me in our sessions what had been lurking deep inside of him before we ever met. He was about to face reality and look for new ways to cope with his life.

VICTOR

Now we're up to the part of change that has to do with *accepting the truth* of what is. Hmmm. Reality is not always a fun place to be. Yep, it can be liberating to stop the pretense, but nevertheless, facing it can be a real pain. Just ask Victor who, at the place where we peer into his therapy, was trying desperately to keep up a charade with his mom.

In Victor's case, I was more directive than I am with most. I urged him, "Victor, your mom knows. Didn't she find those photographs? Come on. You might as well get it over with. Talk to her. Tell her the painful truth. Clear the air between the two of you. You both know what's true. Why should both of you play make-believe games. You now accept your being gay. Isn't it time she does too? Unless you bring it up, you know she won't."

Boy, did I lay it on. I brought this up maybe six months before he probably would be ready for termination of treatment. The first time I broached it, ultimately, I elected to drop the topic, because he was too frightened of the consequences.

Wait. Allow me to step back for a moment to give a bit of history leading up to my intervention.

I asked Victor, "Did the feelings you had when your food prep teacher called attention to your serving plate remind you of how you felt when you read your mother's letters?" (I see that look in your eyes, dear Reader. You're right. Boy, do you learn fast. That was a close-ended question. So, sue me! I had my reasons!)

I was referring to the letters his mother wrote whenever he was away, the ones where she said, "I love you," and he felt it to be unnatural. For his mother to love him meant she might want sex with him. Sex with Mother or any woman meant getting hurt and being converted into a woman himself.

As if what he was thinking had nothing to do with our discussion at hand, Victor blurted, "I was afraid I'd be a momma's boy. I'm embarrassed to say it."

The choice of the word, "embarrassment" often indicates anxiety over sexual thoughts. Victor's use of the word was a confirmation of what I had surmised about his fear of sexual interaction with his mother…

In one session, Victor showed me a picture he painted as a house-warming gift for a friend. I commented, "It is soft, yet emotional, different from other work of yours."

I had moved over to the chair opposite Victor, the one he looked at longingly from time to time, the chair that, to him, had loomed empty. I pulled the chair over closer to where he was sitting. As we viewed the painting, we sat side by side. After I gave my comments, he looked at me. (Was he seeing me for the first time?) I thought I saw a glimmer of something new in his face and posture. A strange sensation overtook me—strange only because I'd never felt it with him before. I thought, *He's really a handsome man.*

Immediately, I took note of my inner response. I always learn so much from using myself as an instrument to learn about my patients (This is kind of a variation on the *internal camera method* I described earlier, the one that you can use to learn about the origin of a seemingly irrational or irrelevant feeling that pops up out of nowhere.) *Why now,* I thought, *am I noticing his physical attractiveness? What message is he sending me?* Now since he had returned to treatment, he experienced more centeredness and security, and he carried himself differently. And suddenly, I could more clearly see Victor as a strong, adult male. Periodically, I was catching glimpses of Victor's self-assurance. He had given up much of the haze that had once been his companion. I often view people as if they are in a photograph, painting, or cartoon. When they appreciate their uniqueness, their "lines" are more in focus, the picture of them is clearer, and the colors are more vibrant—you get to see their real beauty. I remembered back to our first meeting. We had come a long way, and this thought further enhanced the optimism I presently felt.

Almost as if he read my mind and wanted to impress me, without hesitation and in contrast to those first few years of treatment, Victor initiated the discussion.

"I'm mad at my boss for not letting me take off for the holidays."

"Why don't you discuss it with him?"

"I'm afraid to talk to him, because he might get mad."

"You use the word mad as if it's a rejection of you 'the whole person' rather than just one emotion your supervisor might feel toward you at any one moment." (I was helping Victor to accept other people's anger toward him as an emotion rather than as he seemed to experience it, as abandonment.)

He said, "I think I got it from growing up with my mother. When Mom is angry, she appears disgusted. It's the same dirty look she makes when she talks about homosexuals and other minority groups. It's a look of total rejection, as if gays were evil people…"

Almost two years after we had resumed therapy for the second time (his new lover at the time, Joe, had given him an ultimatum), Victor brought a videotape for me to borrow. It was a TV movie I had been unable to record on my own. He felt it was a very good portrayal of a young homosexual man who tells his parents he's gay. As painful as it was for all concerned, the outcome proved positive. Victor was jealous of the man who could confront his parents with the truth.

Shortly after we discussed the movie, Victor brought up the idea of ending therapy. He was feeling confident and relaxed. His relationship with his new lover, Joe, had changed; he was more assertive with Joe but no longer the openly rebellious adolescent he had been two years ago when he was with Tom.

I was directive for the second time in our therapy. "There's one more thing you need to do for your own sake and for the sake of your career."

I paused for effect. "You need to tell your mother about being gay."

I created this hiatus, because I expected a big reaction from him. Instead, he looked at me blankly. I couldn't read his face. It had the facade of a man who is peering out of a window, but there is nothing visible on which he can focus.

"You are holding back part of yourself for fear of being exposed, and therefore, you cannot be as creative as possible, because as long as you hold back one part of yourself, you will have to hold back everything. Restraining most of your thoughts is your way of trying to insure you won't inadvertently reveal your gay lifestyle. It's like holding your stomach tight in case you get punched there. If you're holding it together, all your energy goes to protecting yourself, and you can't think of anything else. If someone then punches you in the arm, you're completely unprepared and cannot come up with creative ways to defend yourself. In the same way, if you don't tell your parents you're gay, your efforts will go toward keeping the secret, and you won't be free to create new recipes or produce awarding winning food trays. I know you want to move on in your life, Victor. The time is now. You've acknowledged your lifestyle to your co-workers, and you are no longer ashamed. How about it?"

He liked the idea but didn't make a commitment. In many ways, he seemed too agreeable, sort of brushing off the recommendation.

He brought up some other issues in the next few sessions, but since he was so close to ending, I pressured Victor to set a date for when he would tell his parents he was gay.

"I remember when we talked about it last time, Phyliss. You said if I tell my parents, it would be like telling myself there really was no hope for me, that my homosexuality was irreversible. I remember how you said it. You said I was convinced I would be dogged by my homosexuality for the rest of my life. I knew that even though I had been gay for years, I still wanted to fight the obvious. And anyway, if I fully accept my homosexuality, then I have to accept that I'll never have a child. That is the worst of it."

This time around, he was more comfortable with his lifestyle; he had discussed it with his co-workers, and they all concluded he should tell his parents. He agreed to tell them the following Thursday.

He and I both had some scheduling difficulties, so we wouldn't be meeting for four weeks. I was looking forward to our next session because of his promise to talk to his parents. I was hopeful that as a result of this action, Victor would feel tranquil and secure, having finally confronted a seventeen-year, long-awaited challenge. Consequently, I was completely stunned when before our next scheduled appointment I received a call from Victor.

"Phyliss, I have to talk to you right away. Something has happened to me that has never happened to me before. I must speak to you right away..."

What he was to tell me was that he had made love to a woman, Aimee, a beautiful girl who had been his friend for years, with whom he had gone out and by the end of the evening, had found himself in bed with her! "It was so natural. I was just excited. I wasn't even scared. It was only *afterward* that my insides turned upside down!"

After he had talked to his parents, as Victor thought about it, he concluded that I kept urging him to tell his parents because I was noticing how much more positive he felt about myself.

Victor had been resistant at first. "I'm afraid of what my mother will say. I kept putting it off."

A few weeks after he revealed the truth about himself, when he and I were reviewing what had transpired, he said he was surprised at his reaction. "I knew I liked you, Phyliss, and I wanted to please you, but I was so afraid of my mother. I couldn't believe I'd risk my mother's rejection so as not to disappoint *you*! What I didn't realize then was that over time new feelings had been creeping up on me, emotions from deep inside. These new feelings were for you, my therapist."

You see how open Victor had become! Despite my urging patients to tell me everything on their minds and that I'm trained not to take things personally, rarely will they reveal feelings specifically about me.

Victor said, "I was surprised also, because just minutes before I committed myself that I would tell my mother, I had been very angry with you. To myself, I kept saying, 'You have no right to force me to reveal my secret to them.' I felt it was none of your business. You didn't have to face these people. You only had to sit in your big chair and direct me. The angrier I became, the more the blood pumped faster through my veins. 'Why is she making me do this?' I understood that I would probably be more comfortable after I told them, but maybe not. Maybe my parents would disown me and withdraw all their love from me. I felt that, in the long run, the decision to tell them would be beneficial, but it never seemed the right time. Without you, there probably never would've been a right time.

"I kept rehearsing a few things, and then I remember blurting out, 'Phyliss, you know she'll be upset. I can just picture that look of disgust on her face.' But you looked so sure of yourself. I remember the look on your face when you said, 'Come on, Victor, she already knows. She and you have just been trying to deny the reality of the situation. After all, she did see those pictures years ago.'"

I was reminiscing too. I said, "You blurted out, 'I'm scared. I'm shaking just thinking about it.'"

"But as much as I shivered, you wouldn't let up. You didn't seem worried about it. I was shaking, and you were like a statue, looking at me so intently. You had kind of a soft look too, though. It was when you leaned forward, the way you always do, and rested your face on your hands. Then you smiled and said, 'I'll bet your mother won't even look visibly upset. I bet she changes the subject.' Then I told you maybe you're right. I had never told you until that day about this sick feeling inside I always used to get when I thought of her being disgusted with me.

"Then, Phyliss, you said, 'You'll have to be assertive and persistent. Just keep bringing her back to the topic and explain to your parents how important it is to you that you not have the secret anymore.'"

Victor was demonstrating how accepting and embracing the truth can bring you to new heights. So what happened after he told his parents he was gay and subsequently made love to Aimee? The proximity of the two events was more than a coincidence; I'm convinced. I'll tell you more about how we put the pieces together as to why his telling his mother then gave him impetus to allow himself to love a woman.

Sometime soon after Victor told me he had made love to Aimee, he compared lovemaking between gays to lovemaking between heterosexuals. He said that he was able to have multiple orgasms with Aimee but never had been able to do that with men. He had always had trouble climaxing from oral sex with men but had no trouble with Aimee. He said that for the past year, whenever Joe was away, he rented heterosexual movies. At the time, he told himself the men were more attractive in the heterosexual movies and the only reason he wanted the movies was to look at the men. He now realized that he was actually identifying with the men as they made love to the women.

"I've let people manipulate me into doing what they wanted me to do." Victor was relating this to how he first began to engage in gay behaviors in the first place. Each time he dated a young woman in high school, the "real fun would begin" after he took her home, when he went to gay bars.

(He always had the feeling he had somehow been manipulated into this lifestyle. Starting way back from the first time his mom put makeup on him to see how her new face powder would look, to the times when the kids called him "Pretty Victoria" to his father's keeping Victor's gay magazines, which Victor interpreted as his father's possible interest in men, to his own internal feelings that he was defective.)

"Last week, on the way home from the session, I cried. I was so happy. I thought about where I've come from and where I am now."

We talked about the factors that had affected his change. I proposed the following: when Victor told his mother about his being gay, she accepted him, nevertheless. She had always been prejudiced against gays, and he previously feared her rejection of him. Now he felt better about himself. Also, since he had the irrational fear that his mother might have incestuous feelings toward him, he felt safe being gay, because then she might "curtail" those unnatural feelings toward him. Once she accepted him as a gay person, he reasoned, he could allow himself to love her without fearing she would act on her feelings. This would free him to love other women. Also, remember his feelings toward me, another woman in his life, played a part in releasing him from his fear of females.

One big change after Victor's transformation revolved around his gaining perspective on his mother's true feelings for him. As soon as Victor told his mother about his change, "She hugged me, and it felt different. I wasn't threatened. Then she put her hand on my hair. At first she said, 'It'll be all right.' Then she said something odd like, "We'll have to do something about your hair!'" She was referring to his pony tail.

Victor pulled away and said, "Leave my hair alone." Victor was reacting to his mother in the same way he had been behaving at work. No longer worried about pleasing everyone just to be able to fit in, Victor didn't tolerate people's mistreating him.

In subsequent sessions, we started putting more things together. Victor said, "After I told my mother about being gay, I felt released, and I wasn't afraid of women anymore… I think I became gay to get even. First of all, my mother was disgusted by gays. My father wouldn't do anything to stop my mother from being prejudiced or from emasculating me. Neither of my parents knew how to raise a child. You know, I rarely laughed with my father, and you can see how I love to laugh. He'd tickle my sister but not me. From my time here in therapy, I realize my being gay was also a way to act out what I thought were my father's wishes. I took my cues from the idea that he had those magazines, that he was afraid to touch me, that he allowed me to play with dolls—all that stuff."

"Victor, do you think you sought other men as a father substitute?"

"I always had lovers who were older, who made more money than I did." I think this statement was Victor's way of saying, "Yes, maybe."

Why am I talking so much about Victor? It's because when I talk about the change process, I can't think of anyone whose story exposes the process more than Victor's. As Victor put it, "I feel like I've lived my whole life here in this office. I went from a small child to an adult, and I did it with you."

We've talked about his accepting reality and then moving on. Now that he had made the change, he entered reluctantly into trying out his newfound image of himself. The night after he made love to Aimee, he went to a gay bar. It was as if he were trying to see what it was like now that he had broken through the barrier of his fear of women. Since his live-in lover, Joe, was away, he drove home with a guy he picked up at the bar. Whenever Joe was away, Victor did this just as he had done with Tom and any other short-term boyfriend. But on the night of which we speak, he was befuddled. He had just made love to a woman. What was he doing back into his old tricks?

He told me, "The next morning, I was so shook up, more than ever in my whole life. I had to nurse a hangover and try to put my actions into perspective. This was a turning point in my life. I had absolutely no idea Aimee was going to enter my life. I just wanted to check myself out. Was it true I wasn't gay anymore? How was I supposed to act now? You know what I mean. Could the impossible really happen to me?" He felt trapped, as if he were in a cage and the door would open only if he pushed on it hard and fast.

The next time he was with Aimee, he had to constantly remind himself that he wasn't dreaming. He kept wondering why Aimee would be so attracted to him.

"The first few times Aimee and I were together, I actually felt taller, as if I grew overnight. I was so proud and happy to be with her. I was dizzy. I could finally go out in public and be proud of myself without having to hide anything."

However, his new label "heterosexual" was overwhelming to him. His inestimable life ahead was presently a mystery to him.

He was overjoyed, yet he felt shook up. He kept asking himself, "Who am I really? Why am I so sad at a time when I also feel elated? Can I hold onto Aimee, or will I wake up from a dream and find myself alone? What about Joe? I hurt him. I still care about him."

So Victor went from the acceptance of his inevitable change (*acceptance of reality*) to experimenting with his new identity (*testing*) then way back to the first stage of being shook up and *overwhelmed*. His heart never stopped pounding; his stomach did constant flip-flops; he had bouts of spontaneous crying; sometimes he laughed aloud for no apparent reason. He felt a little crazy. It was very scary.

Part of him wanted the old Victor back so he could feel integrated again. At the same time, he was elated, high, joyful. He didn't have enough words to describe a feeling so new to him. He told me how his face was sometimes sore from grinning.

So two weeks after he first slept with Aimee, he called me. Through his sobs, he finally got the whole story all out. Even though he was overjoyed, having woken up from a dream of being cursed and stuck in a lonely, isolated life of searching for the right man, he felt raw and exposed. He was lost. Where was the old Victor, the one who mechanically knew the correct behavior and emotions?

Proudly, and through torrents of emotion, he said, "Oh my Aimee, my beautiful Aimee was the woman who has changed my life... And, Phyliss, it is my greatest joy to share this moment with you!

"Oh you should meet her, Phyliss. She asks me questions the way you do. We talk for hours... Why can't I stop crying? I'm so happy. I feel silly crying. I'm scared. Joe, what will Joe do? I didn't mean to hurt him. I tried to love him. You know it, right, Phyliss?"

"Yes, Victor, I do know it!"

"What do you think he'll say?"

"I'm sure he'll feel hurt and angry, and it will take a long time to get over losing you."

"I wish I could do something about it! I cry so much lately. I'm so mixed up. She's taken me over somehow. I like it. But it's so new. To love a woman. I can even be a father... Oh my, I thought it would never happen."

The tears were rolling freely down his cheeks. I smiled when he smiled and became neutral with my head to one side in my listening pose when he told me of his fears about Joe's reaction.

Our time was almost over. He looked pleadingly at me.

I said, "Victor, if you need me, please feel free to call. This is a major change in your life, and it takes time to work through changes. Sometimes you need to check in with someone else. Remember: I'm here."

"Thanks...should I be there when Joe gets home?"

"I think you can handle yourself, Victor. You're strong. You don't have to allow Joe to hurt you, and also you can be respectful of Joe's feelings."

"Phyliss, that feels right."

He cried some more. He got up to leave. As I gulped down my words, I'm sure he heard me say, "Hang in there, Victor."

Quietly, he said, "Thanks for being there, Phyliss."

You see how change can make you so crazy you start going back to carry out old behaviors just to return to the status quo? For months after this visit, we worked on how it would be now that Victor had joined the straight life. He was like a little kid in a strange theatre, and he wanted to be taught how to behave. We had to take it slowly...

Victor said he still hadn't talked to his father about their way of expressing affection with each other. Frustrated, his mouth tight, Victor said, "I wanted to say to my father, 'If only you would have touched me when I was growing up, maybe I wouldn't have been gay.'" He paused. His face brightened. "You know, I've been thinking. I'm so happy now, and I realize I've gone through a lot.

But suppose my father had touched me. Maybe I would've been straight, and maybe then I would've married and cheated on my wife the way so many men do. You know, of all the men I've been with, I bet at least half of them are married. I could have been one of them. I might have been unhappy. Even though it's been terrible for me, maybe all the events leading up to my present life had to happen for me to be where I am now, and I wouldn't give up this happiness for anything. Besides, I really don't want to blame my father."

"Victor, maybe you do blame your father and you're afraid to acknowledge it."

"Well, lately I have been having angry thoughts, but I've been trying to pretend they're not there."

Victor's turmoil provided the momentum for him to reexamine his relationship with his father, an endeavor that terrified him. At the same time, he was trying to gain control by searching for and assigning positive meaning to his life history.

Stay tuned. I'll bring Victor back to you soon.

AGNES

We need our tension and anxiety to spur us to new heights. Agnes searched for answers as to why she had been struck down by a disease hardly anyone ever heard of. After the session where she decorated her walker and subsequent to it, she told me she now loved this helpful aluminum companion. It was essential to her getting around. She had fun telling me about ways in which her newfound attitude was facilitating her adventures in the outside world. In fact, she kept the decorations on for months. Gradually each visit, her walker had shed more and more of the crepe paper and pom-poms. We joked about it every chance we got until one day, there was one little piece of scotch tape remaining that hadn't gotten wet in the rain. At this point, she had begun to pursue new activities and make more friends.

Agnes needed to move on. Her need sharpened up her problem-solving juices, and she found a solution. The way she moved, even though slowly and methodically, I imagined her as a large, graceful bird scudding across a vast lake just skimming the mirrored surface so as not to get wet.

After a while, she decided to volunteer at the library to be a storyteller. As the children snuggled onto her lap, she imagined her heart turning to liquid as if it could shed big red droplets of joyful tears. Here was something that brought value to others; she could sit while doing it; she could enhance herself by getting out into the world and by connecting with children.

One day, she said, "If this disease hadn't come along, maybe I wouldn't have been able to give so much to children. Now that I have the problem, I might as well do what I can with it."

Her verbalization is a perfect example of the concept of validating newly recognized realities by trying to figure out why you consciously or unconsciously change.

Now we're ready to look at internalization. We'll get to this in a little bit of a roundabout way, but we'll get there. Human beings will do almost anything not to feel anxious or scared. Many suffer from what I call "The Perils of Positive Thinking."

SARAH

Sarah, the woman who found out she had breast cancer and kind of left me out of the loop for a while, who later had a mastectomy and tried to "think" herself well, through bright, salty eyes verbalized her wishful stance often enough for me to remember. The way I rephrased it for her was as follows: "Mind over body. Fight the disease. Don't let it break you. Think positive thoughts, and you can control the poisons that threaten your body. Keep your thoughts straight, and your mind will heal you."

Sorry, Sarah, I don't buy it! If you subscribe to this form of thinking, then you subscribe to a system of false control: as long as you control what's in your mind, all will be well. However, the idea that "I'll think myself well" can betray you and turn into, "I'm not strong enough," or, "I don't have enough faith," or, "I'm bad." As long as you are on the positive side, when, for example, you go into remission from chemotherapy, you feel powerful and "right." But when your disease spontaneously returns, you feel weak, inadequate, ashamed, and responsible for having caused more bad things to happen to you.

The same is true when you try to "think" yourself out of your feelings. You talk yourself out of sadness, anger, doubt, jealousy. But if you haven't truly worked through the feelings and you've been putting up a false front to yourself and others, your unresolved issues are likely to express themselves in other ways through headaches, stomach aches, high blood pressure, depression, anxiety, general discontent, and the like.

In addition, this self-protective, automaton stance of "thinking rather than feeling" may be isolating, because it distances you from others. Somehow, people get the message, "Stay away!" Or at least they figure, "Don't get into too many topics beyond the superficial stuff with Sarah. She doesn't like to get too deep."

Yes, "deep" would mean getting too close to Sarah's depression and anxiety. No one would want to hurt her. Besides, most human beings are more than willing to comply with anything that means escaping other people's painful emotions, feelings which are too close to their own discomfort. Most people would prefer the din of emotional neutrality.

This is why I had to crack through Sarah's denial and join with her on safe but scary terrain. She just couldn't see how her anxiety, which she thought "came from nowhere," emerged from her feelings about her cancer. She saw these feelings as "bad." Sarah's mommy had told Sarah it was silly to be afraid. You were supposed to trust your mommy to take care of you; then nothing would ever go wrong. If something did go awry, it was because you weren't listening to your mommy.

I've been on a soapbox for years about this idea of self-robotic control over cancer. I once got so incensed over a TV show called *ER*, which I felt was promoting the idea of being positive or you die, that I wrote a letter to the editor of our local newspaper so at least my neighbors who might have watched the show would be spared of possibly going along with this upbeat-at-all-costs myth.

You know, not everything you see on television is true. Sometimes situations as depicted on TV influence the way we deal with our own lives. I find it troubling when ideas are promoted that are misleading but viewers may take as truth.

On *ER* I was disturbed by the way Dr. Elisabeth Corday reacted to Dr. Mark Green's use of dark humor over his recent diagnosis of terminal brain cancer. These conversations occurred as they waited to see a specialist who might be able to save him. At the time of this episode, I was too shaken to record Green's exact words, but he joked about his demise as being inevitable. Furious, Corday yelled something like this: "Mark, you and I are doctors. You know what we've seen, and you absolutely must not talk like that if you want to get well. You know the people who get well are the ones who are positive about their illness."

Mark Green retorted, "I thought joking was a healthy way to cope with it!" But then he quickly apologized as if he had actually done something wrong, and due to his grave error, he might just die on the spot!

I was so annoyed with this travesty; I threw paper balls at the screen. I yelled, "Get off it! Stop making everyone who gets cancer feel like criminals!" I remonstrated these make-believe TV heroes even before I was diagnosed with cancer years ago, so it wasn't just a personalized thing with me.

Isn't this incriminating message to cancer patients similar to a raped victim's plight? She not only suffers the shame of the uninvited intrusion; now we say she's the one who led him on? Come on. Get real. Unfortunately, whether we like it or not, things are impinged on us from outside our realm of authority, and we are not at fault.

Of course, given your cross to bear, you want to try to protect yourself from the psychological crush to your psyche, and it's true the more positive your outlook, the better chance you'll comply with your treatment recommendations. You'll help those around you to cope better as well. You'll feel better. Why not? But face it: you're a human being. You need a way to be honest with yourself and release your sad, hurting, and even angry feelings, or you will indeed suffer more—and alone. Suffering alone is not very humanistic, wouldn't you say?

May we please allow afflicted people to deal with their feelings about a catastrophe without their having to artificially reverse themselves, turn their minds inside out, and twist their distress into lovely floral designs on contrived landscapes just for our sakes? While we're at it, they shouldn't have to feel guilty besides.

Here's another fallacious way of coping with problems: people refer to the positive word "courageous." You hear this a lot when the media reports on a movie star's being diagnosed with cancer. These artificial heroes are our role models. Why can't we see them cry? They would be doing us a greater service.

People usually think of "courageous" as a word that means brave and tough, or "I'm not going to take this anymore!" Courageous may also mean allowing loved ones to be there for you when you are hurting, sharing your fears about your own death, verbalizing your anger that this had to happen to you, crying, leaning on others, reaching out, sharing. If you believe the only "right way" to deal with feelings is the positive-thinking kind of courageous as opposed to the more difficult "sharing your feelings" courageous, then you further the idea that any response which is not positive is weak, non-courageous, and might cause more bad things to happen to you.

If you're trying so hard to be "courageous," then you miss your chance to discharge your fears, anger, and regret. By sharing these emotions with others, be it through humor or direct expression of doubts, you allow loved ones to be there for you when you are hurting.

Some of you have taken the valiant approach of feeling your feelings rather than "fighting" them. You are not weak. You are doing your best to cope with uncontrollable circumstances of day-to-day living. And you have as much of a chance as anyone to get well.

SARAH

Sarah did go through many of the stages we've discussed. Once, she loosened her stiff upper lip, and she broke down hysterically as she lamented the loss of her breast. She felt unattractive to her husband who, in reality, was being very supportive. She claimed she was marred for life and her life wasn't even worth saving. Through trills of tears, Sarah faced her terror over dying, her shame over disfigurement, and her grief over the loss of her old carefree life.

But as it is with people who hang in there and don't give up on therapy, themselves, or me, Sarah did internalize a change in attitude about her body. Here's how it finally became evident to me. From the beginning, Sarah had always complained about the rubber tree plant in my waiting room. She said it bothered her; it was always tilted and appeared deformed. (I'm really bad about taking care of plants. My botanical skills are definitely lacking.)

Toward the end of her therapy, I predicted (to myself) that we were close to termination when in one session, she declared, "Today, the plant didn't look misshapen. Today, I realized that it's just a tilted plant!"

She later was able to say that she was no longer a defective woman with a missing breast. Just as the plant that used to be deformed and now had a uniqueness about it, so Sarah now saw herself as a one-breasted woman.

She had redefined herself. She had internalized a change in self-perception.

Whether change comes because your natural internal ripening process says, "Give it up already!" or because bad news or tragedy slaps you in the face and says, "You've got no choice, buster. You've got to deal with this," ultimately, you are compelled to adjust in a sane way. Or, yep, what else is there to do? Go nuts? Most people manage by taking a reasonable approach, but haven't we all considered taking escape routes whenever feasible?

You work your guts out to feel okay about a not-so-okay situation, and you notice that as you change the other significant people in your life, the ones with whom you have had the most conflict, are changing too!

Incredulously, Jenny one day elaborated on how her mother had become more understanding. It reminded me of when Margaret had said her husband was being more loving lately. Earlier, you and I talked about how Victor's transformation of his feelings about himself was probably responsible for the fact that his father finally gave up his aloof stance and affectionately touched Victor by massaging Victor's shoulders in the same way Father interacted with other friends and family members.

I'll quote Agnes now, but she wasn't the first nor the last person to say, "Since I began coming here, it seems that my parents have changed. What a coincidence!"

I playfully retorted, "Yes, isn't it fascinating? You go into therapy and do all this work while everyone else, who has done nothing of the kind, is making all the changes!"

Although your loved ones often initially protest and might even sabotage your transformation, invariably they accommodate to the new you, and their own modifications in reaction to you are usually favorable.

Also, relating back to our discussion of hearing your parents' imaginary whispers and no-no's in your ear, when you figure out who you are as a distinct, separately functioning individual with your very own needs, wishes, idiosyncrasies, as well as rights to breathe the air and think your thoughts, your life gets brighter, and other people treat you differently.

I remember fondly when Kevin said, "It's a funny thing how I've hardly changed, but everyone around me seems to be different. Maybe they're all in therapy!"

In some ways it's almost true that without initiating therapy, those around you modify their behavior as if you were their therapist. In any event, you definitely become their change agent, because your change creates a need in them to accommodate to your alteration. This need produces tension in them. You know what tension does to you? That's right. It motivates you to change.

When you are motivated to change, now you regress backward to an earlier way of coping. (I know this is starting to sound repetitive, but it's a good review.)

Think of how a child, who had already given up sucking her thumb, starts to suck her thumb again as soon as a new baby comes into the household. Look at how Victor changed because he made love to one female in a sea of frightening women. Yet, due to engaging in a shift in his usual practice, he regressed to his old place of going to gay bars for a quick trick.

You accommodate to the change by making some kind of adjustment to the stress or threat. For example: you deny feelings, fight, compromise, avoid, spend money, smooth things over, eat too much, abuse drugs, yell at innocent loved ones, rationalize, make jokes, cry, reach out to loved ones, and the like.

Then you integrate or get to the point where the crisis actually *feels* different from the way it felt the first time. For example: you are devastated by divorce. Eventually you make a new life for yourself, settle down, and are able to move on.

In order for the process of healing and accommodation to work, you need to strike a balance between active striving and passive "letting it be." Put it this way: does it help to brace yourself against the cold? Isn't it easier to tolerate the blustery cold air when you relax your muscles and take in stride what comes your way? Or what if you hold on tightly to the arms of the dentist chair? Are you actually helping the dentist to do his work? If you fight pain and stress, then the outside stressor regulates you rather than your taking charge of it!

Risk taking is a part of self-actualization. The only way you grow is by stretching yourself. One of the anonymous sayings I have posted on my waiting room wall is: "A ship that stays in the harbor is safe, but ships were not made for that purpose."

Sometimes I see change in therapy as a person's needing to submit to the change. Just before the final stage, you establish a last holdout of old habits or behaviors before giving yourself over to the new behavior. Just before my children developed a new skill, they would be very cranky. They appeared to be exhibiting an internal battle, like a tantrum, so as not to move on to the next stage of growth. The next day, they might, for example, take their first step.

I have observed in patients that change is about to take place just at the point where they say, "I can't take this therapy anymore! It's making things worse, not better!" Very soon after this declaration, a new behavior or attitude emerges, one they had been unconsciously resisting.

HARRY

Even though Harry and I shared a lot of amusement yukkng it up over his neurosis, there came a day when he had had it. "I think

I'm done," he announced one day at the end of a session just as he was walking out.

Patients will often do this. They fear my response about something they are thinking and wish to avoid. So what do they do? They save it to the very end, when I won't have time to question them. They make their declaration and then they hit-and-run.

Anyway, Harry wanted out. Of course, I had no inkling, because lately we had been moving by leaps and bounds. Sometimes I do get fooled. From my perspective, I'm here to help people change. I forget that their change is something they dread. They want to feel better, but they don't necessarily want to do it if it means venturing into new territory.

To his pronouncement on the other side of the doorway, Harry added, "This will be the last session."

Oh boy. Delicacy here, Phyliss. You don't want to plead with the guy. You've been here before with premature enders. "How about coming in one more time to talk about it? In therapy we don't make sudden decisions without talking about it first. Besides, endings are wonderful. We learn so much—even as we say good-bye." I sensed that Harry was afraid of just such a situation, saying good-bye to me.

However, I think Harry was just waiting for me to say this, to rope him back in for one last time. How would he know that I cared if I didn't stick my neck out and ask him to come back?

"Okay, I'll be back on Wednesday, but that's it."

Phew! A reprieve from the chance he would have missed out on all we were yet to accomplish!

Harry returned for his regularly scheduled appointment the following week. If he had had his way, he probably wouldn't have brought up the topic of his termination, or if he did, it probably would have again been at the last minute. I didn't wait to find out. I brought up the issue as soon as Harry sat down.

"So, Harry, you mentioned you wanted to end therapy."

As if I had pushed a button on an electronic toy, Harry blurted out, "Look, I'm finished. Sally is happy with me as I am. I'm tired of this. It's taking up too much of my time."

"Therapy does take a lot of time. That's true. But Harry, it still won't hurt to talk about it."

"Okay." He seemed to comply more for my approbation than because he heeded my words.

I asked, "If it weren't for the money for therapy and the time, what else would stop you from continuing therapy?"

Harry didn't miss a beat. "Look, I'm getting too analytical. All I ever do is question why this and why that. Why do I feel this way? Why did Sally say that? I'm turning into *you*, Phyliss. I want my old self back. I used to be a happy-go-lucky guy. Nothing ever bothered me. My friends are asking me what's wrong. I'm not the fun guy I used to be." He took out a tissue from his pocket (rather than from my box, I observed) and dabbed at the beads of perspiration beginning to form on his upper lip.

I pursued his concern. "What will happen if you continue changing and become more analytical?"

As we continued this research into Harry's seeming impulsive wish to end his therapy, we determined that Harry was afraid of what he had turned out to be.

"Sally's starting to expect me to listen to her now. After dinner, she turns on the teakettle, puts out the tea bags and the sugar bowl, and sits down as if I should now be with her for the rest of the night. This is getting ridiculous."

"You don't like to sit with her after dinner?"

"Actually, it's been interesting, and I find it softens her up for sex later on, something she used to avoid." He paused contemplatively. "If my buddies from back home could see me now, they'd be ripping me to shreds for what I've become."

"And what have you become, Harry?"

"A wus!"

"It sounds like you are not so much upset with how you've essentially changed as much as you are disturbed by what other guys would think about you now. I think also you're old self would never have approved of a guy like this. Your old self would have laughed at a guy who spent time with his wife, talked to her, and had tea and crumpets together."

"I don't know. Sally's being so affectionate with me. I'm not used to it."

"Sounds like you're shook up about it?"

The features on Harry's face seemed to droop all at once. The color drained from his skin almost instantly. I had never before seen such a rapid and unpredictable makeover of someone's face in such a short time.

"I kind of feel guilty about this, but last week, just before our session, I saw something Sally had written on an e-mail. Listen, I don't snoop around and read her mail or anything, but it was right on the screen when she left the house. I caught a few words, mainly my name, so I couldn't help myself. I wanted to see what she was saying about me. I even printed it out." Harry stopped to study my face, which I'm sure had remained motionless. "I have it with me. I've been carrying it around since last week, so I forget what it really said, because I haven't looked at it since then."

"Let's look at it together," I suggested.

He was quick to comply with my request. I think he needed my company as he looked at it a second time. He pulled it out of the photo section of his wallet. It was crumpled and folded many times as if he had been trying to make it as small as possible. Therefore, it took a while for him to unfold it and get it into a readable position. He reached out and handed to me.

"Why don't you read it to me?" I said.

When patients bring things they've written or articles that are meaningful to them and when they want to share it with me, I frequently ask them to read it to me. I want to hear their inflection. I'll not only glean the words but which ideas are the important ones for them. It's similar to my not wanting to make assumptions about what people say; therefore I ask all those questions. After they read it, I usually like to look at it myself, because I am a visual more than an auditory person. Being a writer, I like to actually *see* the words.

As is true with other patients, Harry implored me to read the e-mail rather than his reading it aloud. I complied and figured we would look into why he resisted his own recitation of it later on. Here is what I read out loud to Harry. It was an e-mail to her friend Peg, the one who had fixed them up on a blind date when they were both working in New York.

> Peg, you'll never guess what! Ever since Harry and I started therapy, he has really changed. He's still a funny guy, thank goodness that didn't change, but he really listens to me now!!!!!! He even tells me things that are bothering him at work. I can't believe it!!!!! It was the best thing we ever did, going into therapy. He even sees the therapist, her name is Phyliss, on his own!! Harry?!!! Do you believe it? Of all people. This is the best thing I ever did for us. It was hard getting him to go. I'm really patting myself on the back for how I pushed him into it. I told him I wanted him to come to a session and tell Phyliss all about me because Phyliss wanted to meet him. He came to the first session and made jokes the whole time, but at least he showed up! It's been all up hill from there.

Apparently there was more to be written, because there were a few more sentences with news about Sally's mother's Alzheimer's condition, and then it sort of broke off in midsentence. Sally was obviously planning to return to the computer, complete the letter, and send it off.

After I finished reading it, I looked up at Harry, whose eyes had widened expectantly. When I didn't comment beyond what I had read, with his lip quivering almost imperceptibly, he said, "She thinks she can cut off my balls like that, huh?"

I asked him to talk about any feelings he may have toward me about my part in his attending the first session at Sally's and my behest and any suspicions he might have about my being in cahoots to try to get him to change (emasculate him). He had difficulty with this, so I didn't push it. I knew I would have us revisit the topic later.

We went further into his anger over his belief she had intentionally tried to castrate him by manipulating him into becoming what she wanted him to be. Then I went into a soliloquy to reveal to him what I was thinking about the letter she wrote and his subsequent need to end therapy.

"I think it would be a good idea for you to tell Sally what you saw in her letter and how you felt about it. We can do that in here if you'd like, or maybe you can talk to her after dinner tonight. But I'd like to tell you my take on what has happened here."

In preparation for my proclamations, Harry readjusted himself by pressing down on his hands as if he were going to spring out of the upholstered chair in which he had wedged himself. He peered down at his feet, wrung his hands and in slow motion, he lifted his head to help his eyes meet mine. His flushed face burned as if he had just been intimate with Sally and the perspiration continued to flow like a leaky and rusty pipe.

"Because you changed into a gentler, more compassionate support for Sally, she was impacted by your new behavior, and this gave her the impetus to change accordingly. Remember when she used to complain that you never listened to her? You just made jokes when she was trying to be serious? Then she went through the phase of noticing you were different, but she kind of doubted you. I remember one time when I asked her how she felt about the new Harry, and she said she wasn't sure. She had wanted you to soften up, and now that you were able to share your feelings with her, even cry with her, she got kind of scared you weren't her big strong he-man any more. She acknowledged the impact your change was having on her. That was very open and vulnerable of her to share with us. Because of it, she eventually acclimated to your new behavior, and it sounds from what you're describing that she not only adjusted to the new you, she really likes you this way."

"She does like me this way. She tells me all the time."

"So what's the problem, Harry? Is it what other people will say about her having power over you to make you change? No one can make another person change. You can't control others. You can only take charge of yourself. Would you give up how much better you feel, how much more fulfilling your relationship with Sally is so you can say to yourself and others, 'Oh no, I didn't let Sally change me. I'm impervious to her demands on me'?"

"Okay, Phyliss, I see your point."

I'd say Harry was conflicted. He had a half smile, half grimace on his face.

"I think I have to think about all this."

"Sounds good to me," I said as I leaned forward and slowly raised myself up from my chair.

Harry knew this as the signal that our time was up. Pensively, he walked slowly to the door as if he had more to say but didn't know quite what it was. He kind of slipped in a "good-bye" and walked out. I didn't even say anything such as, "See you next week." I knew he would be back, and someday soon, we would finish what we had set out to do.

What have we learned from all this talk about change? Here is my take on the whole topic. You know I don't give advice too often, so take heed. First of all:

Use anxiety (or other feelings) as an energizer to motivate you to find new ways to cope, to stretch yourself into new behaviors, attitudes, and actions that are more satisfying than your old ways of managing your life.

Don't take action merely for the sake of anxiety reduction. Then you never have the opportunity to work through the problem. You need anxiety to motivate you to understand what makes you "tick." Jumping into action relieves you temporarily. Because the anxiety is dormant for the moment, you don't have the anxiety available to you to help you learn about and permanently work through the problem.

For example: let's say you feel depressed because you're getting older and you haven't even come close to the goals you set for yourself years ago. The action that has always helped you to feel better in the past is buying something very special. You are not exactly aware as to why you have this overwhelming need to buy a new car, but suddenly, you find yourself rationalizing all the reasons why it would be the best action at this time. So you buy the car.

For a week or so, you feel exhilarated, showing your new purchase to your friends and finding reasons to go on errands. But then, slowly, the depressed feeling creeps back in. Now your original anxiety and depression return to your consciousness. You have more anxiety because you've strained your budget. You aren't any closer to understanding why you impulsively went out to buy the car, and because you don't understand what was underneath the urge to ward off your depressive episodes, the next time you are depressed, you will probably do something similar. You need to resolve the original reason for the anxiety, or you will find yourself repeating the same destructive actions again and again without knowing why.

Embrace the anxiety. Shake hands with anxiety. "Hi there. Here you are again, my old friend!" Compare your nervousness to a fever. A fever is necessary. Think of your disquiet as a fever designed to raise the blood temperature so the germs are burned out. Look at coping with change as an *actively passive approach.* Just knowing what occurs in the change process can be helpful. Allow it to happen. Allow the natural process to take you over. Don't fight it, but be very attentive to it and aware.

When people feel anxious or depressed, they often ask, "What should I do?" As it turns out, the answer sometimes is, "Do nothing." In other words, actively decide to be passive. Don't be passive by default.

People are naturally resilient. You may say that if you were in the same situation as someone you know who just heard bad news, you'd never be able to handle it, but the reality is, if you have to deal with it, you will. I remember a holocaust survivor friend of mine who questioned, "Why do people treat me like a hero? I did what I had to do. I stole food like everyone else!"

Time heals all wounds. This saying is trite but true; you need time to incorporate, internalize, and confirm for yourself, "See I've changed." You need time to adjust to the "new me."

Be wary of the fantasy that when you grow up it's supposed to get better. Who said you weren't going to confront crisis and change and that when you grew up all would be well? Life isn't always fair; no one said it had to be. The emphasis has to be not so much on growing up but on learning strategies to deal with crisis, growth, and change.

Make coping with change a challenge rather than a crisis. Stress can be used for your benefit. You can learn to transmute change into energy. As you work with stress, you force it into a new identity, a new shape. It is a clash between who you were and who you want to be. Life cycles are like cocoons within each of us. From inside, eventual stress builds up and grows, and a butterfly emerges.

Okay, that does it for now. We came back full circle from your own change to how your change affects someone else, which in turn affects you. This is how you grow. I'll conclude this part of our conversation with a poem I wrote back in 1976.

GROWING PAINS

Sometimes, I hurt so badly,
I think I'll never make it through—
Another day.
Sometimes, the world seems right,
And I wonder when the bad part was:
Yesterday or tomorrow.
Sometimes, I feel myself changing,
And then I wonder if I'm still me—
Wanting to meet myself again.
Sometimes, I question my life,
Then I get frightened again—
Wanting to be saved.
Sometimes, I feel my aloneness,
And I shiver coldly—
Waiting for my death.
Sometimes, I feel joyous oneness,
With others around me:
I savor the encounter.
In my life are many sometimes moments.
I feel myself—as a friend:
A friend of me.
Maybe, I'll make it to the end.
I'll be all grown up someday—
Sometimes I am.

SAYING GOOD-BYE

Oh no! We're finally here at the end of our conversation. Time to say good-bye to each other. Yep, you, my friend in the stuffed chair across from me in the living room by the fireplace, and I. Remember how we started way back on page one?

As with all beginnings, I knew when I started the finality of yours and my relationship would come to pass, and we would have to say good-bye but carry each other within ourselves forever. Yes, I knew this, but I courageously embarked on our adventure in any case for the pure joy of it, and I set aside my eager apprehension of the heart-wrenching sensation I would feel at our termination.

It looks as if I'm in the same mess I get into with my patients. When people share themselves with me as my patients do, handing over their souls to me, and when they trust me with their precious spirit, how do I then say farewell, have a good life, and may we never meet again? Why can't we be friends?

Boundaries, boundaries, and more boundaries. That's the name of the game—or should I say, the name of my emotive, but sometimes stirringly difficult profession. What in the world is a person like me doing in a field of practice where you say good-bye almost before you say hello, where you fall in love while preparing to boot someone out the door—nevermore, nevermore?

Your and my conversation has been a slow dissection and reconstruction of my life. You had to learn about me the way I've learned about my patients, in dribs and drabs, piece by piece, like little dots on a printer that join together in various patterns to form a person's life.

The people I've presented here in our conversation are every day persons like you and me who developed ways to deal with their early hurts, and when they reached adulthood, they didn't readjust flexibly to their new world. Without having their families available to dictate by example how to cope, they had trouble finding their own way.

These were the ones who came to me (and you) as perfect strangers. The more you have understood what makes them tick on the inside, the more you've grown to love them. How could you not, as I did, embrace their humanity, especially as they present their verbal offerings as an act of faith and trust?

These folks we have come to know present one picture to the outside world. But to me (and you) during our conversation, they showed us the cross-stitches underneath the embroidery of their lives.

Except maybe for hardened criminals, we are all good folks just trying to make our way in a tough world where we struggle to love and hold onto the people we want in our lives. You see how at first you didn't know my hand-drawn characters in our conversation, but as they continued to return over and over into your and my conversation, you looked forward to the next time you would "see" them again so you could witness their inner workings like a spectator and participant in their journeys?

I think of the visitors to my office as sculptures that start out as slabs of beautiful stone. Gradually, we carve away the excess, unnecessary cover and into their inner core. A statuesque figure emerges, one that we would have never guessed actually existed in the depths of the hidden marble. Oh, to be a witness and invited participant in the sculpting process! Now you have a glimpse into why I love my job and why I have learned so much from the unique and lovely individuals who have informed my life.

I believe I told you already I've loved every person with whom I've worked.

You may ask, "You loved everyone you ever saw, but did you *like* them?" Here's how I will answer that question:

I have liked most of my patients, and a few of them I have to say, I found the task of helping them to be a tedious one. Frequently, these were individuals who used a lot of denial and/or rationalized their feelings as a way to tolerate or escape their inner turmoil. They isolated their feelings, meaning they couldn't quite get in touch with their emotions and compartmentalized the unwanted intrusions as if they could control when their emotions should make an appearance and when to hide away in some vessel walled off in their hearts. When I attempted to give them back much of what I had absorbed from their words, they would tell me I was way off base and they couldn't possibly feel the way I suggested they were feeling.

I know myself well enough to know that I'm not usually off the mark, and even if I get it wrong, I'm not too far amiss. In addition, when I would sit with these people, I could feel a physical sensation as if a wall of wavy lines, the kind you see just above a scalding pot of boiling water or above a blazing fire, separated us. Sometimes I visualized this barrier more like a semi-translucent gray cloud.

With people like this, I used an indicator of progress for them. It came when I found myself liking them more. I knew then that we were getting somewhere. Our therapy had somewhat progressed from my sharing my perceptions and feelings as I received them from the patient and he or she thwarting the communication line by saying, in essence, "No, no, no." Session after session working with this kind of person can bring about in me a sensation of "ennui." My tedious task engenders a sleepy feeling as I wait and wait and wait some more to be accepted into their world, or better yet, for them to agree to enter mine.

Through the years, I have learned to pay attention and ask myself why I am now feeling drowsy. I immediately wonder if it's just that I didn't get a good night's sleep last night, or is this person pushing me way far away from the heart of the matter by being defensive. I use the term "defensive" not as a pejorative term but more as recognition of their need to protect their fragile selves from the likes of an emotional ogre like me! It seems that people who cause this reaction in me also have a way of thrumming their message, droning on and on as if they really do want to put me to sleep.

MARGARET

At some point, depending on our relationship, on how long we've been meeting, and the level of trust I believe we have, I may bring this reaction they cause in me to the surface for discussion. In these cases, we can go very far in a short amount of time because of what comes up as a result. In Margaret's case, she finally got an answer to why many people turned their eyes away from her when she spoke and why people didn't seem to seek her out for conversation. It also helped her husband, Don, who admitted that she bored him.

Margaret had just been given the gift of clarity. Rather than believing her whole self was being subtly rejected as people turned off of her, she saw that the way out of her distant cave was to acknowledge her feelings rather than walling them off for fear she might drown from their intensity or others would be frightened away. In fact, it was the opposite: Show your vulnerability, your humanity, your fragile hold on your own right to be on this earth and thereby make contact with those around you so that soon they will seek you out just for the company and the human connection. When you are with them, they will look you in the eye begging for more of you rather than trying to find a way to get away from you the way one does at a cocktail party, supposedly listening to you but circulating their eyes as they try to pretend they are not patently searching the room to make contact with anyone, anyone other then you!

Dear Reader, please think about this for yourself. I'm not trying to suggest that you are a bore, just that you might be acting in a way that steers people away from you when the very thing you crave is the opposite—human connection.

Through my imagination, I conjured up the lives of the characters in our play, because my ethical profession prevents me from presenting the "real" people who have inhabited my life for the last forty years. I made a covert pact with my partners in pain to never reveal their closeted treasures. If I were to go against my creed, we could not have had the rapport and mutual sharing we did have. I hold their secrets very dear, and I will protect them forever.

These people in our present conversation you've come to know could easily have authentically existed and could have been my real-life patients. Their dilemmas are as genuine as they come. Their problems are ours to take into our own hearts and draw an elastic link with the hope both they and we can mend.

We're all lumped together now, my real patients whom I haven't discussed with you, my make-believe ones whom you've come to know, the ones who gave me permission to share their anecdotes, their therapist, and *your* interviewee. How I wish I could have added your name here too. Since you've been the listener or receptor, we couldn't throw your feelings and thoughts into the mix. Rest assured, I have imagined you in front of me and many times "heard" and "seen" your input—in my mind.

I do wish to know you. For this reason, please don't hesitate to get in touch with me. Tell me how you're doing. How did our conversation impact your life? I'd love to hear from you.

Add the following to the list of what you already know about me: I have this thing where when I'm out in a crowd, say, as I walk through the streets of New York City or in Center City, Philadelphia, or in a mall or just about anywhere, I peer into people's faces. I eavesdrop on conversations, and I make up stories about those individuals.

For example, I was walking in the opposite direction of two men. I heard one man say, "… die a terrible death…" Then it was muffled, and I heard, "I'm not afraid of dying…"

I filled in the pieces. Was this man saying he didn't fear death per se; he worried about the *way* he would die? He didn't want to die a painful death. How I wanted to run after those guys and— you know—talk.

I experience this with almost anyone walking the streets, sitting on a train or a doctor's office; you name it. It isn't just curiosity. It manifests itself as a clutching, reaching, almost disconsolate pleading as I yearn for connection with all those strangers in the world. I quickly submerge this longing. If I didn't diminish my ties to most human beings in the world, I would fill up too much with emotion, and then I'd never be able to exist!

In our good-bye sessions, my patients and I not only sum up what we've learned, but we also learn from the good-bye itself. We learn how they characteristically feel when things end or when they lose someone. We learn how they handle joy, let's say, the joy of ending a process where they opened up their hearts, struggled with reality, and naturally resisted the change but changed in spite of themselves. We talk about their feelings toward me and how hard it is to say good-bye to someone with whom you've shared so much.

Let's look in on a few of these good-bye scenes. Chrissy was one of the first to whom we began, so let's say good-bye to her first.

CHRISSY

Trying not to look at me lest she sob uncontrollably, Chrissy focused her eyes in a needlepoint pattern, darting up and back from her bangle bracelet to her wristwatch. Chrissy and I had come a long way, but we both knew we were to be robbed of our chance to complete our work together. In the last few months, I observed our speech patterns changing. It was as if we believed we could cram more progress into a compressed period of time if we motorized our verbalizations.

Why the rush? Chrissy's husband, Jack, had been laid off and was now taking another job in the trucking industry. Unfortunately, this meant they had to move to Georgia. Chris had been getting along much better with Jack and knew the two of them were in the marriage to stay. She simply had to join him. She would be able to get a nursing job almost anywhere she relocated, but he didn't have the same kind of vocational independence.

Her relationship with Jack had improved so much that sometimes in my office she dropped her formality and referred to him as Spanky. This was the moniker his friends used to call him in college before he dropped out and tried to start a business. Jack had been a real go-getter in those days, giving up his education to seek out the mighty buck. Somewhere along the way, as things got rough, his confidence waned, and he relinquished his former ability to stick with his pursuit.

She reported that at home, when Chrissy called him Spanky, it sparked in him the old feeling of pride. When she recited his nickname, he moved closer to her, and if she could tolerate the idea of having him treat her in this loving way, she would repeat this term of endearment for the expressed purpose of having him give her more of the same. But the day she first used this affectionate name in our session, she inadvertently allowed me to peer into the changing inner world into which her psyche had been taking her.

For at least three months, Chrissy and I had known this last day was to be inflicted on us. I think both of us wanted to pretend it would never really happen. The travesty of it was that in order to reach her goals, Chrissy probably would not have needed to put in much more time beyond the date her therapy was to be so rudely terminated.

In these last few sessions, we had been summing up our trek through Chrissy's therapeutic life. We had periodically forgotten her original reason for consulting me. It was because she was suffering from what her doctors had called Chronic Fatigue Syndrome. We had gone far beyond her presently diminishing physical symptoms. Chris no longer smiled when she wanted to cry; she had come to terms with Daddy's death; she was working toward no longer blaming herself for her mother's misery and subsequent death. This last issue continued to clutch onto her, but she was trying very hard to confront it. Also, Chris continued to hold onto her own misery, but her grip had been loosening. Just as she began to slacken in her gratification of pain for its own sake, Jack announced their need to move away. Here was yet another reason to concentrate on her gloomy despair, something Chris needed whenever she felt compelled to justify any good things that happened to her.

Chris and I had talked many times about her fantasy that she didn't deserve to be happy. Why? Because she was the cause of her mother's wretchedness (particularly because she had left home at sixteen and "stuck" her mother with the household responsibilities as well as the other kids). Even at the end of her mother's life, Chris saw herself as the agent of death. She believed that because she had refused to succumb to her mother's manipulation on that one occasion when her mother said she wasn't feeling well, her mother died on the spot! Well, almost.

Just recently, Chris had broken through her resistance to share negative thoughts and feelings. In the last session, she blurted out, "Phyliss, I'm really not happy with what you did to me!"

"What do you mean?" I gently probed.

As she frequently did when she was very uncomfortable, she combed her hair with her fingers. When she sighed and exhaled, her whole body seemed to deflate. In the big stuffed chair in front of me, she actually looked smaller than her real self. "I used to be able to cover it up when I was upset. Now I cry in movies, and the other day, I even cried while watching a commercial of a woman greeting her husband who was returning from a business trip! What have you done to me, Phyliss?"

I actually fought back an urge to laugh. No, I didn't feel like laughing *at* her; I just found the way she expressed herself so endearing. I loved the idea that she could tell me in so many words she was angry with me. Also, what she was saying was very familiar to me. Many of my patients, as much as they feel better or see their symptoms melting away, are not immediately thrilled with what often accompanies such progress: the arrival on the conscious scene of the dreaded emotions they had worked so hard to suppress.

This is a recognizable stage in therapy where you "defrost" from your numb existence, cease to be a cardboard figure in a three-dimensional world, and come alive! To come alive is to recognize the emotional breezes that used to brush by your face, but now these linger and press on your skin, so there is no pretending your reactions to what you see and hear aren't there. Your heart is pumping intensely, and it awakens from lethargy almost any time you nod off as you try to deny what is. Now you are capable of feeling joy, but, yes indeed, as Gibran so aptly told us, you can't have joy without sorrow. The more you learn to handle the sorrow, the more likely you will be a candidate to absorb the joy that pervades the air but can only be seen by those who are willing to grasp it.

Ralph Waldo Emerson said, "He has seen but half the universe who has not been shown the house of pain."

As with all good things in life, you don't arrive at a peaceful haven without experiencing some pain. In this case, the pain is in the fear that you won't be able to turn off the newfound and very sensitive emotional needle, which points right into your heart.

The worst part of it all is that you know you can't turn back. You won't allow yourself to get away with kidding yourself any longer. As the comic strip characters in Li'l Abner used to say, "Put 'em back the way thee was!"

So here was watery-eyed Chrissy, about to leave me, about to take off for strange and new places. Here was Chrissy in the tenderest state of mind. This was our last session. We had toyed with the idea of her calling me and continuing our relationship on the phone. We decided to wait until she arrived in Georgia, settled in, and then I would help her find someone local with whom she could consult, or we would determine if it would be feasible to continue our therapy on the phone. I recommended that we treat our ending as if it were final. I wanted her to get the full flavor of our parting and to deal with all the feelings therein. If it turned out we were going to work together later, we would redesign our plan accordingly and deal with her feelings of reunification.

Because this was our last session, rather than allowing Chrissy to remain raw and open for the purpose of being able to process her feelings over time, I felt a responsibility to help her close herself up within a protective shell, kind of like a cocoon. She was to hibernate for a while so she would have the fortitude to ready herself for the challenges she faced. These were survival issues such as moving into a new home and learning about a new location and all that goes with it. She needed her psychic energy to literally find her rightful place in the world. I also would have rather encouraged her to express her anger toward me regarding her change, but this was our last day. It would be cruel to leave her in a lurch, devastated by frustration and guilt for having given me her anger. Therefore, as opposed to my usual practice, I educated and comforted her to help her close up rather than prodding and disturbing the status quo as a way to open her up for more emotional upheaval.

"Chris, I know you are feeling raw right now. It's new for you to feel such strong emotion. This hypersensitivity will lessen after a while. You need time to acclimate to it."

"Really?" She had a little girl look on her face, wide-eyed and pleading. Her lips, which had been pressed tightly together, quivered slightly.

"Yes, Chris, really. It's good that you can now feel your feelings rather than have to numb yourself to them. That's why you used to be so tired all the time."

"Yeah, but at least when I was tired I didn't feel weepy."

"You didn't ever feel happy either."

"Yeah, it's true, but I don't know, maybe it was better to be oblivious."

I straightened myself in my chair. I knew I was going to do a lot of talking this session. I guess I was gathering up my energy for the task ahead of me. "I'm sure it is better to be oblivious at times. I wish that for myself once in a while."

"Really?" Her open mouth assumed an almost puppy dog expression as I noted the rhythm of her breathing. It was as if she were an excited pet who runs around in circles and then idles up closer to you with non-stop panting.

"Sure. I don't particularly enjoy feeling painful emotions either."

"Wow!" is all she could muster.

"Yep, many times I have to fight my own impulses to turn myself off. If I did allow myself to block my emotions, then when something good happens, in order to keep the cover, I would have to mute my internal feelings bank. This would mean I'm turning off my capacity for joy as well."

"I like the way you said that," Chris said affectionately.

"Chris, now that you've come alive and you feel your feelings, how is it going? How are you doing with our ending today?"

"It's horrible," she cried out as her head bowed on the way to her hands. Then she muffled some words into her hands, which totally covered her bent face. Her elbows that dug into her thighs supported her hands.

"Chris, go ahead and have a good cry." I paused. "Then please repeat what you said. I had trouble hearing it."

By now, she had grabbed the familiar tissue box, straightened up, and stared at me through the remaining liquid crystals that lingered in her lower eyelids. Her lips curled, and she stumbled through the words, "You have been the mother to me I should have had... There, that's what I said. It was hard to say it out loud. I'm kind of embarrassed."

"I can see why you might be embarrassed. You're not used to expressing your feelings so directly, especially positive ones. I want you to know I appreciate your telling me that, Chris. I would have loved to have you as a daughter."

Then she really took off and allowed the dam to burst. I didn't go over to her to physically comfort her. I was being careful not to foster our attachment. If I were too "wonderful," it would be even harder for her to make the break. I wanted her to experience the grief. This is healthy. However, I had to be responsible about it. I wanted her to know, even as we sat in my office, she could handle these feelings, and she didn't need me to hold her. This is how it would be when she left. She needed to know she could rely on herself to manage her emotions.

At this point, I went into a soliloquy about how she would feel the sting of our ending for a while after she left today, but gradually, as with any loss, she would acclimate to it, and it wouldn't feel so intense. She needed to know this from her surrogate mom. She would have to take me with her in her mind and hear my words even after she left me.

I saved a lot of time at the end of the session for a slow good-bye. But before that, I endeavored to anchor her back to the real world of things as opposed to emotions. I asked her to tell me the color scheme and decorating considerations in her new house. Yes, I was deliberately "walling" her up. She was to go out of my office into a world where no one would have any clue as to what she was experiencing. She was now in touch with all the emotions stored up in her own life. Add to those her feelings about leaving me, feelings only I would understand, the person whom she would have consulted if she needed validation and support, the person whom she would never see again. What a tall order!

I knew she could do it. Again, to detoxify her feelings and help her adorn a protective shield as well as to help her plan for after our good-bye, I asked her, "What will you do when you leave here today?"

She said she planned to go to the bookstore and then to her sister's for lunch.

I smiled. With an upward inflection in my voice, I said, "Chris, that's great. You're taking good care of yourself. You will get through today and all the days to follow. You will feel grief and anger about having to leave, but you will also be able to feel joy and eagerness about fixing up your new home, meeting new friends—the adventure of it all. And it will be good. You will be okay."

She nodded through her tears and managed a smile, a real one. The upturned lips were not there to make me feel better; I'm convinced of it. It was a smile of love and connection.

We embraced and held on to each other for a long time. Through my body motions, she knew it was time for her to release her hold on my shoulders.

"I have so enjoyed working with you," I said while brushing my hand over my cheeks to catch the rivulets that were streaming there.

"Thanks," was the only word she could rally.

Then she was gone.

If you are feeling the way I am right now, you probably would welcome an opportunity for a little break. At the moment, you wouldn't want me to tell you yet another wrenching good-bye story.

Perhaps you would rather walk along a rocky pier jutting into the ocean and hear the waves smashing violently against the black-striated formations. Maybe you would want to inhale the salty moisture and remind yourself that you are still alive, that you can't always have it your way, that people leave your life, and just as the sea gulls noisily return to the shore for more food searches, so you will always look for other forms of nourishment in the many corners of your world.

Rather than attending to your twisted reverie, you might want to trek up Provo Canyon Falls in Utah or escalate up Snow Mountain in the summer time or watch a sunset along the shoreline in Taos, New Mexico, or clamber up the mountains in Big Sur, California, and peer at the streaming sunbeams radiating through the molten-producing apertures. Would you prefer to ascend Dunn's River Falls in Jamaica or snorkel in the ocean off the Cayman Islands? Maybe you'd like to soak in the sunlight as it reflects off the ancient stone structures in Monteriggioni, Italy, or allow white, powdery sand to trickle through your toes in Playa del Carmen, Mexico. You could kayak through the Mangrove trees in Key West, Florida, or take a cruise and swish and sway over the seas in wonderment. It's fun to dream, isn't it?

Having taken the liberty of nature's respite, we are necessarily compelled to move on and finish my story, but now, hopefully, we will tolerate the passions we feel as we enhance the reality of what happens when you open your heart to perfect strangers and after months and years of intimate exchange, they are strangers no more.

DICK

You already know about the final good-bye I had with Dick. It was at his funeral. But there was a last session where he said good-bye to me, although neither of us knew it was the final good-bye. With him and me, every session was a "maybe." It was a "maybe this is farewell," although neither of us ever said it aloud.

I remember very well the last session before he landed in the hospital, because the usual glossy-clean Dick smelled like lemons that day. His skin had a yellow hue. It was difficult not to imagine a warm summer's day and the fragrance of refreshing lemonade.

Dick proudly told me how much more assertive he was becoming. He had demanded from Alice that she not harp on him so much; in a restaurant, he had sent back something he thought was spoiled. He actually told the men's group leader he was upset they had changed the meeting room while he was gone and no one had told him.

"I can't believe I did that. It's so unlike me to say anything. I told them I just wanted to get it off my chest." I took note of the way he said, "off my chest," since it was true his heart could give out if things got too heavy.

Dick felt the other group members didn't validate what he was saying, and the leader intimated Dick had been told about the change. This really frightened fifty-five-year-old Dick. He looked at the ceiling, took in a deep breath, and begged the question, "Could I be slipping the way my mother did at the end of her life?" He pulled on his Santa Claus beard as if he would pluck out each stiff white hair one by one.

I wondered about it myself. Could it be that Dick wasn't getting enough blood to his brain to enable him to function properly? This was a little worrisome to me.

Then he talked about the party the family gave him for his fifty-fifth birthday. "They went all out. It was very expensive the way they rented a bus and everything. I feel so down about it."

"Do you think you didn't deserve all that attention?" I asked.

"I don't know. Maybe that's it. I wish someday I will be able to tell them how much it meant to me. To have them all there with me at the opera, my favorite thing, and then back to a restaurant afterward. Can you imagine how much they spent?"

We both sat still for a few minutes. He went on. "I always feel insecure. I guess this isn't any different."

"How long would you say you have felt insecure?"

"Probably all my life, but I think it really got bad after my father died when I was fifteen. I wish I had known he was going to die. I know I would have been nicer to him... But I think he left this world because of the way my mother acted. She was like a witch at times, pushing him around, never satisfied."

I conjectured, "Do you think he dropped dead suddenly because he had had all he could take from her?"

"Yes, I do. It was wrong to do. Really selfish. Like he took care of himself in preference to taking care of me. How could he leave a fifteen-year-old boy behind? And he basically abandoned me, leaving me to deal with her."

"When you grew up, you married a very dependent woman. I wonder what that was about." I was referring to Alice who was depressed most of the time and afraid to go out alone.

Dick quickly retorted, "But she wasn't that way when I married her."

We talked about some other things, and then he brought up Alice again. "What is she going to do when I die?"

"She'll have to figure out a way to get along. Does this frighten you, Dick?"

"Oh yes, it sure does. How can I leave her in a lurch like that?"

"Kind of like the way your father left you, you mean?"

"Uh huh."

Knowing what I did about Dick, I pursued another line of inquiry. "Do you discuss these feelings with Alice?"

"No way. She would start worrying that I'm gonna die tomorrow. Anyway, she always asks me what you and I talked about in our sessions, and I make up something. In fact, now I'm so used to it, I make it up on the way home."

"Why do you fabricate what we talk about? Aren't you allowed to discuss your feelings about her being dependent on you?"

"No. I'm not. She won't like it. She'll say I'm making her look bad to you. Anyway, when I tell her things we talk about, the ones I make up, she always says she thinks I'm lying."

"So you lie about lying?"

"Um…I guess I do."

"How does this fit with what you used to do when you were fifteen and tried to get around your dad?"

"It's a matter of survival with me."

"How do you feel after you lie to her?"

"Not so good but better than if she found out that I'm trying to learn how to be more in charge in our relationship."

"Yes, it's interesting, isn't it, how you feel pushed around by her, yet she's so dependent on you!"

"I never thought of it that way before."

"Let's try to look at how your fear of her reaction to you causes you to lie and what effect that has on you. Also, you were telling me in the beginning of our meeting how proud you are that you are asserting yourself. Might you feel better about yourself if you were more assertive with Alice?"

Dick was easy about talking to me. I always noticed how his cheeks reddened the further along in the session we got. He readily answered my questions. "She gets so riled up. Then I have to pick up the pieces because she gets sick or goes to bed early, and I can't get her out of the house after that."

I kept asking questions, but I didn't actually plan where I was going. I was just trying in my usual way to get data. Remember what I said, "Data, give me daaaaaata!" I think Dick knew I wasn't trying to lead him anywhere, just attempting to identify the puzzle pieces and put them together in a new pattern so we could understand him better.

Always cooperative, Dick gave me answers and said he would think about the impact his tiptoeing around his wife had on him.

The next day, I received a call from Alice saying Dick had had a massive heart attack and was in Lehigh Valley Hospital's Cardiac Care Unit. He was very insistent that there should be no extreme measures taken to extend his life. (I thought about his newfound assertiveness even as he approached the finality of his death. I felt happy for him.) At this point, there were no tubes or anything to help him breath, but soon the doctors would be making decisions. That's why it was so important that he state his needs now while he still could talk.

I hung up the phone and called the hospital. I asked how he was doing.

The woman at the other end of the phone asked, "Are you family?"

Never one to lie, I said, "Well no, but I am very close to him." Obviously, due to my ethical position, I wouldn't say I was his therapist.

I couldn't believe it, but she actually brought the phone to him (this was well before all the stringent HIPAA stipulations) after he said he wanted to speak to me. Shook up and sad, I started by saying, "I just called to say hello and to tell you I hope you enjoy your stay there."

He laughed meekly. This was an in-joke with us. We had always talked about how if he was going to die, he should at least "milk" the chance to get TLC and be doted on by everyone. We had planned for his dying moments to be fun.

Dick told me a little bit about his condition and that they were suggesting he have a cardiac exploratory surgery, but he refused. He was waiting to see what was to happen.

I said, "Dick, it looks as if you are back at the usual challenge of trying to flow with things as they happen."

He refrained with an old standby phrase of his, "You betcha." It was soothing to hear him say this.

I told him I would visit him at the hospital tomorrow. I very much looked forward to it. In the meantime, I wrote him a card.

Dear Dick,

Hang in there. I miss you and hope you "enjoy" your "vacation." I'll be here when you get back.

Then that night I got the call. Without our knowing it, he and I had had our farewell session on the phone. He was never to receive my card. It was all over. He was at peace.

KEVIN

Through the window, I observed the sputtering rain; the American flag outside my office was rippling violently and sporadically with each gust of wind. Yet, after locking his car door, Kevin sauntered casually through the parking lot. He didn't even brace himself against the biting cold. He merely swung his yellow slicker over his shoulders and slipped his muscular arms through the sleeves. When he entered my waiting room, I could hear his heavy boots as he stomped them on the welcome mat outside my door.

Upon my silent invitation, he entered my office smelling of new rain that would probably evaporate before it had a chance to become mildew. I would never know the future of Kevin's rainy renovation as he went on to live his life, without me. Little details such as these had no place in my mind's eye anyway.

This thought flashed through my brain as we settled ourselves to make ready for our final session. I was reminded of how my children's every move used to occupy my thinking—what they ate, how may times they moved their bowels, what clothes they should wear that day. Now when we talk on the phone or get together, it's more a question of what they are thinking about these days, how their lives are going for them, what new things their children are doing.

With Kevin, it was even more of a break—a total severance of being in any way part of his existence.

So, we began living out our last forty-five minutes of face-to-face association. From here on, Kevin would change—his hair would gray; his face would crinkle; he might eventually walk with a cane, but just like my cousin T'ai, who died at age twenty-six and never again aged a day in my mind, so fifty-five-year-old Kevin's visage froze in my memory.

By this time, Kevin had divorced Darlene and had been married to Diane for about a year. Around the time of his wedding, he and I had talked about terminating therapy in the near future. That's all Kevin needed to know. He was improved enough to contemplate our ending. He took a down turn so deep I really worried about him for a while.

Many of his old symptoms returned to visit us and seemed to be saying, "Unh unh unh unh! We haven't gone anywhere. We've just been hibernating to fool you into believing all is well."

Kevin had perceived my going along with our talk about ending as an abandonment of him. When he shared his dreams, unconsciously he felt he had done something wrong to induce me to be willing to allow him to leave. His most poignant dream was as follows:

> I was standing on a precipice, and you were on the other side. You said come on over, Kevin. I took a running leap, and as I was in the air, I looked across, and you were laughing and just vanished into thin air. I looked down, saw the deep canyon, and started falling into it.

I asked, "Kevin, how did you *feel* in the dream?"

"At first I was glad to see you. Then as I was falling, I was scared, but I think I was really angry because you had tricked me to leap over to your side, and then you deliberately became invisible."

"Why do you think I would do that, Kevin?"

"I don't know."

"It reminds me of something you might have imagined your mother doing."

"I guess so," he said. He rested his head on the heel of his hand, and his coiled-up fingers resembled a small radiator, which was supposed to warm and defrost his frozen expression of woe.

I reminisced, "I'm reminded of a nightmare you told me you had as a child where a giant with black fingers and toes snuck into your bedroom at your aunt and uncle's house, swept you up, and took you into a car with no windows. They told you you were a bad boy and they were taking you to a place where they take bad boys who hurt their mothers."

"Yeah, I remember that dream. I told you that dream, oh, I bet it was about four years ago when we first started. How did you remember it?"

"At the time, it had a great impact on me. I imagined what a scared little boy you must have been. Remember, we talked about the dream for a number of sessions? Remember we said we thought the giant represented your dad, because your dad always had black grease under his nails from working on cars, and we decided you felt guilty that your dad died? He left you because somehow you had been bad to your mother. We said you put the meaning into the dream ex post facto. You didn't feel negative feelings toward your mom, in actuality, until after your father died and you had the dream when your mother went for rehab the first time. I believe you were furious with her for abandoning you."

Kevin appeared to be appreciative of what I was saying. As he pondered my remarks, the creases on each side of his lips maintained an *S* curve, causing him to look as if he were sneering behind his smile. My impression of his smile fit with the return of his protective, scornful laugh, his flying off the handle at his new wife, Diane, and his mistrust of me and fear of my forsaking him as I did in the dream.

In addition, his melancholy returned. Do you recall our discovery that Kevin often maintained his misery as a way to hold onto other people? You and I talked about this when we got into Kevin's difficulty accepting Diane's physically affectionate gestures toward him such as when she massaged his shoulders and back. Then we talked about Kevin's pathetic facial expression, which he had developed as a boy to encourage his mother to feel guilty and make amends to him for her abusive behavior. Diane and I had nothing about which to feel guilty. Besides, we were both onto him!

This particular session marked the beginning of our journey to get to a deeper level of exploration. Therapy can be like peeling an onion, which gets smaller as you go, but there's always still another layer to unwrap.

It took us a full year to get back to the place where we started.

So, about a year later, on this rainy day, we were once again to face the ultimate parting, and this time, we both felt we were ready to do so.

"I think I'm okay about this," he volunteered before he even sat down. "I thought a lot about these last five years. Wow! Who would have believed I'd ever be here more than twice—which is just about what I told myself when I promised Diane I would try it."

"Yes, Kevin, we've had quite an adventure together, haven't we?"

He wholeheartedly agreed. In fact, his first bending of his head up and down in a nod turned into many repetitions, almost like having a hundred afterthoughts, you know, like the way you agree. Then you really agree. Then the more you think about it, the more you really, really think it's a cool idea. I think of it like a carving where the deeper you chisel, the more intense the reality.

As he moved his face in agreement, I observed Kevin's dimples for the last time. They were the elongated and vertical kind, causing me to question if these were real dimples or merely indentations in his face.

Kevin and I reviewed our mutual memories until finally we had about five minutes remaining.

"I've enjoyed working with you," I told Kevin.

"Me too." He looked over my head, rolling his eyes as if he were peering into his brain. "Phyliss, is it okay if I write to you from time to time?"

"Sure, I'd enjoy very much to hear from you."

"Phyliss, can I ask you a question?"

"Sure."

"Did you enjoy working with me because I was an interesting case or for any other reason?"

Okay, we now have about three minutes left, and he asks a question, which I'm sure is loaded with material to fill up at least three sessions. He waits until the end, so whatever I say, we will have no time to process it or for me to find out how he took it in, what fantasies he has about what I said, or to repair any damage done and to set him straight in his misperceptions. What do I do now?

As always, I try to determine what's behind the question. I know it sounds like a copout or a technique to ask my old standby questions, but I needed to be responsible here. "What do you think, Kevin? Why do you ask?"

He squirmed in his chair, looking as if he had just been slapped. "I knew you wouldn't answer. I was just testing you, I guess. I could tell you really cared about me, especially those times when I saw tears in your eyes. I guess I just wanted to hear you say it."

With no time to process and as a closing-up gesture, I complied, "Kevin, I care about you as person, not just as an interesting case."

His eyes widened. "Thanks, Phyliss. I knew that's what you would say, but it's really nice to hear it."

I seized the opportunity to help him see and appreciate his own progress. "Yes, it's really nice that you are finally in a place where you think enough of yourself to really be able to hear it."

"Diane says that too. She says I take her compliments better, and she feels good when I don't put myself down each time she gives me something. I guess I really have come a long way."

I concurred. "You have. Most definitely, you have."

"Can I call and see you if I have things come up?"

"Sure you can. My door is always open."

"Okay, then. I'm off."

Outside, the rain had stopped. He threw his slicker over his right shoulder. He opened the door to the waiting room, tossed his raincoat on the floor, and turned toward me. He reached out his arms.

We hugged.

He picked up his raincoat. "Bye."

I said, "Bye."

That was it.

POLLY

You already know how I said good-bye to Polly, a bulimic patient, because you were there watching our movie the day Polly's alcoholic father walked out leaving her and her stunned mom in a quandary. Mom literally pulled Polly out of my office. Except for her breaking her mother's grip and running back to me, grabbing my shoulders and saying, "I'm sorry. I'm sorry," I never saw her again. That was a tough one. It's these unfinished therapies that get to me the most.

JENNY

Jenny, another bulimic patient, and I also were unable to finish what we started, at least not in the standard way. I couldn't hold her back from going to college. She was ready. True, she had more work to do, but she had come so far, and she had already been held back from going to college for two years while we worked together. We decided to correspond by e-mail and to schedule phone sessions. Blessed be technology.

EMILY

Emily said good-bye in the usual fashion and went on her merry way. I later learned she was studying to become a psychologist. The last I heard, she was working on her PhD.

MELANIE

Melanie eventually outgrew her belligerence toward her mother, the wrong parent to have lived. Melanie worked through feelings about her father's death. Melanie's mom remarried, which meant that Melanie remained in treatment longer than we originally thought she would. She learned how to get along with her stepdad. She did, however, try very hard to move out of her mom's house. She actually postponed going off to college so she could earn the money to support herself and maintain her independence. We worked a long time on her counter dependence, her ferocious wish to never need anyone and therefore not have to suffer pain when these loved ones didn't come through for her.

When we ended, Melanie had really blossomed. When I work with young people, it's a twofold process. They are changing and growing in therapy while at the same time maturing into adults. It's hard to decipher which is which, the therapy or the natural evolution of growth, but I look at it as sitting alongside of someone who is flowering, and I'm there to make sure they get enough water as they grow into whatever they are supposed to be.

HARRY AND SALLY

After having individual summation and farewell sessions, I said good-bye to Harry and Sally in a joint meeting, the same way we had started. I knew that for the last year, they had been visiting fertility doctors, because after six years of trying to conceive, they wanted help. She was to take hormones for a period of time, and within a few months, they were going to attempt in-vitro fertilization.

Of course, I wanted to say, "Please let me know if you conceive or not," but it wasn't my place. This was the ending. I'm the one who is supposed to be left out in the cold with no further information. Secretly, I hoped they would want me to know their good news.

It has been years since we said good-bye. Except for a thank you holiday card they sent six months after termination, I haven't heard from them. I choose to believe they would have sent me a birth announcement or something. This belief feels good. Yet, on the other side, I feel sad, because by my not receiving word from them, it probably means they gave up the contest. If this is so, how unfortunate for them. They would have made great parents. I grieve for them that they never knew the joy of conception, birth, and child rearing, the latter being the most challenging task any human being encounters in a lifetime.

I hope Harry and Sally had acquired enough coping skills individually and as a team to get them through the rough times. The true test of a marriage takes place during arduous, critical moments.

When they left my office on the last day, they each felt comfortable to reach out for a hug, first Harry, then Sally. Then they walked out single file. Sally deposited her familiar shreds of crumpled tissues into my wastebasket near the door. Both of them turned around simultaneously for a last glance. Reminding me of a little boy, Harry raised his hand in a wave as if his hand were made only for that purpose. I'll never forget his endearing gesture. The memory is like a snapshot in my mind.

VICTOR

Victor told his mother that we were close to ending our sessions. His mother said, "I'll bet you'll miss her, and I guess she'll miss you."

He said yes to both of those statements. He was surprised that his mother was so aware of how he felt toward me.

He looked at me and said, "I *will* miss you." He paused as we both absorbed this very direct, clear assertion of his feelings.

Later that same session, Victor said, "I'm feeling so happy these days now that the weather has broken and the sun is shining. I'm happier than I've ever been. I'm just so happy to be alive."

A few weeks later, we discussed the idea of terminating Victor's therapy. We agreed that neither of us could think of anything needing further work at this time, at least not anything that he couldn't handle on his own. We knew that the process would go on even though we wouldn't be seeing each other in formal therapy. He had the tools now to go on his own.

We decided on one more session…

On the last day, Victor came in, a broad smile on his face. He took his usual chair. We sat there, beaming at each other.

He said, "I feel as though I'm saying good-bye to a close friend."

I responded, "We carry each other within ourselves." As you probably guessed, this is one of my favorite original phrases, but each time I say it or think it, the authenticity of it deepens.

He said, "I was in the waiting room thinking about all we've been through together. Just at that moment, the clouds covered the sun, and I realized I still could see beams of sunlight through the clouds. I thought, *Even when it's cloudy, I can see the sun.* It's just like that in here."

We reminisced for the last time. Victor stretched his eyelids wide as he blinked away tears. "I wonder where I'd be today if I never walked through this door. Thank you, Phyliss, for persevering with me, for never giving up on me, for never thinking I was inferior."

A little awestruck, I said, "Of course, I never saw you as inferior, Victor!"

(Had this not been the last session, I sure wouldn't have stopped there! We could have had a heyday with that statement even though it was stated in a disclaiming way, that I did *not* see him as inferior but he didn't say I saw him as equal or superior. It was more of a 'not-feeling" than a positive feeling. When people say what I'm *not* thinking, I'm sure it's what they thought I *was* thinking. If I tell you *not* to think of the color red, immediately, what color do you see looming before you? Do you see what I mean here? So much was behind his utterance of relief of my not putting him down. As I think about it now, I can see that even though I wasn't going to pursue his statement, I reacted way too quickly. I personally hated the idea that he would even consider my seeing him as inferior. I had to be careful. This was the last session. I couldn't allow myself to be overly protective. I'm sure you can see how I overstepped myself on that one.)

As he squirmed, I got a whiff of his after-shave lotion and this reality that he was still here helped me straighten myself out and give myself an internal warning to take heed. Yes this was the end and he was vulnerable but darn it, so was I!

We chatted further, and a little later, he paused, straightened his long-sleeved shirt, and pondered, "I don't know if I could have done this with a male therapist. I think I would have been too afraid."

"Maybe you would've worried you might love him."

Victor readily agreed, "Yes, I think that's true."

"With me, a woman, you thought you were safe, because you thought you could never love a woman."

Victor nodded.

We were both lost in silence for a few minutes. Like the old days, I was the one to break through the stillness.

I joked, "Well, I guess I tricked you, Victor."

We both laughed heartily.

We talked about the doctor who Victor had consulted, the one who had recommended him to me and how thankful he was to Dr. Watkins. He reviewed how much he and Dr. Watkins had been through with his injuries from abuse, sexual diseases, and his overwhelming fear of physical damage. He said that once Dr. Watkins had said, "One of these days, Victor, you're going to come in here, and I'm not going to be able to cure you."

He felt the doctor was being thoughtful, caring. Dr. Watkins was worried that if Victor didn't stop being so promiscuous he was going to get AIDS, a newly publicized disease, which was beginning to devastate the gay population.

The last time Victor went to see Dr. Watkins was when he had the flu a few months ago. He told the doctor he was going to be married and was now in love with a woman. Dr. Watkins said, "That's really very nice. Can you just answer me one question, please, Victor?"

Victor said, "Sure."

"Why do you still wear an earring in your ear?"

Victor said, "It's just style," and laughed. (Victor was non-defensive about his appearance.)

Toward the end of our session, Victor told me he was going to paint a picture and somehow incorporate it with a poem he had written. He wanted me to have it.

I said, "My goodness, that would be so nice, Victor."

Victor smiled proudly the way my son had just done that morning. "Then you could have it in your house. It would be yours."

Throughout the session, there were periods of silence. We just looked at each other, tears brimming in our eyes. Then he broke each hush by expressing an emotion in a poetic way.

At one such point he said, "I can hear the birds in this office from the outside. Birds sing in here." At another point he said, "I grew up here."

I hadn't noticed the change, but that last day, he looked very handsome to me. What was different about him? Then I realized that his face was relaxed. And I wondered when he had stopped smirking like a giggly school girl. He looked manly and serious, as he put it, "someone to be reckoned with."

Victor talked about years ago when he had stopped treatment. During the year and a half, he thought a lot about me and looked for me in stores. He remembered my having said that we might never see each other again, but perhaps we'd bump into each other in a mall or something. "During that year-and-a-half absence, I used to imagine that you were saying things to me." The process of therapy was still going on. Victor had been making many changes during our separation.

We talked about the future and what it was going to feel like saying good-bye to each other this time. He said, "I will always think about you."

Finally, I said, "Well, I think this is it. We have to do it."

We hugged. We held onto each other, squeezed, and cried. Then we released each other.

Victor said, "Thank you."

Victor and I started out at separate points in the universe. Almost as if by a miracle, we met at a summit, and through our relationship with each other, our lives have changed, even as we move on and we separate from each other.

Victor began to see me as real, as human, and then he could love me in a mature way. He no longer confused his love for me, the nurturing caretaker, for the love a mature man has toward a woman, the concern he experienced whenever he felt affection for his mom. His fear of his mom's potentially incestuous feelings toward Victor were actually Victor's own unconscious impulses toward her that he couldn't tolerate in himself so he projected them onto her and imagined she was wanting him in a sexual way.

Only when he accepted himself as deserving to be on this earth as I deserve to be here, could he move on. Yes, as is true with so many of my patients, I had to become an integral part of his change. Even though he and I were worlds apart in lifestyle, profession, and status, we were actually united as one person. He no longer was an anomaly of society. He was, in his own words, "a somebody."

I agreed with him when he said, "I grew up in your office," because when I last met him more than six years prior, I saw him as an infant, and I "lived with him" through his maturation. I supported him when he was the rebellious, giddy adolescent resisting the idea of being alone with me, blanking out rather than sharing thoughts with me, trying on new behaviors, new fashions, and testing out his individuality to see if I would continue to accept him nevertheless. I "lived with him" when he left "the nest" for periods of time—when he removed himself from therapy for a year and a half. We reached the final emancipation: termination of the formal therapy. We went through the preparation for his ultimate "leaving home."

Victor taught me so much. For starters, he reinforced the idea that a psychologist needs to be willing to wait. A psychologist must never underestimate her patient. The goals of treatment must be based always on the individual's inner resources, which will reveal how much that person wants to achieve, how far he or she wants to go. The psychologist does not set out to "change" a person. The therapist must always take the cues from the patient. Victor reaffirmed that given the right environment, a person can learn to allow his creativity to be unleashed, can learn to take himself seriously, can find inner strength as he discovers his ability to survive.

I've been reminded that love is not always achieved by showering someone with reassurance, platitudes, pep talks, or strong assertions of love. Rather, love sometimes needs restraint, patience, letting go, sharing of one's own feelings, doubts, concerns, and joys in relation to the loved one.

Of course, I learned a great deal about the gay world too. I'm even more sensitive now to the torment of how it must feel to wake up each day, and whether conscious of it or not, be aware that your sexual identity somehow makes you different from others. Even if you surround yourself with only gay friends, you still live in a straight world. Although there are many gay individuals who work through the discrepancy of who their parents had expected them to be and the identity they eventually developed, for many others, their eventual determination can be experienced as an unfair strike of life!

Another significant learning from my work with Victor was my reexamination of the power of parenting. When I think about parenting, I see power and forgiveness as going together. Parents have the power to mold and determine the course of their children's lives, and yet parents don't always realize they have that power, nor can they control it, because no one really knows what effect any particular behavior or situation will have on a child. After our children have already exhibited for us the results of the mistakes we've made, the parent has to live with that knowledge. Parent power has affected the child in a way that the parent had not necessarily predicted.

The parent has to deal with the adolescent the way he is now. The adolescent is trying to make his own way and fighting back against all the "mistakes" the parent made in the first place. Can the parent now forgive the child for turning out different from what was imagined in dreams? Does the parent go on to "put down" the child for exhibiting "defects" that might be nearly identical to those possessed by the parent himself? Victor's parents openly forgave Victor for turning out gay, and I believe this action was a strong influence in his final self-acceptance.

And Victor, too, forgave his parents. He analyzed his background and came to understand enough to be capable of exonerating them. He was so happy at the time; he actually questioned whether he would have wanted his background to be any different, because then he might not have ended up where he is now.

Given all the therapy, Victor is still the same man but now allowing innate parts of himself to be expressed. To be who he is today, he had to have absorbed a great deal from his family.

Someone else in the same therapy, who arrived there in the same unmotivated way as Victor, might not have been affected in the same way nor have allowed me in.

Would Victor have altered his identity if he had set out from the beginning to engage in heterosexual activities? It appears that his change of self-image "snuck up" on him. Neither he nor I set out to make it happen. I would have loved Victor had he continued to live his gay lifestyle. I'm sure, though, he could not have loved me (as he wanted to and eventually loved his mom) if he had continued to identify himself as gay. The two ideas were contradictory—being gay and loving me.

Am I saying here that sometimes a person is better off not going after something but instead, allowing change to take him over? Is that the meaning of trust, especially trust in the therapeutic situation? Victor trusted me. He allowed me in, even though neither he nor I were guaranteed any positive outcome of that union.

Victor made himself vulnerable to another human being—me. The fact that I am well adjusted, respectful, and loving further encouraged Victor, the seeker of truth, to go beyond the passive position and take his own risks, to learn his own truths.

Yes, Victor challenged me on every level. It's as if he had allowed me in and then spit me out again when he didn't need me. We both had to go through the process of cutting the umbilical cord and dealing with the feelings involved in the process. We had to allow things to flow even though along with the joys of ending comes the loss and grief.

Some people who knew about his therapy suggested to Victor, "Phyliss must feel good that she helped you to change."

Yes, it is true, to be sure, that I felt good about my part in his growth (having nothing to do with his switch from loving men in a sexual way to loving women). But the real joy is in sharing together, and that's what I miss the most. I even feel a little angry! I helped him unearth a new path, to become happy and independent so he didn't need me any more, and now what does he do? He leaves me just as I had hoped he would be able to do. How dare he grow up! And yet the joy I feel, knowing he has blossomed into a man who takes responsibility for himself regardless of who he loves.

So as much as I may have the urge to put it off, now it is time to end my discussion and say good-bye to Victor, yet again, even as I reminisce about our relationship so many years ago.

Victor, a new "you" was born in my office. You grew up here, and now you are on your way to independence. We have shared the joys of your growth and the grief of all you had to give up in order to become a grownup, a stage you had to reach before you could make choices you had not believed you had the power to achieve. You never believed you had a choice in your life, but now you are free. Even though we are separating from each other, Victor, you and I are still learning. Only now we will each do it on our own. We are both seekers of truth, feelings, and the joys of life. This process will never stop in either of us.

Thank you for giving so much of yourself to me. I am different today because of you. I will never forget you, Victor. Indeed, I will forever miss you…

This conversation with you has been the culmination of my life's work. I thank you for visiting here with me and providing me the opportunity to express my thoughts and feelings to you just as my patients have had the privilege of doing with me.

For sure, I wouldn't be what I am today without the people who have frequented my office. Look how Dick helped me face my own death by allowing me into his dying process; how Katie impressed on me once again the devastation of loss through miscarriage; how Agnes invigorated me to join with her in her loss of function of her leg and her resilience in learning to love her walker and how she permitted me to laugh with her about it; how Victor taught me about the gay world before and after the advent of AIDS; how Chrissy learned to be authentic even at the risk of losing other people's love; how Suzanne learned to face her early life trauma and overcome guilt-ridden decisions to have an abortion and then how she learned to live with the decision she had made as a young woman, which affected her life as a middle-aged woman; how Abe and Esther invited me into their imaginary bedroom so I could join them when they had childish fights; how Melanie gave over her guilt about wishing her mother dead instead of her father; how Kevin, by giving me his bitterness through his scornful laugh, eventually trusted me and was able to move on to the life he deserved (not at my house either, because he no longer needed me to take him there); how Natalie permitted me to go back in our time machine to her four-year-old self to join her in her photographs and become her surrogate mother while we reconstructed her life; how Bonnie went along with my crazy ideas to help her loosen up about her fat body but accepted it at the same time; how Harry literally gave up a life-long shield and weapon in his abuse of humor and trusted me that he could still be a funny guy but have his humor bring him closer *to* rather than alienate him *from* others; how Victor reinforced for me the veracity that I should never ever, ever give up on any one.

Jenny, at the end of her treatment for bulimia, gave me a copy of Karen Carpenter's song, "We've Only Just Begun" (performed by The Carpenters and written by Paul Williams and Rodger Nichols). This song "spoke" to Jenny. The irony is that Karen Carpenter had finally overcome her lifelong bout with anorexia but died suddenly at age thirty-two due to medical complications maybe even because she had put on some weight after years of an emaciated existence. These lyrics belong right here in our conversation on ending therapy. (By the way, therapy never really ends. You just keep growing, questioning, and engaging in internal conflict, but now you have the coping skills to get through it without necessarily journeying with a therapist to do so.) The last line of her song goes like this: "We'll find a place where there's room to grow. And yes we've just begun."

Along the same note as "We've Only Just Begun" is my favorite T.S. Eliot quote, which is posted on my waiting room wall: "We shall not cease from exploration, and the end of all our exploring will be to arrive where we started and know the place for the first time."

After all we've been through together, saying good-bye is so bittersweet. From the beginning, the end is where we wanted to go. But now we must give each other up. As I'm closing the door for the last time, I often say to people, "Have a good life!"

These are the words of a former patient of mine, a "real" patient, not one of the fictitious ones I've presented in our conversation. He gave me permission to publish these thoughts about his experience in therapy:

> Thank you for all that you have done in my "awakening" from a very long dream of nightmare proportions. I feel as though you were my guide with the bright light, and I simply followed you till clarity and light, health and better weather made it possible for me to carry on by my self—at least for now. It also feels good to be awake!
>
> I like the analogy of awakening, but I also like the vision of you standing in the fog holding a lantern of light for me to see in the fog. I always thought that psychotherapy was supposed to unravel your confusion and tell you what to do. In that analogy you would have been standing by the fork in the road pointing which road to take, but you never did. You simply lit up the road and forced me to choose which way was right for me. True, in order to do that accurately you need to see pretty far down that dark highway, and so you need a pretty bright light, and that bright light was you, Phyliss Shanken!
>
> Thank you again for what you did for me and continue to do.

I'm sad to say good-bye, but these characters live within me. I can have them live on in the same way I created them—in my mind. Just as I do with real-life human beings who have enriched me, I can be reminded of them every time I meet someone who has a similar mannerism, such as a smile or a tilt of the head or maybe the way the person folds her tissue or hands me a check or lifts up her hand and says good-bye. I can watch a baseball game and think of Kevin, visit someone in the hospital and secretly hope I'll meet Nurse Chrissy. ("Oh, how are you? How's everything going? I didn't know you worked here.") Maybe I look at photos of children and mothers and think of Natalie. I'll hear of a mafia revenge killing, and my heart will go out to Anna. (Remember her from our "First Encounters" discussion? She feared being killed by her husband if he found out she had told his secret.)

Maybe I'll be walking on a trail in the park and think of Victor, who sometimes met men there. I'll see someone using a walker to get around and wonder about Agnes. A friend might lament that she doesn't see her son as often as she'd like, and I'll hope Kevin finally resolved things with Dirk. I'll see oatmeal raisin cookies on a shelf in the market, and I'll yearn to talk to Dick again. I'll work out on my treadmill and picture Suzanne, who was the one who recommended I buy it from Sears. I'll hear about a suicide and think of Abe and Esther's torment over Stevie's death. I'll say something funny, and people will laugh, and I'll conjure up Harry's smiling face. I'll observe a woman's being made the butt of a joke by her husband, and I'll think of Sally. I'll see a steamy movie, and I'll think of Robert. I'll see a mother and daughter interacting, and I'll think of Cheryl and Courtney.

There will be an endless train of indelible memories that I'll carry with me forever. Now maybe you'll have them too. This is my way of dealing with the loss of precious people in my life. It's really true that we rub off on each other whether we choose to or not.

I choose to—but I guess by now you've figured that out.

A workshop participant sent me a letter thanking me for having impacted her life. She sent along a quote by Sir James Barrie: "Those who bring sunshine to the lives of others cannot keep it from themselves."

I could say the same to my patients who have given me so much. The sun shines brightly for me these days.

Our conversation has taken almost nine months to complete. This is a logical amount of time, don't you think? Time to conceive an idea, take good prenatal care of it, and then give birth to healthy offspring. The fruits of the nurturing have been presented to you here. And it took thirteen years for you to hear my words. Finally. So perhaps this is why I feel the urge to hold onto you a little longer.

However, I think I have procrastinated long enough.

We must now make our break.

Farewell, my friend, my fellow conversant. Thank you for allowing me into your living room and for so willingly receiving my words. For sure, I will miss you.

CPSIA information can be obtained at www.ICGtesting.com
Printed in the USA
BVOW11s0202280814

364644BV00010B/74/P